ASTRONOMY & SPACE

ASTRONOMY & SPACE

From the Big Bang to the Big Crunch

volume 1
A–HER

PHILLIS ENGELBERT

DETROIT · NEW YORK · TORONTO · LONDON

U·X·L
AN IMPRINT OF GALE

Astronomy & Space:
From the Big Bang to the Big Crunch

by Phillis Engelbert

Staff

Jane Hoehner, *U•X•L Developmental Editor*
Carol DeKane Nagel, *U•X•L Managing Editor*
Thomas L. Romig, *U•X•L Publisher*

Mary Beth Trimper, *Production Director*
Evi Seoud, *Assistant Production Manager*
Shanna Heilveil, *Production Associate*

Cynthia Baldwin, *Product Design Manager*
Barbara J. Yarrow, *Graphic Services Supervisor*
Tracey Rowens, *Cover Designer*
Pamela A.E. Galbreath, *Page Designer*

Susan Salas, *Permissions Associate (Pictures)*

Marco Di Vita, Graphix Group, *Typesetting*

Library of Congress Cataloging-in-Publication Data
Engelbert, Phillis
  Astronomy and space: from the big bang to the big crunch/
  by Phillis Engelbert.
      p.   cm.
  Includes bibliographical references and index. Contents: v. 1. A-Her v. 2. Hes-P v. 3 Q-Z
    ISBN 0-7876-0942-0 (set); 0-7876-0943-9 (v.1); 0-7876-0944-7 (v.2); 0-7876-
0945-5 (v.3); (acid-free paper)
    1. Astronomy—Encyclopedias, Juvenile. 2. Outer space—Encyclopedias, Juvenile.
    3. Astronautics—Encyclopedias, Juvenile. [1. Astronomy—Encyclopedias. 2. Outer space—
    Encyclopedias. 3. Astronautics—Encyclopedias.] I. Engelbert, Phillis.
  qb14.a874   1996
  500.5'03—dc20
                                                    96-12522
                                                       CIP
                                                        AC

Printed in the United States of America

10 9 8 7 6 5 4 3 2 1

Table of Contents

Table of Contents

Table of Contents

Table of Contents

Reader's Guide

Astronomy & Space: From the Big Bang to the Big Crunch provides a comprehensive overview of astronomy and space exploration in three hundred alphabetically arranged entries. The topics included in *Astronomy & Space* can be grouped loosely into the following categories: space objects and phenomena (such as planets, black holes, comets, and solar wind); piloted space missions and scientific satellites; famous astronomers and astronauts; the history of astronomy; observatories; and technological advances in the field. Chronologically, *Astronomy & Space* begins fifteen to twenty billion years ago with the Big Bang, and continues on to recent discoveries such as planets beyond our solar system and the possibility of life on Mars. It extends to the future by describing projects—such as the International Space Station and *Pluto Express*—coming early in the twenty-first century and one possible fate of our universe, the Big Crunch.

The approach taken in *Astronomy & Space* is interdisciplinary and multicultural. The writing is interdisciplinary in that it does not merely address the exploration of the cosmos in a scientific sense, but it also places it in a social and historical context. For example, the entry on rockets includes a discussion of World War II and the entry on the space race addresses the cold war. The set is multicultural in that it features astronomers, observatories, astronomical advances, and space programs from around the world.

Scope and Format

The three hundred entries in *Astronomy & Space* are arranged alphabetically over three volumes. Articles range from one to four pages in length. The writing is nontechnical and is geared to challenge, but not overwhelm, students. More than two hundred photographs and illustrations and numerous sidebars keep the volumes lively and entertaining. Each volume begins with a historical timeline depicting major events in astronomy and space. Boldfaced terms throughout the text can be found in the glossary, while cross-references concluding each entry alert the reader to related entries. A cumulative index in all three volumes provides easy access to the topics discussed throughout *Astronomy & Space*.

Advisors

Thanks are due for the invaluable comments and suggestions provided by:

Teresa F. Bettac
Advanced Science for Kids Teacher, Willis Middle School
Delaware, Ohio

Patricia A. Nielsen
8th Grade Science Teacher/Science Fair Director, Todd County
Middle School
Mission, South Dakota

Jacqueline Ann Plourde
Media Specialist, Madison Junior High
Naperville, Illinois

Jan Toth-Chernin
Media Specialist, Greenhills School
Ann Arbor, Michigan

Dedication and Special Thanks

The author dedicates this work to her husband, William Shea, and her son, Ryan Patrick Shea, for their patience, love, and support. Special thanks to Jan Toth-Chernin for her guidance.

Comments and Suggestions

We welcome your comments on this work as well as your suggestions for topics to be featured in future editions of *Astronomy & Space: From the Big Bang to the Big Crunch*. Please write: Editors, *Astronomy & Space*, U•X•L, 835 Penobscot Bldg., Detroit, Michigan 48226-4094; call toll-free: 1-800-877-4253; or fax: (313) 877-6348.

Timeline

15–20 billion B.C.: "Big bang" marks the beginning of the universe.

10 billion B.C.: Galaxies are formed.

4.5 billion B.C.: The solar system is formed.

4 billion B.C.: Amino acids, the building blocks of life, are formed on Earth.

248 million B.C.: Dinosaurs roam the Earth.

65 million B.C.: Dinosaurs become extinct.

100,000 B.C.: First modern humans inhabit the Earth.

10,000 B.C.: Ice Age ends.

8000 B.C.: Archaic Age begins.

c. 3100 B.C.: Construction begins on Stonehenge.

c. 3000 B.C.: Egyptians create the first 365-day calendar.

c. 1500 B.C.: Chinese astronomers create the first star chart.

1300 B.C.: Chinese astronomers note a nova in the constellation Scorpius.

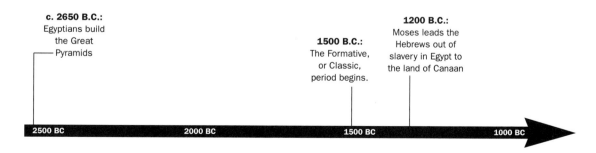

c. 2650 B.C.:
Egyptians build the Great Pyramids

1500 B.C.:
The Formative, or Classic, period begins.

1200 B.C.:
Moses leads the Hebrews out of slavery in Egypt to the land of Canaan

2500 BC   2000 BC   1500 BC   1000 BC

585 B.C.: Greek philosopher Thales correctly predicts a total eclipse of the sun.

c. 330 B.C.: Aristotle writes *De caelo* (*On the Heavens*).

c. 260 B.C.: Greek astronomer Aristarchus proposes that the Earth revolves around the sun.

c. 130 B.C.: Greek astronomer Hipparchus creates a star chart.

46 B.C.: Julius Caesar adds leap year days to the calendar, creating the Julian calendar.

c. A.D. 140: Alexandrian astronomer Ptolemy publishes his Earth-centered theory of the universe.

927: Muslim instrument-maker Nastulus creates the first astrolabe.

1006: Egyptian astrologer Ali ibn Ridwan observes what is considered to be the brightest supernova in history.

1408: Chinese observers note supernova in the constellation Cygnus the Swan, today believed to be a black hole.

1572: Danish astronomer Tycho Brahe observes supernova in the constellation Cassiopeia.

1608: Dutch optometrist Hans Lippershey creates the first telescope.

1609: German astronomer Johannes Kepler publishes his first two laws of planetary motion.

1616: The Catholic Church bans Copernicus' *De Revolutionibus Orbium Coelestium*.

1633: Galileo is placed under house arrest for advocating the sun-centered model of solar system.

1675: Danish astronomer Olaus Roemer measures the speed of light at 76 percent its actual value.

1682: English astronomer Edmond Halley first views the famous comet that is later named after him.

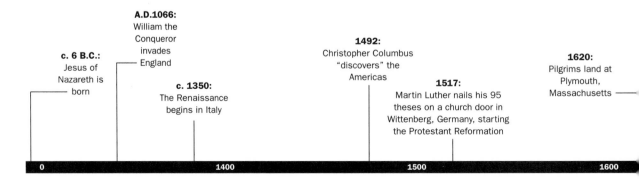

c. 6 B.C.: Jesus of Nazareth is born

A.D.1066: William the Conqueror invades England

c. 1350: The Renaissance begins in Italy

1492: Christopher Columbus "discovers" the Americas

1517: Martin Luther nails his 95 theses on a church door in Wittenberg, Germany, starting the Protestant Reformation

1620: Pilgrims land at Plymouth, Massachusetts

0   1400   1500   1600

1728: English astronomer James Bradley calculates speed of light to be 185,000 miles per second.

1758: French astronomer Charles Messier begins his catalogue of non-star celestial objects.

1772: German astronomer Johann Elert Bode publishes his law of inter-planetary distances.

1781: German astronomer William Herschel discovers Uranus.

1783: English geologist John Michell suggests the existence of black holes.

1800: William Herschel discovers infrared radiation.

1845: English astronomer John Couch Adams and French astronomer Urbain Leverrier co-discover Neptune.

1847: American astronomer Maria Mitchell makes the first discovery of a comet not visible to the naked eye.

1852: French physicist Jean Bernard Léon Foucault proves that the Earth rotates with his famous pendulum experiment.

1877: American astronomer Asaph Hall discovers moons of Mars.

1877: Italian astronomer Giovanni Schiaparelli describes markings called *canali* on surface of Mars, which is erroneously translated to "canals," fueling speculation of life on Mars.

1889: American astronomer George Hale invents the spectrohelioscope.

1895: German physicist Wilhelm Röntgen discovers X-rays.

1905: Albert Einstein publishes his special theory of relativity.

1912: American astronomer Henrietta Swan Leavitt discovers how to use cepheid variable stars as "astronomical yardsticks."

1914: Einstein publishes his general theory of relativity.

1917: Dutch astronomer Willem de Sitter proposes that the universe is expanding.

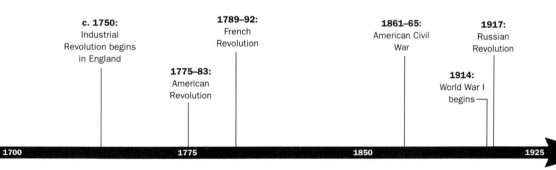

c. 1750: Industrial Revolution begins in England

1775–83: American Revolution

1789–92: French Revolution

1861–65: American Civil War

1914: World War I begins

1917: Russian Revolution

1700   1775   1850   1925

1919: Star observations during a solar eclipse prove Einstein's theory (that gravity bends light) correct.

1923: American astronomer Edwin Hubble discovers that the Andromeda nebula is actually a separate galaxy, establishing the existence of galaxies beyond our own.

1926: American physicist Robert Goddard launches the world's first liquid-propelled rocket.

1929: Hubble pens Hubble's Law, which describes the rate of universal expansion.

1930: American amateur astronomer Clyde Tombaugh discovers Pluto.

1932: American physicist Carl Anderson discovers anti-matter.

1932: American radio engineer Karl Jansky discovers radio waves coming from space.

1939: Ham radio operator Grete Rober builds the first radio telescope in his backyard and maps radio waves coming from throughout the Milky Way.

1943: American astronomer Carl Seyfert discovers bright, violent, spiral galaxies that now bear his name.

1947: The 200-inch Hale Telescope, which for the next thirty years remains the world's largest, becomes operational at Palomar Observatory.

1950: Dutch astronomer Jan Oort suggests comets lie dormant in an "Oort cloud" that surrounds the solar system.

October 4, 1957: Soviets launch *Sputnik 1,* initiating the space race with the United States.

1958: National Aeronautics and Space Administration (NASA) created.

January 31, 1958: *Explorer 1,* the first U.S. satellite, is launched into orbit.

October 4, 1959: Soviet satellite *Luna 3* takes the first photographs of the far side of the moon.

1960: United States launches the *Echo* communications satellite.

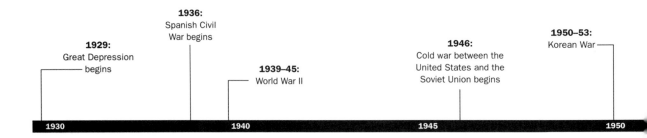

1929:
Great Depression
begins

1936:
Spanish Civil
War begins

1939–45:
World War II

1946:
Cold war between the
United States and the
Soviet Union begins

1950–53:
Korean War

1930   1940   1945   1950

April 12, 1961: Soviet pilot Yuri Gagarin orbits Earth aboard *Vostok 1*, becoming the first human in space.

May 5, 1961: Alan Shepard takes a sub-orbital flight aboard *Mercury 3*, becoming the first American in space.

August 27, 1962: *Mariner 2* is launched into orbit, becoming the first interplanetary space probe.

1963: Construction completed on the world's largest radio telescope, at Arecibo Observatory in Puerto Rico.

June 16, 1963: Soviet cosmonaut Valentina Tereshkova rides aboard *Vostok 6*, becoming the first woman in space.

1967: Irish graduate student Jocelyn Bell Burnell discovers pulsars.

1967: Mauna Kea Observatory, which has the world's largest concentration of optical telescopes, opens in Hawaii.

July 20, 1969: American astronauts Neil Armstrong and Buzz Aldrin become the first humans to walk on the moon.

April 13, 1970: Explosion occurs aboard *Apollo 13* when it is over halfway to the moon.

December 15, 1970: Soviet probe *Venera 7* arrives at Venus, making the first-ever successful landing on another planet.

April 19, 1971: Soviet Union launches *Salyut 1*, the world's first space station.

December 2, 1971: Soviet probe *Mars 3* makes first-ever successful landing on Mars.

March 3, 1972: U.S. probe *Pioneer 10* is launched.

December 7, 1972: Launch of *Apollo 17*, the final mission landing humans on the moon.

April 5, 1973: U.S. probe *Pioneer 11* is launched.

May 26, 1973: *Skylab*, the first and only U.S. space station, is launched.

December 4, 1973: U.S. probe *Pioneer 10* flies by Jupiter.

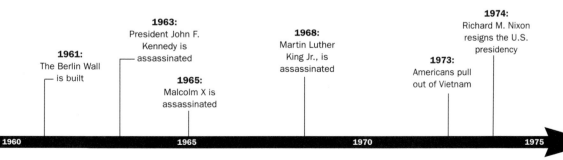

1961: The Berlin Wall is built

1963: President John F. Kennedy is assassinated

1965: Malcolm X is assassinated

1968: Martin Luther King Jr., is assassinated

1973: Americans pull out of Vietnam

1974: Richard M. Nixon resigns the U.S. presidency

1960   1965   1970   1975

1975: European Space Agency founded.

July 15, 1975: *Apollo 18* docks with *Soyuz 19*; Americans and Soviets unite for historic "handshake in space."

August 20, 1977: U.S. probe *Voyager 2* launched.

September 5, 1977: U.S. probe *Voyager 1* is launched.

June 22, 1978: American astronomer James W. Christy discovers Pluto's moon, Charon.

September 1, 1979: *Pioneer 11* becomes the first spacecraft to reach Saturn.

December 6, 1979: American astronomer Alan Guth develops the "inflationary theory" describing the rapid inflation of the universe immediately following the big bang.

1980: The Very Large Array, an interferometer consisting of 27 radio telescopes, becomes operational in Socorro, New Mexico.

April 12, 1981: First launch of a space shuttle: *Columbia.*

June 13, 1983: *Pioneer 10* becomes the first spacecraft to leave the solar system.

June 18, 1983: Sally Ride becomes the first U.S. woman in space, aboard the space shuttle *Challenger.*

August 30, 1983: Guion Bluford becomes the first African American in space, aboard *Challenger.*

November 28, 1983: First Spacelab launched.

January 24, 1986: *Voyager 2* flies by Uranus.

January 28, 1986: Space shuttle *Challenger* explodes just after lift-off, killing all seven crew members.

February 20, 1986: Launch of the Russian space station *Mir,* currently the only space station in operation.

March 13, 1986: First crew arrives at *Mir.*

March 14, 1986: European probe *Giotto* flies in to the nucleus of Halley's comet.

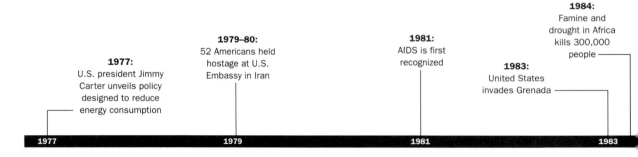

1977:
U.S. president Jimmy Carter unveils policy designed to reduce energy consumption

1979–80:
52 Americans held hostage at U.S. Embassy in Iran

1981:
AIDS is first recognized

1983:
United States invades Grenada

1984:
Famine and drought in Africa kills 300,000 people

1977   1979   1981   1983

May 4, 1989: U.S. Venus probe *Magellan* is launched.

August 24, 1989: *Voyager 2* flies past Neptune and heads out of the solar system.

October 18, 1989: U.S. Jupiter probe *Galileo* is launched.

November 18, 1989: NASA launches the *Cosmic Background Explorer.*

April 24, 1990: The Hubble Space Telescope is deployed from the space shuttle *Discovery.*

August 10, 1990: *Magellan* arrives at Venus and begins mapping surface.

April 5, 1991: Compton Gamma Ray Observatory is launched by NASA to produce an all-sky map of cosmic gamma-ray emissions.

September 12, 1992: Mae Jemison becomes first African American woman in space, aboard the space shuttle *Endeavour.*

December 1993: Astronauts aboard *Endeavour* repair the flawed Hubble Space Telescope.

December 7, 1995: *Galileo* reaches Jupiter and drops a mini-probe to the surface.

December 12, 1995: Solar and Heliospheric Observatory is launched to study the sun's internal structure.

January 1996: American astronomers Geoffrey Marcy and Paul Butler discover two new planets orbiting stars in the Big Dipper and Virgo constellations.

January 16, 1996: A team of astronomers led by David Bennett of the Lawrence Livermore National Laboratory announce their discovery that white dwarfs make up at least half of all dark matter.

March 25, 1996: Comet Hyakutake reaches its closest point to Earth in about 20,000 years.

August 7, 1996: Discovery of possible evidence of primitive Martian life, found in a 4.5-billion-year-old meteorite.

September 26, 1996: Astronaut Shannon Lucid returns to Earth after 188 days in space aboard *Mir.*

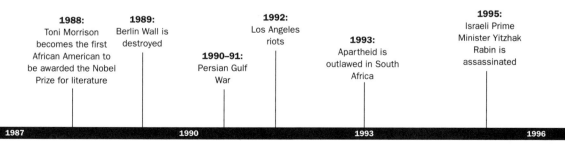

1988:
Toni Morrison becomes the first African American to be awarded the Nobel Prize for literature

1989:
Berlin Wall is destroyed

1990–91:
Persian Gulf War

1992:
Los Angeles riots

1993:
Apartheid is outlawed in South Africa

1995:
Israeli Prime Minister Yitzhak Rabin is assassinated

1987   1990   1993   1996

Words to Know

A

Aberration of light: the apparent movement of stars due to Earth's motion forward into starlight.

Absolute magnitude: a star's brightness at a constant distance from Earth.

Absolute zero: the lowest possible temperature at which matter can exist; equal to -259 degrees Fahrenheit and -273 degrees Celsius.

Absorption lines: dark lines that appear in the **spectrum** of an object, indicating **wavelength**s at which light is absorbed.

Adaptive optics: a system that makes minute adjustments to the shape of a **reflector telescope**'s primary mirror to correct distortions that result from disturbances in the atmosphere.

Aphelion: the point along an orbit of a planet or **comet** that is farthest from the sun.

Apollo objects: the group of **asteroid**s that cross Earth's orbit.

Armillary sphere: an instrument made up of spheres and rings used to observe the stars.

Asteroid: a relatively small, rocky chunk of matter that orbits the sun.

Astrolabe: a primitive star map historically used for timekeeping, navigation, and surveying.

Astrology: the study of the supposed effect of celestial objects on the course of human affairs.

Astrometric binary star: a **binary star** system in which only one star can be seen, but its wobble implies that there is another star in orbit around it.

Astronomical unit: a standard measure of distance to celestial objects, equal to the average distance from Earth to the sun (87 million miles).

Astrophysics: the study of the physical properties and evolution of celestial bodies, particularly concerning the production and use of energy in stars and **galaxies.**

Aurora: a bright, colorful display of light in the night sky, better known as the Northern and Southern lights, that results when charged particles from the sun enter Earth's atmosphere.

B

Big bang theory: the theory that explains the beginning of the universe as a tremendous explosion from a single point that occurred fifteen to twenty billion years ago.

Big crunch theory: the catastrophic prediction that there will come a point, very far in the future, in which matter will reverse direction and crunch back into the single point from which it began.

Binary star: a double star system in which two stars orbit one another around a central point of **gravity.**

Black dwarf: the cooling remnants of a **white dwarf** star that has ceased to glow.

Black hole: the remains of a massive star that has burned out its nuclear fuel and collapsed under tremendous gravitational force into a single point of infinite **mass** and **gravity.**

Blue-shift: the shift of **wavelength**s of an object's light **spectrum** into the blue (shorter wavelength) end of the range of visible light—an indication that the object is approaching the observer.

Bode's Law: the simple yet flawed mathematical formula published by eighteenth-century German astronomer Johann Elert Bode dictating the distances of planets from the sun.

Bolometer: an instrument that can detect **electromagnetic radiation** entering Earth's atmosphere, used in particular to measure **radiation** and **microwave**s from the sun and stars.

Brown dwarf: a small, cool, dark ball of matter that never completes the process of becoming a star.

C

Calendar: any system for organizing time into days, months, and years.

Celestial sphere: the sky, or imaginary sphere, that surrounds Earth and provides a visual surface on which we can plot celestial objects and chart their apparent movement due to Earth's rotation.

Cepheid variable: a pulsating yellow **supergiant** star that can be used to measure distance in space.

Chandrasekhar's limit: the theory that any star with a **mass** greater than one and one-half times that of the sun will be crushed at the end of its lifetime by its own **gravity,** so that it will become either a **neutron star** or a **black hole.** A star below this limit will end up as a **white dwarf** star.

Charged coupling device (CCD): a light-capturing device placed at the end of a telescope that is the modern, computerized version of old photographic plates.

Chromosphere: the glowing layer of gas that makes up the middle atmospheric layer of the sun.

Cold war: the period of tense relations, from 1945–1990, between the former **Soviet Union** (and its Eastern allies) and the United States (and its Western European allies).

Comet: a small body of rocky material, dust, and ice in orbit around the sun.

Command module: the section of the Apollo spacecraft in which astronauts traveled.

Constellation: one of eighty-eight groups of stars in the sky named for mythological beings. Each constellation is bordered by an imaginary line running north-south and east-west across the **celestial sphere,** so that every point in the sky belongs to one constellation or another.

Convection: the process by which heat is transferred from the core of the sun toward the surface via slow-moving gas currents.

Copernican model. *See* **Heliocentric model**

Corona: the outermost atmospheric layer of the sun.

Coronagraph: a modified telescope that uses a black disc to block out most of the sunlight entering its chamber, leaving only the image of the sun's **corona.**

Cosmic dust: solid, microscopic particles found in the **interstellar medium.**

Cosmic rays: invisible, high-energy particles that constantly bombard Earth from all directions. Most are high-speed protons (hydrogen atoms that have lost a electron) although they also include the nuclei of all known elements.

Cosmic string: a giant vibrating strand with tremendous gravitational pull containing trapped **spacetime** from a much earlier period.

Cosmology: the study of the origin, evolution, and structure of the universe.

Cosmonaut: a Russian astronaut.

Cosmos: the universe regarded as an orderly system.

Coudé telescope: a modified **reflector telescope** that has the eyepiece angled so that it keeps the image of an object in view, even as that object moves across the sky.

D

Dark matter: virtually undetectable matter that is thought to account for 90 percent of the **mass** in the universe and acts as the "cosmic glue" that holds together **galaxies** and clusters of galaxies.

Diffraction: deflection of a beam of light.

Dwarf galaxy: an unusually small, faint **galaxy.**

E

Earth's meridian: an imaginary circle on the surface of Earth passing through the North and South poles.

Eclipsing binary star: a **binary star** system in which the orbital plane is nearly edgewise to our line of sight, meaning that each star is eclipsed (partially or totally hidden) by the other as they revolve around a common point of **gravity.**

Electromagnetic radiation: radiation that transmits energy through the interaction of electricity and **magnetism.**

Electromagnetic spectrum: the complete array of **electromagnetic radiation,** including **radio waves** (at the longest-**wavelength** end), **infrared radiation,** visible light, **ultraviolet radiation, X-ray**s, and **gamma ray**s (at the shortest-wavelength end).

Electroscope: an instrument used to detect electrons.

Elliptical galaxy: the most common type of **galaxy** in the universe; elliptical galaxies vary in shape from circles to narrow, elongated ellipses (ovals) and may be spherical or flat.

Emission lines: bright lines that appear in the **spectrum** of an object, indicating **wavelength**s at which light is emitted.

Epicycle: a small secondary orbit erroneously added to the planetary orbits by pre-Copernican astronomers to account for periods in which the planets appeared to move backwards with respect to Earth.

Equinoxes: the days marking the start of spring and fall and the only two days of the year in which day and night are of equal length.

Event horizon: the surface of a collapsed massive star or **black hole.**

Exosphere: the outer layer of Earth's atmosphere, starting about 250 miles above ground, in which molecules of gas break down into atoms and become ionized (electrically charged) by the sun's rays (also called the "ionosphere").

Extravehicular activity (EVA): an activity performed in space by an astronaut attached to the outside of a spacecraft (also called "space walk").

F

Faculae: bright hydrogen clouds often found near **sunspot**s on the sun's surface.

Flare: a temporary bright spot that explodes on the sun's surface.

G

Galaxy: a huge region of space that contains hundreds of billions of stars, **nebulae** (clouds), gas, dust, empty space, and possibly a **black hole.**

Gamma ray: short-**wavelength,** high-energy **radiation** formed either by the decay of radioactive elements or by nuclear reactions.

Gamma ray astronomy: the study of objects in space by observing the **gamma rays** they emit.

General theory of relativity: the theory in which Albert Einstein demonstrated that **gravity** is the result of curved **spacetime.**

Geocentric model: the flawed theory of the **solar system** placing Earth at the center, with the sun, moon, and planets revolving around it.

Geodesy: the study of Earth's external shape, internal construction, and gravitational field.

Geostationary orbit: a special kind of geosynchronous orbit, in which a satellite travels in the same plane as Earth's equator. A geostationary satellite remains more or less stationary over the same point on Earth.

Geosynchronous orbit: an orbit around Earth that takes twenty-four hours to complete.

Globular cluster: a tight grouping of stars found near the edges of the Milky Way.

Globules: small dark patches of concentrated particles found in the **interstellar medium.**

Granules: Earth-sized cells covering the sun's surface that transfer hot gas from the sun's interior to its outer atmospheric layers.

Gravity: the force of attraction between objects, the strength of which depends on the **mass** of each object and the distance between them.

Gravity assist: a technique used by a spacecraft journeying to distant planets, in which it uses the gravitational field of one planet to propel it toward another, eliminating the need for additional **rocket** motors.

Greenhouse effect: the warming of an environment that occurs when **infrared radiation** enters the atmosphere and becomes trapped inside.

Gyroscope: a navigational instrument consisting of a wheel that spins around a rod through its center. The wheel continues spinning in the same direction, even when the direction of the instrument is changed.

H

Heliocentric model: the theory that the sun is at the center of the **solar system** with the planets revolving around it.

Helioseismology: the study of the sun's interior structure and dynamics, determined by measuring the vibrations of sound waves deep within the sun's core.

Heliosphere: the vast region permeated by charged particles flowing out from the sun that surrounds the sun and extends throughout the **solar system.**

Heliostat: a flat, rotating mirror that collects light at the top of a solar telescope tower.

Heliotrope: an instrument that reflects sunlight over great distances to mark the positions of participants in a land survey.

Hertzsprung-Russell diagram: the graph showing the relationship between the color, brightness, and temperature of stars. It places **absolute magnitude** (or brightness) on the vertical axis and color (or temperature) on the horizontal axis.

Homogeneity: uniformity; the state of being the same everywhere.

Hubble's Law: the distance-to-speed relationship showing that the more distant a **galaxy,** the faster it is receding; it describes the expansion of the universe.

I

Inertia: the property of matter that requires a force to act on it to change its state of motion.

Inflationary theory: the theory that the universe underwent a period of rapid expansion immediately following the **big bang.**

Infrared astronomy: the study of objects in space by the **infrared radiation** they emit.

Infrared radiation: electromagnetic radiation of a **wavelength** shorter than **radio wave**s but longer than visible light that takes the form of heat.

Interferometry: the process of splitting a beam of light (or other form of **electromagnetic radiation**) in two, bouncing it off a series of mirrors, and examining its pattern when it comes back together.

Interstellar medium: the space between the stars, consisting mainly of empty space with a very small concentration of gas atoms and tiny solid particles.

Ionosphere. *See* **Exosphere**

K

Kirkwood gaps: areas separating distinct asteroid belts that lie between the orbits of Mars and Jupiter.

Kuiper belt: the proposed cometary reservoir, located just beyond the edge of the orbit of Pluto, containing an estimated ten million to one billion inactive **comet**s.

L

Latitude: an imaginary line circling Earth, parallel to the equator, that tells one's north-south position on the globe.

Launch vehicle: a **rocket** system used to launch satellites and piloted spacecraft into space.

Light-year: the distance light travels in one year, about 5.9 trillion miles.

Longitude: an imaginary line circling Earth, perpendicular to the equator, that tells one's east-west position on the globe.

Lunar eclipse: the complete or partial blocking of the moon by Earth's shadow that occurs when Earth passes between the sun and moon.

Lunar module: the section of Apollo spacecraft that detached to land on the moon.

M

Magnetic axis: the imaginary line connecting Earth's, and other planet's, magnetic poles.

Magnetic field: the area of a planet affected by magnetic force.

Magnetism: the property of a body to produce an electrical current around itself.

Magnetosphere: the region around a planet occupied by its magnetic field.

Mass: the measure of the total amount of matter in an object.

Mass-luminosity law: the law describing the relationship between a star's **mass** and brightness; the more massive a star, the greater the interior pressure and temperature, and therefore the greater the brightness.

Mesosphere: the middle layer of Earth's atmosphere, existing between 40 and 50 miles above ground.

Meteor: also known as a "shooting star," a meteor is a small particle of dust or a small rock left behind by a **comet**'s tail.

Meteor shower: periods of increased **meteor** activity from a common point in the sky, caused by Earth's passage through the orbit of a **comet** or the debris left behind by a comet.

Meteorite: a large chunk of rock, metal, or rock-and-metal that breaks off an **asteroid** or a **comet** and survives passage through Earth's atmosphere to hit the ground.

Meteoroid: the term that collectively describes all forms of meteoric material, including **meteor**s and **meteorite**s.

Micrometer: a device used to measure minute distances or angles.

Microwave: a subset of **radio waves**, those with the shortest **wavelength**s (less than three feet across).

Milky Way: our home **galaxy,** which contains the sun and billions of other stars, possibly one or more **black hole**s, star clusters, planets, glowing **nebulae**, dust, and empty space. It is approximately 100,000 light-years in diameter and 2,000 light-years thick.

Molecular cloud: a cool area in the **interstellar medium** in which molecules are formed.

N

Nebula: a cloud of interstellar gas and dust.

Neutrino: a high-energy subatomic particle with no **mass,** or such a small mass as to be undetectable, and no electrical charge.

Neutron star: the extremely dense, compact, neutron-filled remains of a star following a **supernova.**

Nova: a sudden, intense, temporary brightening of a star.

Nuclear fusion: the merging of two hydrogen nuclei into one helium nucleus, accompanied by a tremendous release of energy.

Nutation: the slight shift in the angle of tilt of Earth's axis due to the gravitational tug of the moon as it orbits Earth.

O

Oort cloud: a region of space beyond the **solar system,** about one light-year from the sun, theoretically containing trillions of inactive **comets.**

Open cluster: a loose grouping of stars found toward the center of the **Milky Way.**

Optical interferometer: a series of two or more optical telescopes that are linked together electronically, with a viewing power far greater than the sum of the individual telescopes.

Ozone layer: the layer of Earth's atmosphere, between 25 and 40 miles above ground, that filters out the sun's harmful rays.

P

Parallax: the observed change of a star's position due to Earth's motion around the sun.

Payload: the passengers, instruments, or equipment carried by a spacecraft.

Penumbra: the lighter region surrounding the dark, central part of the moon's shadow that sweeps across Earth during a **solar eclipse.**

Perihelion: the point along an orbit (of a planet or **comet**) that's closest to the sun.

Period-luminosity curve: the graph that enables one to find the distance to a **cepheid variable.** It places **absolute magnitude** (brightness) on the vertical axis and period (days to complete a cycle) on the horizontal axis.

Photometry: the measurement of the properties of a light source. In astronomy, it pertains to the measurement of the brightness and colors of stars that, in turn, are indicators of stellar surface temperature.

Photosphere: the few-hundred-mile thick innermost layer of solar atmosphere that constitutes the sun's surface.

Planetesimals: ancient chunks of matter that originated with the formation of the **solar system** but never came together to form a planet.

Plasma: a substance made of ions (electrically charged atoms) and electrons that exists at extremely hot temperatures.

Plasma theory: the theory that the universe was born out of electrical and magnetic phenomena involving **plasma.**

Probe. *See* **Space probe**

Prominence: a high-density cloud of gas projecting outward from the sun's surface.

Propellant: an energy source for **rocket**s that consists of fuel and an oxidizer. Types of fuel include alcohol, kerosene, liquid hydrogen, and hydrazine. The oxidizer may be nitrogen tetroxide or liquid oxygen.

Proper motion: the apparent motion of a star resulting from both its actual movement in space and the shift in its position relative to Earth.

Protoplanet: the earliest form of a planet, plus its moons, formed by the combination of **planetesimals.**

Ptolemaic model. *See* **Geocentric model**

Pulsar: a rapidly spinning, blinking **neutron star.**

Q

Quadrant: an ancient instrument used for measuring the positions of stars.

Quantum mechanics: the study of the behavior of subatomic particles.

Quasars: extremely bright, star-like sources of **radio wave**s that are the oldest known objects in the universe.

R

Radiation: energy emitted in the form of waves or particles.

Radio astronomy: the study of objects in space by observing the **radio waves** they emit.

Radio interferometer: a system of multiple **radio telescope**s linked electronically that act as a single telescope with a diameter equal to the area separating them. Powerful computers combine their information and create detailed pictures of objects in space.

Radio telescope: an instrument consisting of a large concave dish with an antenna at the center, tuned to a certain **wavelength**. It receives and processes **radio wave**s and produces a picture of the source emitting the radio waves.

Radio wave: the longest form of **electromagnetic radiation,** measuring up to six miles from peak to peak.

Red dwarf: a star that is 10 to 70 percent smaller in mass and much cooler than the sun.

Red giant: the stage in which an average-sized star (like our sun) spends the final 10 percent of its lifetime. Its surface temperature drops and its diameter expands to ten to one thousand times that of the sun.

Red-shift: the shift of an object's light **spectrum** toward the red-end of the visible light range—an indication that the object is moving away from the observer.

Reflector telescope: a telescope that uses mirrors to bring light rays into focus. It works by directing light from an opening at one end of a tube to a mirror at the far end. The light is then reflected back to a smaller mirror and directed to an eyepiece on the side of the tube.

Refractor telescope: the simplest type of telescope; light enters through one end of a tube and passes through a glass lens, which bends the light rays and brings them into focus. The light then strikes an eyepiece, which acts as a magnifying glass.

Retrograde motion: the perceived backward motion of the outer planets (those farther from the sun than Earth) as Earth overtakes them along their respective orbits around the sun.

Rocket: a tube-like device containing explosive material which, on being ignited, releases gases that propel the device through the air.

S

Schmidt telescope: a combined refractor-reflector telescope that has a specially shaped thin glass lens at one end of a tube and a mirror at the other.

Service module: the section of Apollo spacecraft in which supplies and equipment are carried.

Sextant: an early navigational instrument used to measure the angle from the horizon to a celestial body.

Seyfert galaxy: a fast-moving, spiral-shaped **galaxy** characterized by an exceptionally bright nucleus.

Singularity: the single point at which pressure and density are infinite.

Solar eclipse: the complete or partial blocking of the sun that occurs when the moon's orbit takes it in front of Earth.

Solar system: the sun plus all its orbiting bodies, including the planets, moons, **comet**s, **asteroid**s, **meteoroid**s, and particles of dust and debris.

Solar telescope: a modified reflecting or refracting telescope capable of directly observing the sun.

Solar wind: electrically charged subatomic particles that flow out from the sun.

Solstices: the two days each year when the sun is at its highest and its lowest points in the sky.

Soviet Union: the former country in Northern Asia and Eastern Europe that in 1991 broke up into the independent states of Armenia, Azerbaijan, Belarus, Estonia, Georgia, Kazakhstan, Kyrgyzstan, Latvia, Lithuania, Moldova, Russia, Tajikistan, Turkmenistan, Ukraine, and Uzbekistan.

Space age: the modern historical period beginning with the launch of *Sputnik 1* in 1957 and continuing to the present, characterized by space travel and exploration.

Space probe: an unpiloted spacecraft that leaves Earth's orbit to explore the moon, other bodies, or outer space.

Space race: the twenty-year-long contest, from the mid-1950s to the mid-1970s, for superiority in space travel and exploration, between the United States and the **Soviet Union.**

Space shuttle: a reusable winged space plane that transports astronauts and equipment into space and back.

Space station: an orbiting spacecraft designed to sustain humans for periods of up to several months.

Space telescope: a telescope placed on board a satellite that can make observations free from interference of Earth's atmosphere.

Space walk. *See* **Extravehicular activity (EVA)**

Spacetime: a four-dimensional construct that unites the three dimensions of space (length, width, and height) and a fourth dimension, time.

Special theory of relativity: Albert Einstein's theory—applicable to situations in which the rate of motion is constant—that space and time are not fixed, but change depending on how fast and in what direction the observer is moving.

Spectrograph: an instrument that photographs light **spectra** of celestial objects, making it possible to learn their temperature and chemical composition.

Spectrohelioscope: a combined telescope and **spectroscope** that breaks down sunlight into a colorful display of the sun's chemical components.

Spectroscope: an instrument used to break down **radiation** into its component **wavelength**s.

Spectroscopic binary star: a **binary star** system that appears as one star that produces two different light **spectra.**

Spectroscopy: the process of separating the light of an object (generally, a star) into its component colors so that the various elements present within that object can be identified.

Spectra. *See* **Spectrum**

Spectrum: the range of individual **wavelength**s of **radiation** produced when light is broken down by the process of **spectroscopy.**

Speed of light: the speed at which light travels in a vacuum—186,282.397 miles per second.

Spicules: narrow gas jets that characterize the outer edge of the sun's **chromosphere.**

Spiral galaxy: a **galaxy** with old stars at the center, surrounded by a band of star clusters and an invisible cloud of **dark matter,** with arms spiraling out like a pinwheel.

Steady-state theory: the theory of the origin of the universe stating that all matter in the universe has been created continuously, at a constant rate throughout time.

Stellar nurseries: areas within glowing clouds of gas and dust where new stars are in formation.

Stellar spectrophotometry: the study of the intensity of a particular spectral line or series of spectral lines in a star's absorption or emission **spectrum.**

Stratosphere: the second-lowest layer of Earth's atmosphere, from about 9 to 40 miles above ground.

Sundial: a primitive instrument used to keep time by following the sun's passage across the sky.

Sunspot: a cool area of magnetic disturbance that forms a dark blemish on the surface of the sun.

Supergiant: the largest and brightest type of star, which has over fifteen times the **mass** of the sun and shines over one million times more brightly than the sun.

Supernova: the explosion of a massive star at the end of its lifetime, causing it to shine more brightly than the rest of the stars in the **galaxy** put together.

T

Thermosphere: the layer of Earth's atmosphere, between 50 and 200 miles above ground, in which temperatures reach 1800 degrees Fahrenheit.

Transit: the passage of an inner planet (Mercury or Venus) between the sun and Earth.

Tropical year: the time it takes Earth to complete an orbit around the sun.

Troposphere: the lowest layer of Earth's atmosphere, in which weather patterns are formed.

U

Ultraviolet radiation: electromagnetic radiation of a **wavelength** just shorter than the violet (shortest wavelength) end of visible light **spectrum.**

Umbra: the dark, central part of the moon's shadow that sweeps across Earth during a **solar eclipse.**

V

Van Allen belts: doughnut-shaped regions of charged particles encircling Earth.

Variable star: a star that varies in brightness over periods of time ranging from hours to years.

Visual binary star: a **binary star** system in which each star can be seen distinctly.

W

Wavelength: the distance between one peak of a wave of light, heat, or energy and the next corresponding peak.

White dwarf: the cooling, shrunken core remaining after a medium-sized star ceases to burn.

X

X-ray: electromagnetic radiation of a **wavelength** shorter than **ultraviolet radiation** but longer than **gamma ray**s that can penetrate solids and produce an electrical charge in gases.

Picture Credits

The photographs and illustrations appearing in *Astronomy & Space: From the Big Bang to the Big Crunch* were received from the following sources:

On the cover: Hans Bethe (**AP/Wide World Photos. Reproduced by permission.**); Annie Jump Cannon (**UPI/Corbis-Bettmann. Reproduced by permission.**); Percival Lowell (**Lowell Observatory. Reproduced by permission.**); *Atlantis* space shuttle (**Corbis-Bettmann. Reproduced by permission.**).

Corbis-Bettmann. Reproduced by permission.: pp. 1, 18, 27, 28, 32, 34, 39, 41, 43, 48, 52, 69, 74, 80, 84, 111, 142, 154, 157, 178, 181, 215, 217, 262, 265, 295, 297, 309, 310, 325, 385, 413, 436, 459; **UPI/Corbis-Bettmann. Reproduced by permission.:** pp. 3, 30, 82, 91, 95, 139, 141, 162, 163, 168, 170, 186, 189, 243, 244, 251, 255, 284, 286, 301, 320, 330, 381, 392, 429, 508, 517, 533, 540, 547, 551, 559, 601, 610, 618, 658; **AP/Wide World Photos. Reproduced by permission.:** pp. 5, 24, 45, 54, 57, 93, 103, 129, 175, 176, 191, 202, 205, 208, 213, 269, 303, 322, 327, 352, 360, 408, 420, 424, 492, 497, 500, 505, 510, 519, 585, 588, 637, 645, 664, 669, 675, 677, 689, 697, 700, 704; **Frank Rossotto/Stocktrek Photo Agency. Reproduced by permission.:** pp. 37, 64, 88, 97, 126, 135, 148, 150, 173, 375, 383, 388, 405, 457, 488, 529, 570, 615, 625, 655, 672, 684, 691; **Mullard Radio Astronomy Laboratory/Science Photo Library, National Audubon Society/Photo Researchers, Inc. Reproduced by permission.:** p. 62; **Courtesy of the Library of Congress:** pp. 68, 514, 648; **Archive Photos. Reproduced by permission.:** pp. 71, 166, 258, 307, 315, 343, 394, 398, 544, 634; **Chris Butler/Science Photo Library, National Audubon Society/Photo Researchers, Inc. Reproduced**

by permission.: pp. 77, 502; **Frank Rossotto. Reproduced by permission.**: pp. 101, 346, 350, 354; **Stav Birnbaum Collection/Corbis-Bettmann. Reproduced by permission.**: p. 109; **Tommaso Guicciardini/INFN/Science Photo Library, National Audubon Society/Photo Researchers, Inc. Reproduced by permission.**: pp. 116, 410; **Dr. Charles Alcock, Macho Collaboration/Science Photo Library, National Audubon Society/Photo Researchers, Inc. Reproduced by permission.**: p. 124; **Illustrations reprinted by permission of Robert L. Wolke**: p. 146; **SETI Institute/Science Photo Library, National Audubon Society/Photo Researchers, Inc. Reproduced by permission.**: p. 158; **Courtesy of U.S. National Aeronautics and Space Administration (NASA)**: p. 194; **Hans & Cassidy. Courtesy of Gale Research.**: pp. 196, 537; **Mehau Kulyk/Science Photo Library, National Audubon Society/Photo Researchers, Inc. Reproduced by permission.**: p. 219; **Science Photo Library, National Audubon Society/Photo Researchers, Inc. Reproduced by permission.**: pp. 260, 552, 567; **© NASA, National Audubon Society Collection/Photo Researchers, Inc. Reproduced with permission.**: p. 275; **JLM Visuals. Reproduced by permission.**: pp. 289, 640, 641; **Courtesy of National Optical Astronomy Observatories**: p. 299; **Royal Observatory, Edinburgh/Science Photo Library, National Audubon Society/Photo Researchers, Inc. Reproduced by permission.**: p. 312; **Lowell Observatory. Reproduced by permission.**: p. 332; **Sovfoto/Eastfoto. Reproduced by permission.**: p. 339; **Reuters/Corbis-Bettmann. Reproduced by permission.**: p. 341; **The Bettmann Archive. Reproduced by permission.**: pp. 363, 416; **UPI/Bettmann. Reproduced by permission.**: pp. 367, 370, 378, 438, 441, 462, 522, 549, 599, 613, 616, 630, 662, 681; **NASA. Reproduced with permission.**: pp. 454, 581; **Julian Baum/Science Photo Library, National Audubon Society/Photo Researchers, Inc. Reproduced by permission.**: pp. 564, 628; **Reuters/Bettmann. Reproduced by permission.**: p. 577; **Finley Holiday Film/U.S. National Aeronautics and Space Administration. Reproduced by permission.**: p. 595; **David A. Hardy/Science Photo Library, National Audubon Society/Photo Researchers, Inc. Reproduced by permission.**: p. 621; **Courtesy of the University of Wyoming**: p. 693.

Adams, John Couch (1819–1892)

English astronomer

For John Couch Adams astronomy was a lifelong pursuit. Even as a teenager he constructed his own sundial and plotted solar altitudes. He is best known for his discovery of the planet Neptune.

Adams was born near Launceston, England, into a poor farming family. His early knowledge of astronomy was self-taught. In 1839, he entered Cambridge University on a scholarship. In addition to his studies, he worked as a tutor and sent his earnings home to his family.

John Couch Adams.

Adams spent all of his free time studying the irregular orbit of Uranus. Since William Herschel's discovery of Uranus in 1781, astronomers had wondered if that planet's fluctuating orbit was caused by the presence of another planet's gravitational field.

By 1843, the year that Adams graduated first in his class in mathematics, he had completed his calculations of the location of the unknown planet. Adams' data indicated that the other planet was about the same size as Uranus, orbited in the same plane as Uranus, and was located about thirty-nine **astronomical unit**s from the sun. (An astronomical unit is thirty-nine times the distance of the Earth to the sun.)

In 1845, Adams presented his findings to England's highest authority on such matters, George Airy, the Astronomer Royal. Airy paid little attention to Adams' work. Some authorities think that Airy ignored Adam's discovery because he was working on his own theory to explain Uranus' orbit. Airy's theory on the idea that **gravity** no longer had any effect in space beyond Saturn's orbit. Another possible explanation for Airy's lack of interest was that Adams had no social status.

One year later, Airy was forced to reconsider. A French astronomer named Urbain Jean Joseph Leverrier announced that he had determined the position of the new planet. Leverrier's calculations placed the planet at almost the exact location as had Adams. Scientists at the Cambridge Observatory and the Berlin Observatory confirmed the findings of both men.

Leverrier was initially given credit for discovering the planet, which he named Neptune. However, John Herschel, a scientist who knew about Adam's work, soon published an article giving credit to Adams. It seemed as though the only two members of the scientific community who stayed out of the debate as to who deserved the credit were Adams and Leverrier, who had become fast friends.

In 1851, Adams was named president of the Royal Astronomical Society, and in 1858 he became a professor of astronomy at Cambridge University. Adams spent much of his later years studying the orbital motion of the Leonid's, the swarm of meteors that are visible in the sky for two nights each November. Adams died at Cambridge in 1892.

See also **Bode, Johann Elert** and **Leverrier, Urbain**

Advanced X-ray Astrophysics Facility

The latest in a series of satellites to study **X-ray** sources in space is scheduled for launch by the year 2000. Originally set to be launched in the late 1980s, the Advanced X-ray Astrophysics Facility (AXAF) has been the victim of drastic budget cuts within the National Aeronautics and Space Administration (NASA). In addition to suffering from across-the-board reductions, the AXAF project has had funds redirected for the repair of the originally flawed Hubble Space Telescope. Many astronomers are very much disappointed that AXAF is not yet operational.

If and when AXAF gets off the ground, it will be by far the most powerful tool for detecting and analyzing X-rays in space. X-rays are a type of **electromagnetic radiation** with wavelengths much shorter than that of visible light. When examining the sky through specialized instruments that detect X-rays, scientists get a much different picture than they do from any other type of radiation. Some objects that give off X-rays are **galaxies, quasar**s, **pulsar**s, and **black hole**s.

The Earth's atmosphere filters out most X-rays. This fact is fortunate for humans and other life on Earth, since a large dose of X-rays would be deadly. On the other hand, the atmospheric filter makes it difficult for scientists to observe the X-ray sky. Radiation from the shortest-wavelength end of the X-ray range, called hard X-rays, can be detected at high altitudes such as heights that can be reached in a hot-air balloon. The only way to see longer X-rays, called soft X-rays, however, is traveling beyond the Earth's atmosphere and using special telescopes placed on satellites.

Advanced X-ray Astrophysics Facility

Artist's depiction of the X-ray Astrophysics Facility, probing the X-ray portion of the ***electromagnetic spectrum*** *and gathering information on such mysterious items as quasars,* ***neutron stars, and black holes.***

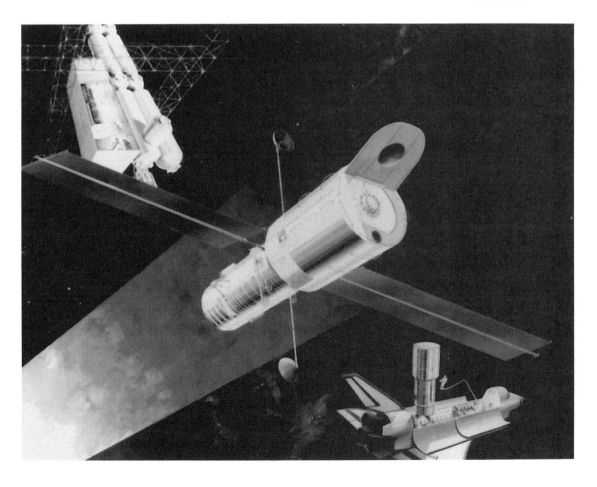

A series of X-ray telescopes had been deployed on satellites beginning in 1970. The first of these telescopes, *Uhuru,* produced a detailed map of the X-ray sky. Then in 1977, the first High Energy Astrophysical Observatory (HEAO) was launched. During its year and a half in operation, it provided constant monitoring of X-ray sources, such as individual stars, entire galaxies, and pulsars. The second HEAO, also known as the Einstein Observatory, operated from November 1978 to April 1981. It contained an extremely high resolution X-ray telescope, which found that X-rays were coming from nearly every star. The Einstein Observatory was followed by the 1990 launch of ROSAT, an international X-ray satellite that continues to make general observations of the **cosmos,** as well as detailed studies of individual objects.

AXAF promises to be one hundred times more sensitive than its predecessor, the Einstein. Plans for AXAF include the construction of a complete X-ray diagram of the sky, the study of X-rays in the sun's **corona,** and the search for quasars. The satellite's equipment should be strong enough to identify the approximately three hundred individual stars in the Pleiades cluster, as well as many stars in the nearby galaxies called the Large and Small Magellanic Clouds.

One of AXAF's most important missions will be to penetrate the dust that occurs everywhere throughout the **Milky Way** and provide us with pictures of uncharted regions of our own galaxy. In addition, AXAF's designers claim it will be capable of detecting X-ray objects so distant as to shed light on the formation of the universe.

Once launched, AXAF is expected to operate for five-to-ten years before running out of fuel.

See also **High Energy Astrophysical Observatories** and **X-ray astronomy**

Aldrin, Buzz (1930–)

American astronaut

Opposite page:
Buzz Aldrin.

Edwin Aldrin was born in Montclair, New Jersey. As a child, his sister called him "Buzz," a nickname that has stayed with him to this day. Aldrin's mother, whose name, ironically, was Marion Moon, was the daughter of an Army chaplain. His father, Edwin Eugene Aldrin, was a

student of **rocket** pioneer Robert Goddard and one of the first flight pilots. Although Aldrin has led a life full of achievements, he is best known as the second man to walk on the moon.

Aldrin received his schooling at West Point Military Academy, graduating with honors in 1951. He then served in the Korean War as a fighter jet pilot, after which he entered a Ph.D. program at the Massachusetts Institute of Technology. There he wrote his graduate thesis on "Manned Space Rendezvous." The techniques Aldrin described have been used on various U.S. missions where two vessels linkup in space, including the 1975 docking of the U.S. *Apollo 18* spacecraft with the Russian *Soyuz 19*.

In 1963, Aldrin was selected by the National Aeronautics and Space Administration (NASA) to be among the third group of Apollo astronauts. His first space flight came three years later, as pilot of *Gemini 12*. During this four-day mission, Aldrin completed the first successful s**pace walks**, spending a total of five and one-half hours outside the craft in **extravehicular activity (EVA)**. In 1968, Aldrin served as backup **command module** pilot for the *Apollo 8* mission, the first piloted spacecraft to orbit the moon. As such, he was assigned the pre-flight task of reworking the operational procedures for the navigational system.

The *Apollo 11* Flight

It was only through a series of accidents, setbacks, and changes in schedule that Aldrin landed a prized position on board the first piloted spacecraft to land on the moon. On July 16, 1969, *Apollo 11* took off with Aldrin, Neil Armstrong, and Michael Collins on board. Four days later, Armstrong and Aldrin climbed into the **lunar module** and landed on the moon. Armstrong was first to set foot on lunar soil, followed by Aldrin.

The *Apollo 11* flight to the moon, viewed by the largest international television audience to that date, is considered by many to be the greatest achievement of the modern world. For his part on this mission Aldrin was presented with numerous awards, including the Presidential Medal of Freedom.

The *Apollo 11* flight was Aldrin's last spaceflight. Upon returning to Earth, he and the rest of the crew spent three weeks in isolation while scientists watched for signs of any strange microbes they may have picked up on the moon. After that, Aldrin embarked on a goodwill tour around the world. He then returned to NASA to work on early designs for the **space shuttle.**

In 1971, Aldrin resigned from NASA and returned to military service, this time to run the Test Pilot School at Edwards Air Force Base in

Return to Earth (1976)

Originally made for television, this drama is based on the autobiography of astronaut Edwin "Buzz" Aldrin. It tells about Aldrin's nervous breakdown following the historic *Apollo 11* lunar landing mission, his mid-life crisis, and his battle to overcome alcoholism.

California. The following year, however, he had a nervous breakdown and was forced to retire. Three years later, in his autobiography entitled *Return to Earth,* Aldrin described his mid-life crisis, including his problems with and recovery from alcoholism. Ever since that time he has been a public voice in the fight against substance abuse.

Aldrin's Later Life

For the last two decades, Aldrin has worked both in private industry and as a professor at the University of North Dakota. In 1989, he wrote a book about the Apollo program entitled *Men From Earth.* In his current travels and lectures, Aldrin encourages the continuation of piloted missions for space exploration.

On July 20, 1994, twenty-five years after his historic walk on the moon, Aldrin spoke before fellow astronauts, members of Congress, and space travel enthusiasts at a conference in Washington, D.C. "I believe a whole people must have the humility to nurture the Earth and the pride to go to Mars," said Aldrin. "Let us proclaim a resounding commitment to the continued human exploration of our **solar system,** a challenge that can bind together nations, inspire youth, advance science, and ultimately end our confinement to one vulnerable world."

See also **Apollo program**

Ancient Chinese astronomy

Some of the world's earliest astronomical observations were made by the Chinese. Perhaps as early as 1500 B.C., Chinese astronomers created the first rough charts of the heavens. Then in 613 B.C., they described the sighting of a **comet.** Within a few centuries Chinese astronomers were

A n c i e n t
C h i n e s e
a s t r o n o m y

keeping track of every eclipse, **sunspot, nova, meteor,** and other celestial phenomenon they observed.

One reason that we have such detailed records of ancient Chinese observations is that the Chinese language was developed very early. The first dictionary in the language dates back to A.D. 121. In addition, Chinese is one of the few languages in which pictographs were used as written characters that remain essentially unchanged to this day.

Ancient Chinese astronomers worked for the emperor, who was believed to have divine powers connecting him with the heavens. Their observations were used primarily for forecasting the fate of the emperor, his enemies, and the empire and for providing useful information about wars and harvests.

Thus, Chinese astronomers worked also as astrologers, making predictions based on the "omens" they viewed in the sky. Their dual role as astronomers and astrologers often meant that coming up with pleasing information was more important than making accurate observations, making some Chinese records from this period unreliable. Astronomers served the emperor in this way for over two thousand years, which restrained much of their potential for real scientific advancement.

Even so, Chinese astronomers still made numerous contributions to the field. For instance, they studied the question of the Earth's motion and created one of the first **calendars**. Another feat that distinguished the Chinese from other ancient astronomers was that they created a primitive map of the **celestial sphere.** On this map they placed stars in relation to the sun and the North Star. Chinese astronomers were also the first to observe the sun by looking through tinted crystal or jade.

Beyond that, however, ancient Chinese analysis of the skies had little in common with what we in the modern Western world consider "scientific." They associated celestial objects with various animal spirits and opposing forms of energy called yin and yang. Yin is male energy related to heat and the sun. Yang is female energy related to cold and the moon.

Around the second century B.C., the emperor hired large numbers of sky-watchers and put them to work in separate government departments called "astronomy" and "**astrology.**" These departments each had more in common with modern-day astrology than modern-day astronomy, and the differences between them were relatively insignificant. "Astronomers" were assigned to look for omens in the planets, sun, and other bodies beyond the Earth's atmosphere, as well as to be the official keepers of time.

"Astrologers" sought signs in the weather, such as the clouds, wind, and **aurora**e.

By the fourth century B.C., astronomers had produced a number of star charts, which depicted the sky as a hemisphere. This form of mapping is understandable, since we can only see half the sky at any one time. It took three hundred more years for Chinese astronomers to regard the heavens as an entire sphere, a sign that they were then aware of the Earth's own spherical shape, as well as of the Earth's rotation about its axis.

The Sung dynasty, which began in the year A.D. 960, was a period during which astronomical discoveries were greatly encouraged. Around this time the first astronomical clock was built. It was during this period also that mathematics was first introduced into Chinese astronomy.

Astronomer Shen Kua proposed a geometric model of planetary motion based on the **geocentric** (Earth-centered) **model** of the **solar system.** Kua described planetary orbits as circular paths, each with a small, leaf-shaped area attached to one side. According to this model, a planet travels along the circle, take the detour, and then continues on. This model is similar to other explanations of **retrograde motion,** the perceived backward movement of Mars, Jupiter, and Saturn in relation to the Earth.

Chinese astronomy saw its final golden age during the Yuan dynasty, from 1260 to 1368. It was during this period that the great astronomer Kuo Shou-Ching wrote his *Calendar of Works and Days, 1281.* Shou-Ching also oversaw the construction of a bronze-plated **armillary sphere** (an instrument made up of spheres and rings) and a stone tower used to study the **solstices.**

Ancient Egyptian astronomy

The term ancient Egyptian astronomy usually refers to the period prior to 3000 B.C. During that time, astronomy was virtually inseparable from religious beliefs and folklore, in particular the cycle of death and rebirth. Astronomical observations were largely the domain of priests, who used their findings to forecast the future. When compared to the beginnings of astronomy in Greece in the seventh century B.C. and Babylon in the second century B.C., the ancient Egyptian study of the skies appears to have had little scientific value. Another way of assessing its worth, however, is by the criterion of "astronomical awareness"—in other words, the importance of celestial phenomena in peoples' daily lives. In this regard, the ancient Egyptians were very astute observers of the sky.

At least three significant scientific astronomical accomplishments are usually attributed to the ancient Egyptians: the 365-day **calendar,** the 24-hour day, and the Great Pyramid. As early as 3000 B.C., the Egyptians created the first standardized **calendar,** consisting of 12 months, with 30 days in each month. Then they added 5 days to the end of each year, to bring the total to 365 days.

This addition of 5 resulted in a far more practical calendar than the one created some five hundred to one thousand years later by the Babylonians. In the latter case, months were determined by lunar cycles (from one new moon to the next), which are each shorter than 30 days. Thus, 12 lunar months combined fell far short of the **tropical year,** the time it takes the Earth to complete an orbit around the sun. The Babylonians accounted for this difference by inserting an extra month into their calendar every 2 or 3 years.

To make matters worse, standards varied between individual cities in the Babylonian empire. There was no way of knowing the date for certain, which made it difficult for people in their day-to-day affairs. The Egyptian calendar proved much easier to use. Their year, called a "civil year," was based on months of fixed lengths of time, independent of the moon's position in the sky. A similar system is still in use today, albeit with major modifications such as interspersed 31-day months and leap years.

Defining the 24-Hour Day

The ancient Egyptians were also responsible for establishing the 24-hour day. They based this system on nightly observations of a series of 36 stars (called decan stars), which rose and set in the sky at 40 to 60 minute intervals. For ten days, one particular star would be the first to appear in the sky, rising a little later each night until a different decan star would be the first to rise.

"Hours" (although they varied between 40- and 60-minute periods) were marked nightly by the appearance of each new decan in the sky. Depending on the season, between 12 and 18 decans would be visible throughout a night. The number of and the particular decans visible varied with the Earth's changing position along its orbit. The official designation of the hours came at midsummer, when only 12 decans, including the brightest star in the sky, Sirius, were visible. This event coincided with the annual flooding of the Nile River, a crucial event in the lives of valley-dwellers. Thus the night was divided into 12 equal parts. The daylight hours, which also numbered 12, were marked by a sundial, a notched, flat stick attached to a crossbar. The crossbar cast a shadow on successive notches as the day progressed. The combination of the 12 hours each of daylight and darkness resulted in the 24-hour day.

The ancient Egyptians' most famous achievement was the construction of the Great Pyramid in about 2650 B.C. Many scientific and spiritual functions have been attributed to the pyramid, although it is difficult to know for certain what it represents and how it was used. The pyramid is most impressive as an engineering and architectural feat, as well as a spiritual center, while its astronomical functions appear to be more primitive.

The only obvious connection the pyramid has to astronomy is the orientation of its sides and two internal passageways. Each side faces a cardinal direction—north, south, east and west, to a great degree of accuracy. This layout is quite remarkable, considering that the pyramid was built from over two million two-ton limestone blocks, and that determining the four directions at that time was quite a complicated process.

In addition, two passageways inside of the pyramid follow the north-south path across the sky of two bright stars at that time. The two stars are Thuban, near the North Star's current position, and Alnilan, a star in the "hunter's belt" in the **constellation** Orion. These passages would seem to be ideal for observing these and other north-south moving stars. Yet there is a bend at the end of each shaft, blocking the view of the sky. A more likely explanation for their configuration is a religious one. Ancient Egyptian lore describes the journey of the pharaoh's soul to the heavens, to meet Osiris, the underworld god of rebirth. And since the Egyptians believed that Osiris was linked with the constellation Orion, it is possible these shafts were built for the passage of the pharaoh's soul.

No evidence exists to suggest that the Egyptians made systematic and comprehensive observations of the sun, moon, planets, and stars. However, the contributions of the Egyptian astronomers to modern civilization—the tropical calendar and the 24-hour day—continue to remind us of the ideas they developed more than five thousand years ago.

See also **Ancient Greek astronomy** and **Calendar**

Ancient Greek astronomy

According to records that have survived the ages, the ancient Greeks were the first people to question the nature of the universe. This most likely was related to the fact that theirs was a democratic society, made up of distinct, sovereign cities, in which all points of governance were hotly debated by ordinary citizens. It stands to reason that out of this environment of free thought and intellectual challenge would come attempts to understand and describe the universe.

The earliest Greek astronomers, beginning in the seventh century B.C., were more like philosophers than scientists. They sought to answer grand questions about life and the human condition as opposed to seeking factual knowledge about the material world. The first of these philosophers was Thales (624–546 B.C.), who rose to fame with his correct prediction that a total eclipse of the sun would occur in a particular year. This may have been due to his knowledge of the tendency of **solar eclipse**s to occur every forty-seven years, coupled with the fact that he had heard of one that took place forty-seven years earlier. He was incorrect, however, in his assertion that the Earth is flat and floats on water.

Thales' student, Anaximander (610–547 B.C.), proposed a theory that the Earth is shaped like a cylinder and is surrounded by a sphere of stars. Whereas no one took much notice of the cylinder theory, the "sphere" notion was very popular among astronomers. Anaximander's ideas formed the basis of a "sphere theory" that depicted the Earth as a huge ball at the center of the universe, surrounded by "spheres" or circles. Each sphere carried a celestial object—such as the moon, sun, planets, or stars—around the sky. Spheres were considered central to the structure of the universe for the next two thousand years.

Another influential Greek thinker was Pythagoras (c. 582–c. 497 B.C.). He proposed an elaborate scheme in which the center of the universe was occupied by a fire that drove the motions of the celestial bodies. He placed the Earth nearest to the fire and the orbits of the moon, sun, planets, and stars farther away. Pythagoras also suggested that the universe is filled with music, which we are so used to hearing that we no longer notice it.

Heraclitus (540–480 B.C.) pronounced that a new, one-foot-wide sun rises every day. Parmenides (512–400 B.C.) was correct in his assumption that moonlight is reflected sunlight. Around the same time, Anaxagoras (500–428 B.C.) authored a number of interesting theories, including that colliding planets were the source of **comet**s, the mind controls the universe, and that the Earth is flat, among others. Anaxagoras was correct in his assessment that the sun is farther away from Earth than is the moon.

Plato's student Eudoxus of Cnidus then proposed a modified sphere theory—that the universe was comprised of twenty-six rotating spheres (with the Earth, of course, at the center). His student Callipus, in turn, hypothesized that thirty-four spheres were involved. This paved the way for Plato's most brilliant student, Aristotle (384–322 B.C.), who carried the sphere theory to new heights.

Aristotle wrote in his book *De caelo* (*On the Heavens*) that the Earth sits at the center of a great **celestial sphere,** made up of fifty-five successively smaller spheres. Each of these spheres carries a celestial body around the heavens in a perfectly circular motion around the rotating Earth. The closest sphere to Earth (and hence the smallest sphere) contains the moon. The area below the sphere of the moon has five components: earth, air, fire, water, and the "quintessence," a transparent element from which the spheres are formed. Aristotle also felt that the Earth, with its imperfections, was an exception to the rule that all other celestial bodies are unchanging and flawless.

Aristotelian theories dominated scientific thought for nearly two thousand years. While Aristotle is widely considered one of the world's earliest and greatest philosophers, his teachings in the area of astronomy turned out to be far from correct. For this reason, many historians feel that Aristotle ultimately did more to hinder our understanding of the **cosmos** than to advance it.

Contributions of Hipparchus

One hundred years after Aristotle came Hipparchus (c. 190–120 B.C), considered to have been the greatest ancient Greek astronomer. Hipparchus simplified Aristotle's system of spheres and was the first to offer a detailed explanation of how objects move throughout the **solar system.** For this reason he is considered the true author of the **geocentric** (Earth-centered) **model.**

Hipparchus' created a diagram that consisted of seven large spheres— for the sun, moon, Mercury, Venus, Mars, Jupiter, and Saturn—with the Earth in the center. Hipparchus was the first to introduce the concept of **"epicycles,"** small secondary orbits that accounted for the periods in which the planets appeared to move backwards (called **retrograde motion**) with respect to the Earth. The inclusion of epicycles in Hipparchus' diagram turned the planetary paths from circles into elaborate figure-eight patterns.

Hipparchus is known for making a number of other contributions to astronomy as well. For instance, he created a catalogue of the stars and grouped them into forty-eight **constellations.** He also established some of the basics of trigonometry; studied the solar and **lunar eclipse**s, as well as the **solstices** and **equinox**es, in order to create a **calendar** based on a year containing 365.2467 days; estimated the relative sizes of the sun and the moon (although his values cannot be found); and calculated that the moon is 29.5 Earth radii from the Earth, a figure only off by about 2 percent from the value accepted today.

Some ancient Greek astronomers promoted a **heliocentric** (sun-centered) **model** of the solar system, but they were in the minority. Among the first of these astronomers was Philolaus (c. 480 B.C.–?), a mystic who advocated a unique brand of heliocentricity. He proposed that the six planets, sun, moon, and sphere of stars all traveled around a central fire, of which the sun was a reflection. He added a tenth body to this system—the Earth's invisible twin—which caused his colleagues to regard his theory with a high degree of skepticism.

A more convincing argument for a heliocentric solar system was made by Aristarchus of Samos in 260 B.C. He believed that the sun was much larger than the Earth and that, therefore, it made sense that the Earth as well as the other planets should revolve around the sun. His contemporaries debated the merits of this idea for a century, but ultimately rejected it.

If there were any question as to the dominance of the geocentric model, Ptolemy, around A.D. 140, put an end to that. He essentially retold Hipparchus' version of the universe in a 13-volume catalogue entitled *Megale mathematike systaxis* (*Great Mathematical Compilation*), while claiming all the credit, for which many accuse him of plagiarism. Ptolemy's book was so influential that, although the geocentric model originated centuries before him, it is today known as the **Ptolemaic model.**

Ptolemy was also known for his work in **astrology.** In Ptolemy's time, this field was considered as legitimate a field of study as any other field. In his four-volume book *Tetrabiblios,* he attempted to show how patterns of stars influence human events. Ptolemy charted the stars using antiquated instruments called a plinth (a stone block with an engraved arc used to measure the height of the sun) and a triquetrum (a triangular rule).

The geocentric model of the solar system was accepted as true throughout Europe until the Renaissance in the mid-1500s. Then a Polish astronomer named Nicholas Copernicus presented convincing new arguments for a sun-centered solar system. Despite official attempts to silence Copernicus and censor his writings, the **Copernican model** was undeniably sound and eventually became accepted within the scientific community.

See also **Aristotle**; **Copernicus, Nicholas**; and **Ptolemy**

Astronomy on the World Wide Web

The World Wide Web, also known as the Internet, is an invaluable source for learning about a wide range of topics in astronomy. On the Web, you can find everything from recent photos of Pluto taken by the Hubble Space Telescope, to updates on evidence of primitive life on Mars, to information on celestial objects currently visible in the sky. The National Aeronautics and Space Administration (NASA) posts lots of information about space projects past, current, and present, and a slew of astronomy clubs and university astronomy departments display their latest findings and activities.

There are two ways to plug in to astronomy on the Web. One is to enter an address of a given web page; the other is to search for a particular topic using one of the Web's numerous search engines. To get you started, here is a short list of Web addresses for very general topics, each with links to many other pages.

http://galaxy.einet.net/galaxy/Science/Astronomy.html

Provides links to a large number of observatories, organizations, news articles, events listings, and periodicals.

http://www.jsc.nasa.gov/Bios

NASA astronaut biographies.

http://www.osf.hq.nasa.gov/interest.html

"Space Hotlist"—information on satellites, space probes, piloted space missions, astronauts, and more.

http://www~groups.dcs.st~and.ac.uk/~history/BiogIndex.html

Index to biographies of famous astronomers throughout history.

http://www.w3.org/pub/DataSources/bySubject/astro/astroweb/P-history.html

Provides links to subjects relating to the history of astronomy.

http://www.ksc.nasa.gov/shuttle/missions/missions.html

NASA guide to space shuttle missions.

http://seti-inst.edu

News and information from the Search for Extraterrestrial Intelligence Institute (SETI).

Ancient Mayan astronomy

Mayan Indians have inhabited the region that is now Mexico's Yucatan Peninsula and Central America since about 3000 B.C. They built a civilization of city-states that grew at a tremendous rate between the years A.D. 300 and A.D. 900. Then they faced competition from the Toltecs, a native group from the Valley of Mexico, interested in expanding their own empire. Although its growth slowed, the Mayan civilization continued to prosper until the Spanish Conquest around the year 1560. The arrival of the Spaniards marked the end of a society that had developed, in addition to astronomy, advanced mathematics, art, and architecture; a system of writing; a **calendar**; and an extensive set of religious rituals and beliefs.

Today, Mayas still live in the Yucatan, Belize, Guatemala, and western Honduras, but in isolated villages and in far fewer numbers. Most of them are Roman Catholic and speak Spanish, although many still practice their traditional religion and speak the Maya language.

In the ancient Mayan civilization, priests and astronomers were one and the same. They did not pursue skywatching solely as a quest for scientific understanding. Rather they linked phenomena in the sky with their spiritual beliefs. They closely associated the heavens with their ancestors and rulers, both of which groups were elevated to a god-like status.

The motions of celestial objects were used to determine the fates of individuals, cities, and even entire nations. Certain astronomical alignments could signal the time for the selection of a new emperor, the start of a war, or even human sacrifice.

The most visible link between religion and astronomy in ancient Mayan culture is their temples and pyramids, many of which have been excavated and are now tourist attractions. These sites, where rituals were held, were constructed in such a way as to align with significant celestial phenomenon. One example is the huge pyramid at Chichen Itza, in the northern Yucatan peninsula. At sunset on the spring and fall **equinox**es, a shadow resembling a diamond-backed serpent inches its way up the steps of the pyramid called El Castillo.

Records of Mayan Astronomy

While we know that the ancient Mayan people predicted eclipses and planetary motion to a high degree of accuracy, we can be certain of little else in terms of their accomplishments. The reason for this uncertainty is that all but three books, along with virtually the entire Mayan civilization, were destroyed by the Spaniards. Most of the information that remains is in the form of hieroglyphics etched on the stone walls of temples and notes taken by the European explorers and priests who first encountered the Mayans.

The three remaining records from what is believed to have been an extensive Mayan library are books constructed from bark. One of these books is a now-famous work called the "Dresden Codex." The Dresen Codex is so-named because it was discovered in the late 1800s in the archives of a library in Dresden, Germany. It includes observations of the motions of the moon and Venus and predictions of the times at which **lunar eclipse**s would occur.

The most remarkable section of the Dresden Codex is a complete record of the orbit of Venus around the sun. Mayan astronomers had correctly calculated that it takes Venus 584 days to complete a revolution. They arrived at this figure by counting the number of days that Venus first appeared in the sky in the morning, then the days when it first appeared in the evening, and finally the days that it was blocked from view because it was on the opposite side of the sun. They marked the beginning and ending of the cycle with the heliacal rising, the day on which Venus rose at the same time as the sun.

The Maya associated both Venus and the sun with warfare, sacrifice, fertility, rain, and the harvest. They considered the heliacal rising—the coming together of Venus and the sun—to be a sacred event. On that day they would often perform human sacrifices of enemy warriors they had captured during battle.

Andromeda galaxy

Andromeda is the most distant object from Earth, and the only one beyond our **galaxy** that we can see in the night sky without a telescope. It is four times more massive than our own **Milky Way.** At 2.2 million **light-year**s away, it is also the closest major galaxy. The Milky Way and Andromeda together dominate the Local Group (regional cluster) of galaxies.

Hundreds of billions of stars reside within Andromeda. Many of them are part of the six hundred or so **globular cluster**s located on the edges of the galaxy. Each one of these nearly spherical star systems contains anywhere from tens of thousands to millions of stars.

Andromeda shares many characteristics with the Milky Way. It is the same shape and about the same age, contains many of the same types of objects, and is believed to have a **black hole** at its center. The two galaxies are also the same size, each about one hundred thousand light-years across.

The Milky Way and Andromeda are both **spiral galaxies.** Spiral galaxies have a group of objects at the center (mostly older stars), surrounded by a halo and an invisible cloud of **dark matter,** with arms spiraling outward like a pinwheel. The spiral shape is formed because the entire galaxy is rotating, with the stars at the outer edge forming the arms.

Astronomers continuously study Andromeda, in part seeking clues about our own galaxy. Despite its distance from us, Andromeda is still ac-

*Andromeda galaxy,
also known as M31.*

tually easier to study than the Milky Way. The reason is that from Earth's position in the middle of the Milky Way, many parts of our own galaxy are blocked from view by dust.

Early Studies of Andromeda

Andromeda is also known as M31, referring to its position as the thirty-first non-star object to be catalogued by French astronomer Charles Messier in 1774. Another nickname given to the galaxy because of its size is "the Great Galaxy."

Messier credited astronomer Simon Marius with the 1612 discovery of Andromeda. Marius was the first to describe the galaxy as seen through a telescope. Records show, however, that ancient Persian astronomer Al-Sufi observed the galaxy as early as A.D. 905 and called it the "little cloud."

Not until the present century was Andromeda shown to be a galaxy. Previously, astronomers had considered it a **nebula** within the Milky Way. In 1912, American astronomer Vesto Melvin Slipher analyzed Andromeda with a spectrometer, an instrument that breaks light down into its component wavelengths. He discovered that Andromeda's **spectrum** did not match that of any known gas, but was more like the pattern made by starlight.

Slipher also discovered the Andromeda's spectrum was **blue-shift**ed, meaning that light from the galaxy was shifted toward the blue (shorter wavelength) end of the range of visible light. A blue-shifted object is one that is approaching the observer. Slipher calculated that Andromeda was moving toward Earth at a speed of 186 miles (299 kilometers) per second, a speed that was later revised downward to 31 miles (50 kilometers) per second.

In 1924, American astronomer Edwin Hubble first proved that Andromeda is indeed a separate galaxy. Hubble identified twelve **cepheid variable** stars in Andromeda and determined that they were at least eight hundred thousand light-years away. This distance is much greater than the farthest reaches of the Milky Way. Thus, Hubble concluded that Andromeda was a separate galaxy. Twenty-five years later, German-born American astronomer Walter Baade looked through a telescope twice as powerful as the one used by Hubble and came up with a more accurate measurement of its distance of two million light-years away.

In 1991, the Hubble Space Telescope photographed Andromeda and revealed that a double nucleus lies at its center. A nucleus is a dense group of stars at the midpoint of a galaxy. The most likely explanation for this discovery is that at some point Andromeda absorbed a smaller nearby galaxy, the nucleus being the only remaining part of that galaxy. Another possibility is that a lane of interstellar dust runs through the middle of one wide nucleus, giving it the appearance of two separate nuclei.

See also **Galaxy**; **Hubble, Edwin**; **Milky Way galaxy**; and **Spiral galaxy**

Anglo-Australian Observatory

The Anglo-Australian Observatory (AAO) consists of the Anglo-Australian Telescope (AAT), the UK Schmidt Telescope (UKST), and a laboratory. Both telescopes are located at the Sliding Spring Observatory in New South Wales, Australia, at the edge of Warrumbungle National Park. The laboratory is in Epping, a suburb of the Australian capital, Sydney.

The AAO was established in 1975. It is jointly funded by Great Britain and Australia, and astronomers from the two countries share observing time equally. The AAO is one of the few observatories in the Southern Hemisphere. From its location, astronomers can observe regions of the sky that are difficult to observe from the Northern Hemisphere, including the central part of the **Milky Way,** adjacent **galaxies,** and certain **globular cluster**s and radio galaxies.

The AAT, measuring 153 inches (389 centimeters) across, is among the world's ten largest telescopes. (The largest in the world is the Keck Telescope of the Mauna Kea Observatory at 394 inches, or 1,000 centimeters, across.) The AAT is known for its excellent optics and state-of-the-art equipment. It functions as both an optical and an infrared telescope, meaning that it can detect both visible light and longer-wavelength **infrared radiation.**

In most cases, the AAT collects information in a new way, with light-sensitive electronic instruments called **charged coupling devices (CCDs).** The CCDs take electronic "pictures" of objects and store them in computers for further analysis. The AAT also records images the old way with regular photography.

The AAT also contains **spectrograph**s, instruments that break light down into its color components. From an object's **spectrum,** one can determine its temperature, chemical composition, and distance from Earth.

The AAT has a wide field, in which many objects (up to four hundred faint stars) can be seen and analyzed at once. This feature saves time for astronomers who otherwise would have to analyze a greater number of smaller fields, one at a time. And its infrared adaptor enables the AAT to detect some objects that do not shine in visible light, such as **stellar nurseries** (areas where stars are being created).

Sliding Spring's second telescope, the UKST, is also equipped with visible light and infrared detectors. This 47-inch (119-centimeter) telescope was in use at the Royal Observatory in Edinburgh, Scotland, from 1973 to 1988, before being moved to Australia. It also has a wide-angle view and is capable of obtaining light spectra for up to one hundred objects at a time. The UKST has been used together with the AAT to confirm the existence of numerous **quasar**s, the brightest and most distant objects in our slice of the universe.

See also **Infrared astronomy**

Anti-matter

Anti-matter is one of the most bizarre concepts in astronomy. As its name suggests, it is the opposite of matter. Physicist Paul A. M. Dirac first deduced in 1928 that all matter should exist in both positive and negative states. He applied his discovery first to electrons and five years later was proven correct when anti-electrons, or positrons, were discovered.

Perhaps the most troubling feature of anti-matter is that it and matter are supposed to destroy one another on contact. The existence of anti-particles is one thing, but in theory, there are also anti-stars, anti-planets, and anti-**galaxies** are out there. If this turns out to be true, we can only guess at where they are and how they behave.

When Dirac first set out to find the anti-electron, he quickly dismissed what some people may have considered a likely candidate—the proton. This is because the proton, while positively charged, has a **mass** 1,836 times greater than the electron. This violates the rule that particles and anti-particles must be of the same mass.

The positively charged electron was discovered in 1932 by American physicist Carl Anderson. Anderson tracked particles bouncing off a lead plate and found that while all the electrons were deflected in one direction, there was another type of particle that headed off in the opposite direction. This particle had all the same characteristics as an electron, except for its positive charge. Anderson gave it the name "positron." For the discovery of the positron, Dirac and Anderson shared the Nobel Prize.

Two decades later the anti-proton and anti-neutron were discovered. Naturally occurring positrons were detected in 1979, high above Texas, during a balloon experiment. An outpouring of positrons has also been identified near the center of our galaxy (maybe coming from a **neutron star** or **black hole**).

If all matter exists in an anti-matter state, then it's curious why so little anti-matter has been seen. We have detected the anti-forms of sub-atomic particles but where is the bigger matter? In theory, particles and anti-particles are always created in equal amounts, or destroyed in equal numbers in explosions (which are yet to be discovered) of energy and **gamma rays.** This balance between matter and anti-matter is known as symmetry.

One possible reason for anti-matter not being seen is that matter and anti-matter do not exist in equal amounts. There may be far more matter, dwarfing anti-matter in comparison. And maybe matter has already destroyed most anti-matter. Another theory, far-fetched as it may seem, is that matter and anti-matter occupy separate spaces. Perhaps our universe has an anti-universe twin, and the two are somehow, fortunately, kept apart.

Apollo program

In 1961, the former **Soviet Union** beat the United States to the goal of putting the first man in space. In response, the U.S. space program went into high gear. Then-President John F. Kennedy vowed that not only would the United States match the Soviet accomplishment, but that by the end of the decade the United States would put a man on the moon.

The Apollo program was begun for that purpose. It became the focus of the National Aeronautics and Space Administration's efforts during the years 1967–1972. NASA engineers designed a craft consisting of three parts: a **command module** where the astronauts would travel; a **service**

module, which contained supplies and equipment; and a **lunar module,** which would detach to land on the moon. In all, they produced a total fifteen Apollo spacecraft, twelve designed for piloted missions and three for unpiloted missions.

While the Apollo program was quite successful overall, it was not without its snags. In fact, it began with a tragedy. In January 1967, during a ground test of *Apollo 1,* a fire engulfed the command module, killing Virgil Grissom, Ed White, and Roger Chaffee, the three astronauts on board. This accident prompted a two-year launch delay, during which over fifteen hundred modifications were made to the command module.

Later that year and early the following year, three unpiloted Apollo missions were flown. Their purpose was to test the powerful new Saturn V **rocket,** the lunar module, and a variety of new safety features.

The first successful piloted mission, *Apollo 7,* was launched in October 1968. Three astronauts orbited the Earth for eleven days and tried out the ship's new guidance system and other equipment. Two months later, the crew of the *Apollo 8* became the first humans to escape the Earth's gravitational field and orbit the moon. The next two flights, *Apollo 9* and *Apollo 10,* in early 1969, worked out the final kinks and prepared for the next and most significant mission of the series.

Apollo 11 Lands On the Moon

On July 16, 1969, *Apollo 11* was launched with astronauts Neil Armstrong, Buzz Aldrin, and Michael Collins on board. Four days later Armstrong and Aldrin climbed into the lunar module and, true to President Kennedy's promise, landed on the moon. As Armstrong set foot on lunar soil, he stated his now-famous words: "That's one small step for man, one giant step for mankind."

Over the next three years, five more Apollo missions landed twelve more Americans on the moon. One flight, however, the notorious *Apollo 13,* had to be aborted before it reached the moon and nearly ended in disaster. On April 13, 1970, when the spacecraft was already more than halfway to its destination, an explosion occurred. The accident left the crew without enough oxygen, water, and power to continue the mission as planned. The only thing that saved the three astronauts was their decision to ride out the return journey in the lunar module (which still had basic life support systems) and their ability to improvise new methods of spacecraft operation.

Apollo-Soyuz
Test Project

The crew (sitting, from left): astronaut Donald K. Slayton, astronaut Vance D. Brand, and cosmonaut Valerly N. Kubasov; (standing, from left): astronaut Thomas P. Stafford, and cosmonaut Alexei A. Leonov.

Apollo 17, the final mission of the series, flew in December 1972. Three more missions were originally scheduled, but then canceled because of budget cuts and waning public interest. NASA then turned its attention to the development of reusable **space shuttle**s and unpiloted **space probe**s to explore the rest of the **solar system.** To this day, the moon remains the only celestial body to have been visited by humans.

See also **Aldrin, Buzz**; **Armstrong, Neil**; and **Spacecraft, piloted**

Apollo-Soyuz Test Project

The *Apollo-Soyuz* Test Project, in 1975, was the first cooperative venture in space between the United States and the former **Soviet Union.** The first

twenty years of the **space age** were dominated by the **space race,** the fierce competition between the two superpowers to be "first" in a variety of space flight categories. The space race was, in many ways, an extension of the **cold war,** the hostile standoff between the United States and Soviet Union following World War II. In the early 1970s, relations between the two countries entered a phase called détente, a truce of sorts. It was during this time that then-President Richard Nixon and then-Prime Minister Leonid Brezhnev agreed to the largely symbolic link-up in space.

On July 15, 1975, the Soviet *Soyuz 19* spacecraft was launched, with cosmonauts Alexei Leonov and Valerly Kubasov on board. Leonov had earlier been the first man to walk in space. Seven hours later, the American *Apollo 18* spacecraft took off, carrying astronauts Thomas Stafford, Vance Brand, and Donald "Deke" Slayton. *Apollo* carried with it a docking module designed to fit *Soyuz* at one end and *Apollo* at the other, with an airlock chamber in between.

That evening the two spacecraft approached one another and successfully joined. The Americans entered *Soyuz* and the two crews shook hands on live television. They remained docked for two days, during which time they carried out joint astronomical experiments. After separating from each other, *Soyuz* returned directly to Earth while *Apollo* stayed in space for three more days. Both vessels landed safely.

While the *Apollo-Soyuz* Test Project had far greater political than scientific significance, it has led to further joint research ventures. For example, American astronauts are now regular visitors to Russia's *Mir* **space station.**

See also **Apollo program** and *Mir* **space station**

Apollo 13

Apollo 13 is the most famous near-disaster in the history of U.S. piloted space flight. On April 13, 1970, when the spacecraft was more than halfway to the moon, an explosion occurred. The crew, astronauts Jim Lovell, Jack Swigert, and Fred Haise, soon learned that the oxygen tanks had ruptured and most of the ship's systems had been destroyed. They had to give up their goal of landing on the moon and instead had to focus all their energies on making it back to Earth alive.

Apollo 13 (1995)

This re-enactment of the 1970 near-tragic mission of *Apollo 13* was nominated for an Academy Award for best picture. Starring Tom Hanks, Kevin Bacon, and Bill Paxton, it tells the story of the *Apollo 13* astronauts, their families, and their dreams of landing on the moon. It features a nail-biting sequence of events starting with the explosion in the cabin, followed by the three-and-a-half days during which the crew used the lunar module as a lifeboat and cautiously navigated their way home. The story is based on the 1994 book, *Lost Moon,* by astronaut Lovell.

The accident of *Apollo 13* occurred fifty-six hours into the flight. A crew member had unknowingly triggered the explosion by stirring the tanks of liquid oxygen, a routine procedure. Investigators later discovered that weeks before the flight, while the spacecraft sat at Cape Canaveral, the wiring in an oxygen tank had been damaged. Thus, when the tanks were stirred, the faulty wiring shorted out and started a fire. The flames heated the oxygen to boiling, which created enough pressure to burst the tank apart.

Hot gas then entered the **service module** (the portion of the vessel containing supplies and equipment). The drastic increase in pressure there also caused an explosion, blowing out one wall of the unit.

At that point, the spacecraft jerked forward and alarms went off. At first, the crew was aware only that the fuel cells used to produce electricity were not operating properly. But when they looked out the window and saw that the oxygen gas they needed to survive was blowing into space, they realized they had a much larger problem on their hands.

Surviving the Trip Home

There was nothing the astronauts could do to repair the damage. Their only hope was to ride out the journey home in the **lunar module,** which had life support systems of its own. The lunar module was not intended, however, to keep three people alive for three and one-half days. It was meant only to supply two people for two days. Oxygen, electricity, and water all had to be conserved to last the entire journey home. The cabin temperature was maintained at just above freezing and each crew member could drink only six ounces of water a day.

Over the next few days, the astronauts and their supporting engineers at mission control in Houston, Texas, scrambled to figure out how to use the lunar module's engine to bring *Apollo 13* home and how to stretch its limited power supplies. The decision was made that the spacecraft should loop around the moon, using its gravitational field as a slingshot to send the ship back toward Earth.

As the spacecraft finally approached Earth, the astronauts climbed back into the **command module** and cast off the service and lunar modules. They had only very basic navigational methods with which to determine their point of re-entry into the Earth's atmosphere. If they had been off by even a small amount, the ship would have bounced off the atmosphere and back out into space, where it probably would have been lost forever.

Fortunately, the calculations made by the astronauts and their controllers were correct. After a few very tense minutes during re-entry when

The original Apollo 13 *crew (from left to right): Fred Haise, James Lovell, and Thomas Mattingley. Mattingley was later replaced by Jack Swigert when he became exposed to the German measles.*

all contact with them was lost, the crew radioed the command center to announce they had splashed down.

The astronauts returned home dehydrated and in varying stages of hypothermia (lower than normal body temperature), but alive. This "successful failure," as *Apollo 13* has been called, might very well have ended in tragedy if not for the cool-headedness of the crew and engineers and their ability to quickly improvise new methods of spacecraft operation.

See also **Apollo program** and **Lovell, James**

Arago, Dominique-François-Jean
(1786–1853)
French physicist and astronomer

Dominique-François-Jean Arago was the leading French astronomer for the first half of the nineteenth century. He also made important contributions to the fields of optics and electricity and is credited with stimulating the scientific interests of a generation of French students.

*Dominique-
François-Jean
Arago.*

Arago was born in 1786 in Estagel, France, a town where his father was the mayor. After receiving a classical education, Arago planned to enter the military at age twenty. French officials, however, recognized his scientific abilities and instead assigned him to the Paris Observatory, and later to the Bureau of Longitudes.

Arago's second post sent him to southern Europe and northern Africa to survey land in order to determine the curvature of the **Earth's meridian.** The political situation in that region made this work very difficult. After decades of French colonial rule, the native people were largely intolerant of the French. Arago was even taken prisoner for a short time in the former French colony of Algiers, now Algeria.

When Arago returned to France in 1809, he was hired as a professor of analytical geometry at the Ecole Polytechnique and elected to the French Academy of Sciences. Arago also conducted research and lectured in the astronomy department.

Among Arago's achievements in astronomy was his discovery of the solar **chromosphere,** a glowing layer of gas surrounding the sun. He also offered an explanation for the twinkling of stars and conducted research that led one of his assistants, Urbain Leverrier, to discover Neptune.

Arago also entered the debate within the scientific community over the nature of light: was it composed of particles or waves? He originally believed that light was composed of particles, but changed his mind after significant study. Arago believed that to prove light traveled in waves, he would have to measure its speed through two different mediums, air and water. If light were composed of waves, it would travel more slowly through water than through air. Beset by faulty equipment, failing eyesight, and the onset of the French Revolution in 1848, Arago was never able to complete this experiment. (His experiments were completed three years before his death by Jean Bernard Léon Foucault and Armand Fizeau. We now know that light behaves as both a wave and a particle.)

Perhaps Arago's most important work was in the field of electromagnetism. He determined that an electric current produces a magnetic field in a variety of metals, such as iron and copper. His colleague André Ampere developed a mathematical description for the phenomenon, and thus received much of the credit for the work.

In 1830, Arago left his professorship to serve as permanent secretary for the French Academy of Sciences. He also received the political appointment of Minister of the Navy, Minister of the Army, and President of the Executive Committee. During his political tenure, Arago oversaw the abolition of corporal punishment and slavery in the French colonies.

See also **Foucault, Jean Bernard Léon**; **Leverrier, Urbain**; and **Solar atmosphere**

Arecibo Observatory

The Arecibo Observatory, in Arecibo, Puerto Rico, is a joint project of Cornell University and the National Science Foundation. It is best known as the home of the world's largest and most sensitive radar-radio telescope.

The telescope was constructed in 1963 and upgraded in 1974. Also located at the observatory are the Ionospheric Modification Facility (for the study of **plasma** physics) and the Optical Laboratory (for the study of the physics and chemistry of the middle atmosphere).

The telescope at Arecibo has greatly advanced the field of **radio astronomy,** the study of objects in space by observing the **radio wave**s they emit. An optical telescope, the kind most people are familiar with, detects visible light. However, visible light represents just one type of radiation from the **electromagnetic spectrum.** On the longer wavelength end of the **spectrum** are radio waves. Objects that would appear very dim or invisible through an optical telescope may shine brightly through a **radio telescope.**

A basic radio telescope consists of an antenna and a receiver which can be tuned to the appropriate frequency. A reflector dish is often used to collect and magnify the intensity of the radio waves.

*Arecibo Observatory
in Puerto Rico.*

Radio telescopes have been used to map the spiral structure of the **Milky Way galaxy**; to detect **pulsar**s; and even to pick up background radiation coming from throughout the universe. This radiation is believed to be left over from the **big bang** with which the universe began around fifteen billion years ago. The Arecibo telescope has managed to break through the cloud cover on Venus and map some of the planet's surface features.

The reflector dish of the Arecibo radar-radio telescope is a breathtaking sight. Nestled between the hills, on top of a natural depression in the land, it lies on its back with the concave side pointing upward. The dish has a 1,000-foot-diameter (305-meter-diameter) surface (larger than three football fields) made of forty thousand aluminum panels, each about 3 feet (0.9 meters) by 6 feet (1.8 meters).

The telescope itself is suspended 426 feet (130 meters) above the dish on a 600-ton (544-metric ton) platform. It is supported by twelve steel cables, hung four each from three concrete towers. Cables also run from each tower and from each corner of the platform to anchors buried in the ground. The cables hold the platform steady, even in windy conditions.

The Arecibo Telescope in Use

Several antennas (tuned to different frequencies) hang down from the telescope, in the direction of the reflector dish. To use the telescope, an observer must first decide what she or he is looking for. The observer must then choose the appropriate antenna and aim it at a certain part of the dish (corresponding to a particular region of the sky). All the reflective powers of the enormous mirror are then concentrated on one small area of the sky where it picks up very strong radio emissions, in essence creating a radio-wave picture of a slice of the sky.

The Arecibo Observatory is used twenty-four hours a day, seven days a week, by scientists from all over the world. About two hundred scientists annually conduct research in radio astronomy, planetary radar (the technique of sending radio waves out toward a planet to determine its distance from the Earth), and atmospheric sciences. In addition, numerous college students are granted access to the facilities for their projects. Arecibo is also open to the public and receives about fifty thousand visitors, about half of whom are children, each year. As of April 1996, a visitor's center is under construction and plans are underway to upgrade the radio telescope, incorporating the most recent technological advances.

See also **Radio astronomy**

Aristotle (384 B.C.-322 B.C.)
Greek philosopher and scientist

Aristotle, a thinker and educator, lived at a time when the fields of science and reason were still in their infancy. Although many of his theories were later proven incorrect, Aristotle succeeded at something very important— he laid the foundations for later scholars to build on.

Aristotle was born into a wealthy family in the Greek village of Stagira. His father was the personal physician of the king of Macedonia and Aristotle spent much of his boyhood in the royal court. When Aristotle was ten, his father died, leaving him to be raised by friends of the family.

At age seventeen, Aristotle went to Athens to study at the Academy of Plato. There he became Plato's star student and earned a nickname, the translation of which is "intelligence of the school." Twenty years later, Plato died and Aristotle left Athens to travel and conduct research in natural history and biology. Aristotle was then invited back to the Macedonian court by King Philip II, to be a tutor to his son, Alexander (later known as Alexander the Great).

Aristotle, in a painting by Raphael.

In 335 B.C., Aristotle moved back to Athens and founded a university of his own, called the Lyceum. He had a unique style of teaching. In many of his classes he discussed problems and theories while leading his students on strolls through the gardens. There Aristotle and his students conducted research in every existing field of knowledge. They also devised primitive classification systems for plants and animals. This system was used by scientists for almost two thousand years until Swedish scientist Carl Linnaeus replaced it with a more complex and useful system in the late 1700s.

When Aristotle was not looking down at plants and insects, he was looking up at the planets and stars. Aristotle wrote in his book *De caelo* (*On the Heavens*), incorrectly, that the Earth was at the center of the universe. In Aristotle's universe, everything was part of an overarching **celestial sphere,** the outer layer of which contained the stars. Within this sphere was a set of fifty-five spheres that fit inside one another. Aristotle theorized that these spheres carried celestial objects around the heavens in a perfectly circular motion (another mistaken theory) around the rotating Earth.

The closest sphere to Earth (and hence the smallest sphere) contained the moon. The area below the sphere of the moon had five components: earth, air, fire, water, and "quintessence"—a transparent element from which the spheres were formed. Aristotle also felt that the Earth, with its imperfections, was an exception—that all other celestial bodies were unchanging and flawless.

Aristotle was also the first to define the various branches of knowledge. He broke them down into physics, metaphysics (a branch of philosophy), rhetoric (public speaking), poetics, and logic.

In the year 323 B.C., King Alexander died and the political winds shifted. Popular sentiment turned against people from Macedonia and Aristotle was forced to leave Athens. He died a year later in his mother's homeland of Chalcis.

Aristotelian theories dominated astronomical teachings for nearly two thousand years until the Renaissance period, which began in the fourteenth century.

See also **Ancient Greek astronomy**

Armstrong, Neil (1930–)
American astronaut

Neil Armstrong represents one of America's proudest moments in science. He was the first man to walk on the moon, a representative of the first and only country to accomplish this goal. As Armstrong stepped off the Eagle **lunar module** on July 20, 1969, he stated his now-famous words: "That's one small step for man, one giant step for mankind."

Armstrong began life on a farm outside the small town of Wapakoneta, Ohio. For a time, his father's job as an auditor for the state of Ohio required that the family move every year, but they returned to Wapakoneta for Neil to finish high school. He built model airplanes and at age sixteen he received his student pilot's license.

Astronaut Neil
Armstrong, wearing
his spacesuit, talks
with technicians at
Cape Kennedy on
July 16, 1969.

In 1947, Armstrong enrolled at Purdue University with the assistance of a U.S. Navy scholarship. A year-and-a-half later, however, the Navy called him to active duty. He was sent to Pensacola, Florida, where he trained to be a fighter pilot. When the Korean War broke out, Armstrong was sent overseas, where he flew several bombing missions. His tour of duty ended in the spring of 1952, after which he returned to Purdue. In January 1955, Armstrong graduated from Purdue with a bachelor's degree in aeronautical engineering.

Armstrong next moved to Cleveland and went to work for the National Advisory Committee on Aeronautics (NACA), which later became the National Aeronautics and Space Administration (NASA). Soon after, he was assigned to be an aeronautical research pilot at the NACA post at Edwards Air Force Base, California. In this capacity, Armstrong piloted jet and rocket planes on high-altitude test flights.

In 1962, when NASA selected its second group of astronauts, Armstrong became one of the first two civilians chosen for the program. After going through survival training, Armstrong was assigned to work on the Gemini program. He played support roles for three Gemini missions and commanded one his first of two space flights, *Gemini 8*.

Armstrong's first space flight in March 1966 nearly ended in disaster. The plan was for him to pilot a Gemini spacecraft into orbit and dock with an Agena target **rocket.** The exercise was designed to test procedures that would later be used on moon flights. The Gemini launch went successfully, and Armstrong docked the *Gemini 8* with the Agena rocket. But the combined Gemini-Agena spacecraft then began to rumble end-over-end, out of control. Armstrong was able to break the Gemini free from the Agena, but the planned three-day exercise had to be aborted.

Armstrong Lands On the Moon

Armstrong was next assigned to the Apollo program. In 1961, President John F. Kennedy had set a national goal of landing a man on the moon by the end of the decade. The Apollo program was created to achieve this goal.

Armstrong was not initially not slated to command the prized *Apollo 11* flight. Only due to scheduling changes did he end up on *Apollo 11* along with crewmates Buzz Aldrin and Michael Collins.

Apollo 11 lifted off on July 16, 1969. After a four-day journey, Armstrong and Aldrin climbed into the lunar module (a specially designed, removable section of the spacecraft) and descended to the moon's surface. Armstrong was first to set foot on lunar soil, followed by Aldrin. There they planted the American flag, had a telephone conversation with President Richard Nixon, set up science experiments, and collected rocks and soil samples. They left behind a plaque that read: "Here men from the planet Earth first set foot upon the Moon, July 1969 A.D. We came in peace for all mankind."

The *Apollo 11* flight to the moon, viewed by the largest international television audience to that time, is considered by many people to be one of the greatest scientific achievements of the modern world.

For Armstrong, this historic flight was followed by months of public appearances, after which he assumed an administrative post at NASA. Two years later, he retired from NASA to take a teaching position at the University of Cincinnati. Armstrong remained there until 1979, after which he went to work in private industry.

In the mid-1980s, Armstrong was recruited by NASA to serve on the National Commission on Space, whose task it was to develop goals for future space travel. In 1986, following the explosion of the **space shuttle** *Challenger,* Armstrong was named vice-chair of the committee investigating the accident.

Armstrong and his wife, Jan, currently reside in Lebanon, Ohio.

See also **Apollo program** and **Lunar exploration**

Asteroids

Asteroids are relatively small, rocky chunks of matter. They look like stars, in that they shine like dots of light, but act like planets, in that they orbit the sun. While most asteroids are made of carbon-rich rock, some (those farthest from the sun) contain iron, nickel, and a few contain other elements. One asteroid, Pholus, is coated with a red material that may be organic compounds similar to those of which living material is made.

Asteroids vary in size from 579 miles (933 kilometers) in diameter (Ceres, the first asteroid discovered) to less than 0.6 miles (1 kilometer) in diameter. Most are small. Only 120 larger than 81 miles (130 kilometers) across and 10 larger than 155 miles (250 kilometers) across have been found. They are generally irregular in shape and vary in brightness as they rotate.

Scientists once thought that asteroids were remnants of exploded planets. That theory was discarded however, because the asteroids are so small. All known asteroids combined would form an object much smaller than our moon.

Scientists now believed that asteroids are **planetesimals.** Planetesimals are ancient chunks of matter that originated with the formation of our **solar system** but never came together to form a planet. For this reason, asteroids can provide valuable information about the beginnings of our solar system.

Early Discoveries

The first asteroid was discovered by Father Giuseppe Piazzi on New Year's Day in 1801. He saw a star-like body that was not listed in star catalogues. He observed the object over several nights and noted that it moved relative to fixed stars, so it had to be an object that belonged to the solar system. It was moving faster than Mars yet slower than Jupiter, so he deduced it must lie between the two. He named the asteroid Ceres, after the Roman goddess of agriculture.

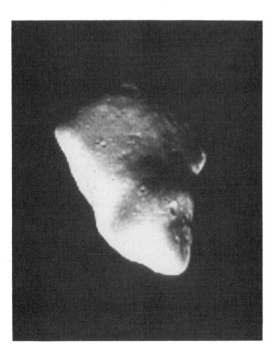

Asteroid Gaspra, shot by the Galileo probe. October 1991.

It was no accident that Piazzi discovered Ceres in the spot that he did. For years, astronomers had been searching the sky in that location for a mystery planet. In the late 1500s, Johannes Kepler was the first astronomer to theorize about the existence of a hidden planet between Mars and Jupiter. In 1766, German astronomer Johann Titius devised a formula for calculating distances between planets known today as **Bode's Law.** (Although Titius devised the formula, it did not receive much attention until Johann Elert Bode restated it in 1772. By that time Titius had been all but forgotten, and Bode got the credit.) Bode's Law predicted the existence of a planet between Mars and Jupiter. The prediction was reinforced in 1781, when William Herschel discovered a new planet, Uranus, in the position that Bode's Law had predicted a planet to be.

The year after Piazzi's discovery, German mathematician Carl Gauss invented a method of orbit calculation, and thus was able to plot the course of Ceres. At about the same time, another German scientist, Heinrich Olbers, found a second asteroid and named it Pallas. In the mid-1800s, with the improvement of telescopic equipment and techniques, many new asteroids were discovered. The all-time champion asteroid hunter in the days before photography was Johann Palisa who found a total of 120.

In the late 1800s, the use of photographic techniques paved the way for the discovery of thousands of asteroids. There are now about five thousand tracked and documented asteroids, an additional thirteen thousand identified, and an estimated total of one million. An estimated one hundred thousand asteroids are bright enough to be photographed from Earth. Only one asteroid, Vesta (the fourth one discovered), is bright enough to be seen with the naked eye.

Asteroid Orbits

Most asteroids are located in belts that lie between the orbits of Mars and Jupiter. These belts are separated by distances known as **Kirkwood gaps.** Kirkwood gaps are spaces in which the gravitational attraction of two or more bodies prevents any object from maintaining orbit. The gaps are named for their discoverer, nineteenth-century American astronomer Daniel Kirkwood.

But not all asteroids are found there. For instance, the Trojan asteroids are located in two clusters, one on either side of Jupiter. This arrangement is a consequence of the gravitational attraction of Jupiter and the sun. Another exception is Chiron, discovered in 1977, which is located between the orbits of Saturn and Uranus. Another class of asteroids crosses the orbits of several planets.

One group of asteroids, called **Apollo objects,** cross Earth's orbit. These bodies may come relatively close to Earth. One member of the group, the asteroid Hermes, swept by along a path twice the distance of Earth to the moon. Some asteroids have even collided with Earth. For instance, in 1908, an asteroid about a tenth of a mile in diameter came through the atmosphere and exploded above central Siberia. The blast caused a mushroom cloud, scorched and uprooted trees for miles around, and wiped out a herd of reindeer. It shattered windows six hundred miles away. Some scientists believe that an asteroid crash caused the extinction of the dinosaurs.

A large asteroid colliding with Earth today could truly be a catastrophe, possibly causing more damage than all the nuclear weapons in existence. And there is a greater chance of Earth being hit by an asteroid than there is of winning a lottery. Asteroids ten times the size of the one that hit Siberia are estimated to hit Earth every few hundred thousand years. This notion keeps scientists busy devising ways to change the path of an oncoming asteroid, before it would hit Earth.

See also **Bode, Johann Elert**

Astrolabe

The **astrolabe** is an instrument used by astronomers to observe the positions of the stars. With some adjustments it can be used for time-keeping, navigation, and surveying.

The most common type of astrolabe, the planispheric astrolabe, was a star map engraved on a round sheet of metal. Around the circumference were markings for hours and minutes. Attached was an inner ring that moved across the map, representing the horizon, and an outer ring that could be adjusted to account for the rotation of the stars.

Astrolabe used by a sixteenth-century astronomer.

To use the astrolabe, an observer would hang it from a metal ring attached to the top of the round star map. They would look toward a specific star through a sighting device, called an adilade, on the back of the astrolabe. By moving the adilade in the direction of the star, the outer ring would pivot along the circumference of the ring to indicate the time of day. The adilade could also be adjusted to measure **latitude** (one's north-south position on the globe) and elevation (height of the land).

Ancient Arabs perfected astrolabes and made regular use of them. With the clear desert sky constantly above them, they excelled in astronomy and used the stars to navigate across the seas of sand.

From the fifteenth century until the development of the **sextant** in 1730, sailors used astrolabes for navigation. Regular use of astrolabes continued into the 1800s.

The newer prismatic astrolabe continues to be used to determine the time and positions of stars and for precision surveying. This instrument consists of a mercury surface and a prism, placed in front of a telescope. It works by tracking the passage of a star from the time it rises in the sky to the time it sets. As the star enters the field of view of the astrolabe, its light rays shine both directly and indirectly on the prism (indirectly by reflecting off the mercury surface). When these light rays all come into focus together, the star's precise location at that moment is recorded.

Astrology

In ancient times, people were filled with wonder by the sun, moon, planets, and stars. They came up with creative explanations for what they saw in the sky. Ancient astronomers, who charted the stars and planets night after night, invested the celestial objects with a host of god-like qualities. They named planets and star groupings after the gods of their particular religion and felt that some of these bodies were, indeed, gods. In this way, the fields of astronomy and **astrology** advanced together for several centuries.

The birth of modern astronomy in the early 1500s was the point at which the two paths went their separate ways. Once Nicholas Copernicus determined that the Earth and other planets revolved around the sun and Galileo Galilei crafted the first telescopes, the skies became much less mysterious. Those who held to the mystical beliefs about the **cosmos** continued on their own, separate quest for greater understanding.

Astrology is the belief that celestial objects influence the course of human affairs. Depending on who you ask, astrology is either a science or a religion; a valid pursuit or a hoax; a source of enlightenment or a superstition that promotes ignorance. According to one believer, an astrologer named Haizen in Arizona, "Astrology is an art and a science that deals with the seasons and the cycles of our lives." He claims that reading one's fate in the stars allows a person to "make use of their strengths and overcome their weaknesses."

Most scientists, however, argue that astrology has no scientific basis and is of no value. "Astrology just doesn't work," states Jay M. Pasachoff, author of astronomy texts. "It is not merely that some people harmlessly believe in astrology. Their lack of understanding of scientific structure may actually impede the training of people needed to solve the problems of our age."

Astrology believers point to tests that prove the merit of their pursuit, while non-believers point to other tests that show that astrological predictions usually fail. So what's the answer? Perhaps it falls somewhere in between the two extremes, or perhaps there is no answer at all. Some questions cannot be tested by traditional scientific means. For example, take the question "Does God exist?" This question, like the validity of astrology, is one that every individual must answer for herself or himself, based on personal convictions and beliefs.

Astrology probably had its beginnings in Babylonia around the year 1000 B.C. Over the next several centuries it spread to Greece and throughout the Orient. Whereas the Babylonians felt that astrology applied only to the lives of kings and nations, the Greeks believed that the fate of every individual was connected to the heavens.

Signs of the zodiac.

The first person to produce a comprehensive written work on astrology was the Alexandrian astronomer and astrologer Ptolemy. His four-volume treatise, called *Tetrabiblios,* was published in the second century A.D. It is still considered the fundamental astrology text and continues to be widely used by astrologers today.

The most popular form of modern astrology is called natal (birth) astrology. Natal astrology involves plotting the positions of the sun, moon, planets, and stars at the exact time of a person's birth, creating a chart called a horoscope. Astrologers believe that the horoscope provides information about that person's traits and the sequence of his or her life events.

When casting a horoscope, an astrologer maps the planets and stars against the backdrop of the zodiac. The zodiac breaks the **celestial sphere** into twelve regions, each one defined by a **constellation** residing within it. The twelve zodiac signs are: Aries, Taurus, Gemini, Cancer, Leo, Virgo, Libra, Scorpio, Sagittarius, Capricorn, Aquarius, and Pisces.

The most important component of a horoscope is the position of the sun, followed by the positions of the moon and planets. For instance, if a person were born at the end of March, the sun would appear in the Aries region and that person would be considered an Aries. A certain set of characteristics is attributed to all Aries, characteristics such as dominance, impatience, and creativity, which all persons born under that sign are expected to share. A person's horoscope becomes more individualized as the astrologer looks at the positions on the zodiac where the planets and the moon appear, individually and in relation to each other.

Astrologers do not agree with each other as to how much influence a horoscope has on one's life. Some feel that our lives are pre-destined, that every second is already accounted for at the moment of birth and can be read in the stars. Others believe that the cosmos is just one influence on our lives among many other influences, such as heredity and environment.

See also **Constellations**

Atlantis

In 1985, *Atlantis* became the fourth member of the National Aeronautics and Space Administration's fleet of **space shuttle** orbiters. An orbiter is a winged space plane designed to transport astronauts into space and back.

Together with solid **rocket** boosters and an external tank, it makes up a space shuttle (officially called the Space Transportation System).

The space shuttle orbiter is a vessel that acts like a spacecraft but looks like an airplane. It contains engines, astronaut living and work quarters, and a cargo bay large enough to hold a bus. The orbiter is launched vertically using its own engines, aided by two attached rocket boosters. The boosters fall away from the orbiter about two minutes after launch and parachute into the ocean, where they are retrieved and used again.

Once in orbit, the vessel can use its own rocket motors to change direction. When it is ready to come back to Earth, the orbiter brakes with its engines. Its delta-shaped wings facilitate its re-entry into the Earth's atmosphere and it glides in for a landing on a specially designed 3-mile-long (5-kilometer-long) runway.

Atlantis was named for the first U.S. ocean vessel to be used for re-

The space shuttle Atlantis lands after completing its third mission, December 1988.

search at the Woods Hole Oceanographic Institute in Massachusetts from 1930 to 1966. The space vessel *Atlantis,* weighing 85.5 tons (77.5 metric tons), completed sixteen flights between October of 1985 and March of 1996.

Atlantis' first flight was a classified U.S. Air Force mission, in which it delivered into space two defense communications satellites. Some of the shuttle's more notable missions since then have been delivery into space of the *Galileo* and *Magellan* interplanetary **probe**s in 1989 and the Compton Gamma Ray Observatory in 1991. *Atlantis* dropped off U.S. astronaut Shannon Lucid at the Russian **space station** *Mir* in March 1996 for a six-month stay, and brought her back to Earth in September.

Of the four original space shuttle orbiters, three are still in use. Besides *Atlantis,* these include *Columbia* and *Discovery.* The fourth, *Challenger,* was destroyed in a tragic accident in 1986. It has since been replaced with the newest shuttle, *Endeavour.*

See also **Space shuttle**

Aurorae

Aurorae (the plural form of aurora) come in two forms—aurora borealis and aurora australis—better known as the northern and southern lights. These bright, colorful displays of light in the night sky are most prominent at high altitudes, near the North and South poles. They can also be seen sometimes at lower **latitude**s on clear summer nights, far from the lights of the city. On a number of nights each year, the northern lights can be seen as far south as the Canada/United States border.

A display of northern or southern lights can be as fascinating as fireworks. It varies in color from whitish-green to deep red and takes on shapes such as streamers, arcs, curtains, and shells.

Aurorae are produced when charged particles from the sun enter the Earth's atmosphere. This stream of particles, a form of **plasma,** is carried away from the sun by the **solar wind.** As the plasma approaches Earth, it is trapped for a time in the outermost parts of the Earth's **magnetic field,** an area called the **Van Allen belts.** Eventually the plasma is drawn down toward the north and south magnetic poles. Along the way, it ionizes (creates an electric charge within) the oxygen and nitrogen gas it encounters in the atmosphere, causing it to glow.

The flow of plasma from the sun is generally continuous, although it occasionally bursts out of holes in the sun's outermost atmosphere. Massive ejections of plasma have also been shown to accompany solar **flare**s, **prominence**s, and **sunspot**s. It is during these periods of highest solar activity that one is most likely to witness aurorae.

Earth is not the only planet with aurorae. They also occur on Saturn and Jupiter. These auroral displays were captured on film by the *Voyager 1* spacecraft as it flew by the planets in 1980. *Voyager 1* found that the aurorae on these giant planets, unlike aurorae on Earth, are not limited to the area around the magnetic poles, but are planet-wide.

See also **Solar wind**

The aurora borealis, otherwise known as the northern lights, as it appeared over New York City on September 18, 1941.

Baade, Walter (1893–1960)
German-born American astronomer

Walter Baade made a number of startling discoveries in his twenty-seven years working in the field of astronomy. He first theorized the existence of **neutron star**s, and discovered the distinction between stars of the inner and outer reaches of **galaxies,** and radically advanced our understanding of the size and age of the universe.

Wilhelm Heinrich Walter Baade was born in Schrottinghausen, Westphalia, Germany. He became interested in astronomy while in high school. At age twenty-six, he received his doctorate at Göttingen, then spent eleven years on staff at the University of Hamburg. In 1931, he moved to California, where he started working at Mount Wilson and Palomar observatories.

One of Baade's first achievements in California, together with his colleague Fritz Zwicky, was to suggest that a **supernova** could produce a kind of stellar corpse other than a **white dwarf:** a neutron star. Baade and Zwicky theorized that neutron stars are extremely dense and compact objects, comprised mostly of neutrons that spin extremely fast.

This theory was proven true in 1968 as a result of observations made by a Cambridge University graduate student named Jocelyn Bell Burnell and her professor Antony Hewish. Bell Burnell and Hewish discovered regular radio pulses coming from the remnants of a supernova. They were able to demonstrate that this pulsating source of radiation, later named a **pulsar,** was actually a rotating neutron star, spewing radiation out of its magnetic poles. Its axis was tilted in such a way that from Earth it appeared as though the radiation was an on-and-off signal.

*Walter Baade at the
Mount Wilson
Observatory, 1939.*

Baade made other significant contributions to astronomy during World War II. Because of his German heritage, Baade was confined by the U.S. government to the Mount Wilson-Pasadena area. While his colleagues were sent away on government assignments, Baade had plenty of time to work with the telescope at Mount Wilson.

Baade Distinguishes Population I and Population II Stars

One night, Los Angeles suffered a power outage and the skies were exceptionally dark. Baade took advantage of this event to study the stars, which appeared particularly bright in contrast. He was able to make a detailed study of the Andromeda galaxy and became the first person to distinguish the stars near its core in fine detail. Previously, only the stars in the galaxy's spiral arms had been resolved, by Edwin Hubble. Baade found that, in contrast to the whitish-blue outer stars, the core stars were reddish.

Baade classified the stars into two groups. He named the stars in the spiral arms Population I and the core stars Population II. The distinction between these two classes of stars had never before been noticed, mainly because the stars at the core of our own **Milky Way** galaxy are hidden by clouds of dust and gas. Astronomers now know that Population I stars have a chemical composition similar to that of the sun. They contain 1-2 percent, by **mass,** elements heavier than hydrogen and helium on the periodic table of elements. They have been created over long periods of time from materials expelled by other stars. Population II stars are older. They were formed long before elements heavier than hydrogen and helium had built up in the universe. Thus they contain only about one hundredth of these elements as are found in Population I stars.

Baade's later discoveries showed that the universe is much larger and older than previously thought. After World War II, Baade used the new telescope at Palomar Observatory to identify over three hundred **cepheid variable**s in the Andromeda galaxy. Cepheid variables are pulsating stars that can be used to determine distance. Using only Population II stars, Hubble had earlier estimated that the Andromeda galaxy was eight hundred thousand **light-year**s away and that the universe was about twenty-six billion light-years in diameter.

Baade, using pulsating cepheid variables in both Population I and Population II, determined that the distance to the Andromeda galaxy was actually closer to two million light-years. And he calculated that the universe was twenty times larger than previously thought.

These changes were significant for several reasons. First, in order to have expanded to the size Baade calculated, the universe had to be much older than scientists had previously estimated. And secondly, if other galaxies were farther away than previously thought, this meant they had to be bigger and brighter, in order to be seen over the greater distances. The perception of our Milky Way galaxy as the biggest in the universe changed. We now know that our home galaxy is only an average sized galaxy among millions of others.

See also **Bell Burnell, Jocelyn** and **Hewish, Antony**

Bell Burnell, Jocelyn (1943–)
Northern Irish astronomer

As a youngster in northern Ireland, Jocelyn Susan Bell Burnell developed an interest in astronomy. Fortunately, she lived near the Armagh Observatory, where the staff encouraged her to learn more. Little did they know she would go on to make the important discovery of **pulsar**s.

Bell Burnell attended the University of Glasgow in Scotland, and earned a bachelor of science degree in 1965. Later that year she moved to London and enrolled in Cambridge University to begin work on her doctorate.

Bell Burnell and her supervisor, Antony Hewish, built a giant **radio telescope** designed to track **quasar**s, powerful sources of radio energy extremely far from Earth. The telescope consisted of scraggly looking antennae linked by wires, spread over a four and one-half-acre field. It was able to detect faint and rapidly changing energy signals and record them on long rolls of paper. Bell Burnell's job was to review every mark made on the paper.

In August 1967, Bell Burnell noticed some strange markings. At first she thought they were the result of interference from local amateur radio operators. She watched the signals as they showed up periodically for three months, and then began to monitor them with a high-speed recorder. She learned that the signal pulsated regularly. This pattern was mysterious because prior to that time the only recorded signals coming from space were continuous ones.

Locating the Source

**B e l l
B u r n e l l ,
J o c e l y n**

Bell Burnell's next task was to locate the source of the signal. It came so regularly (every 1.337 seconds) that at first Bell Burnell and Hewish wondered if it was a message from aliens. They even named the source LGM, for Little Green Men. "We did not really believe that we had picked up signals from another civilization," Bell Burnell later admitted, "but obviously, the idea had crossed our minds and we had no proof that it was entirely natural radio emission. It is an interesting problem—if one thinks one may have detected life elsewhere in the universe, how does one announce the results responsibly?"

But soon Bell Burnell found three other pulsating sources, making it highly unlikely that the signals were from little green men. Thus, Bell Burnell and Hewish renamed the objects "pulsars," short for "pulsating radio source."

Hewish hypothesized that the pulsars might be **white dwarf** stars or **neutron star**s. By the end of the following year, two pulsars were located within **supernova** remnants. This discovery led astronomers Thomas Gold and Franco Pacini to the conclusion that neutron stars were indeed the source of the signals detected by Bell Burnell and Hewish.

Neutron stars, the debris left after the implosion of a massive star, are incredibly dense. The spinning of a neutron star intensifies its **magnetic field,** causing the star to act as a giant magnet. It emits radiation out of its magnetic poles. If the **magnetic axis** is tilted in a certain way, the rotating star's on-and-off signal is visible from Earth.

Hundreds of pulsars have now been catalogued, including many in spots where a supernova is known to have occurred. Scientists now believe that our **galaxy** may contain over one hundred thousand active pulsars.

The discovery of pulsars was so significant that the Nobel Prize was awarded for it. Unfortunately, the prize went only to Hewish and his co-director on the project, Martin Ryle. Although not officially recognized by the Nobel committee, Bell Burnell received much attention for what many considered her discovery.

Bell Burnell then moved on to take a professorship at the University of Southampton, where she worked on **gamma ray astronomy.** She also worked on the British satellite *Ariel V* at the Mullard Space Science Laboratory. In 1982, she was appointed Senior Research Fellow at the Royal Observatory in Edinburgh, Scotland. There she has continued her research on **infrared astronomy,** optical astronomy, and millimeter wave astronomy.

See also **Baade, Walter**; **Hewish, Antony**; and **Pulsar**

Bessel, Friedrich (1784–1846)

German astronomer

Friedrich Bessel, born in Minden, Germany, was a self-taught astronomer. He began working as an accountant at age fifteen, but his true interests were astronomy and mathematics.

At age twenty, Bessel recalculated the orbit of Halley's **comet** and mailed his findings to astronomer Heinrich Olbers. Olbers got Bessel's work published, then helped Bessel obtain a post as an assistant at a private observatory. At age twenty-six, Bessel was appointed by King William III of Prussia to the directorship of the Königsberg Observatory, a position he held until his death in 1846.

Bessel worked tirelessly and had an impressive list of achievements to show for it. He catalogued over fifty thousand stars, developed a new method of mathematical analysis that could be applied to fields outside of astronomy, and created the most precise telescopes of his day.

Friedrich Bessel.

Bessel's greatest achievement was to define the **parallax** of a star. As the Earth orbits the sun, its position relative to any star shifts by up to 186 million miles (300 million kilometers). Thus, the apparent position of any star in the sky changes slightly throughout the year. The amount of the observed change in position is the parallax. Once the parallax is known, it is possible to calculate the distance to a star.

In 1838, Bessel found the parallax for a star called 61 Cygni, the star with the largest known range of apparent movement. He assumed that the star was relatively close to Earth, because the closer an object is, the greater its parallax would be. He calculated that the star was ten **light-year**s away. Although we now know that this distance is actually very close for a star, it astounded astronomers in 1838. They thought the stars were much closer than that. Bessel's work turned out to be the first accurate measurement of the distance to a star, something that astronomers had been trying but failing to do for almost a century.

Discovering the concept of parallax also helped refute the notion that the universe centered around the Earth. Parallax implied that the Earth was moving, which strengthened Nicholas Copernicus' theory that the earth orbited around the sun.

In 1841, Bessel noticed that the bright star Sirius wobbled in its path. The motion was unlike that due to parallax, which would be smooth. He concluded that the wobbling was caused by the gravitational tug of an invisible companion star in orbit around Sirius. Sirius and its companion are an **astrometric binary** system, meaning only one star in the pair is visible. Bessel's theory was shown to be correct in 1862 when Sirius' companion star was found by telescope-maker Alvan Graham Clark. Clark observed a bright, small, dense star known as a **white dwarf.** Since both stars were visible, the pair from then on has been considered a **visual binary** system.

See also **Binary star** and **Copernicus, Nicholas**

Bethe, Hans (1906–)
German-born American physicist

Hans Albrecht Bethe was born in Strassburg, Germany (now part of France), in 1906, the son of two university professors. His father taught physiology, and his mother, medicine. Science was Bethe's passion, but the nature of his work was shaped largely by political events. He is best known for discovering the process of **nuclear fusion** and for his work on the development of the atomic bomb.

Bethe was a brilliant high school student and went on to study physics at universities in Frankfurt and Munich. In Munich in 1926, Bethe came under the wing of Arnold Sommerfeld, an early pioneer of **quantum mechanics,** the study of nuclear and atomic particles in motion. He joined Sommerfeld's brilliant group of scientists which included Linus Pauling and Edward Teller. Bethe's main project in the group was to study the structure of atoms and nuclei.

Bethe finished his studies in 1930. A Rockefeller Foundation fellowship enabled him to spend two years as a visiting scholar at the Cavendish Laboratory in Cambridge, England. He then continued his studies in Rome, working with Enrico Fermi. Bethe returned to Germany in 1932 to teach physics at the University of Tübingen.

Just two months later, Adolf Hitler rose to power. Because of his mother's Jewish heritage, Bethe was fired from his job and had to leave the country. Many of Germany's finest scientific minds found themselves in a similar predicament, and waves of scholars left for the United States, England, Australia, and other countries.

Bethe went first to England, where he taught for two years. He then went to Cornell University in Ithaca, New York, where he teaches to this day.

Hans Bethe, who helped develop the atomic bomb, is shown here lecturing a physics class at Cornell University, 1967.

Bethe Analyzes Nuclear Fusion

Soon after reaching Cornell, Bethe tackled a question that had baffled scientists for centuries: how do stars produce their energy? To arrive at the answer, Bethe combined what he knew about subatomic physics with theories of the high temperatures of stars. This approach led him to understand the process of nuclear fusion. By May 1938, as the Nazi war effort went into high gear, Bethe announced his answer.

Bethe suggested that deep in a star's core, where the temperature is in the millions of degrees, nuclear fusion takes place. He suggested two ways this can happen. In very hot stars, the nuclei of hydrogen atoms can fuse with carbon nuclei. This process begins a complex chain reaction, ending with the fusion of two hydrogen nuclei into a helium nucleus. One recycled carbon nucleus, and a tremendous amount of energy are also produced. In slightly cooler stars, hydrogen nuclei do not fuse with carbon, but fuse together to produce helium and energy.

Our sun contains so much helium that the fusion of hydrogen to helium must have been going on for billions of years. The sun has enough hydrogen to continue producing energy for many more billions of years.

Bethe and the Manhattan Project

In 1939, as the world was headed for war, several prominent scientists visited Albert Einstein, who was living in New York. They convinced him to write a letter to President Franklin D. Roosevelt urging him to begin work on an atomic bomb to help defeat the Nazis. Einstein, who had always been a pacifist (one opposed to war or violence), later called this letter "the greatest mistake" he ever made.

Nonetheless, Einstein's letter set the wheels in motion. In 1942, one year after the Japanese attacked Pearl Harbor, a program known as the Manhattan Project was created to manufacture the atomic bomb. Robert Oppenheimer, one of the the atomic physicists who worked on the project, recruited Bethe to join his research team.

Three years later the bombs were ready. In July 1945, the United States dropped atomic bombs on the Japanese cities of Hiroshima and Nagasaki, and the world was changed forever. The most destructive weapon devised had been unleashed, killing thousands of civilians and leveling entire cities at once, giving new meaning to the nuclear threat.

After the war, Bethe returned to Cornell and resumed teaching and conducting research into the nature of the physical universe. Bethe received the Fermi Award in 1961 for his part in the development of atomic energy and the Nobel Prize in physics in 1967.

See also **Einstein, Albert**

Big bang theory

Fifteen to twenty billion years ago, an explosion occurred, creating the universe. The universe began as an infinitely dense, hot fireball, a scrambling of space and time. Within the first second after the "big bang," **gravity** came into being. The universe expanded rapidly and became flooded with subatomic particles that slammed into one another, forming protons and neutrons. Three minutes later, when the temperature was a mere 500,000,000 degrees Fahrenheit (277,777,760 degrees Celsius), protons and neutrons formed the nuclei of hydrogen, helium, and lithium (the simplest elements).

It took another five hundred thousand years for atoms to form and three hundred million more years for stars and galaxies to begin to appear. Countless stars condensed from swirling **nebulae**, evolved, and died before our own sun and its planets came into being in a **galaxy** named the **Milky Way.** And it was only four and one-half billion years ago that the **solar system** was formed from a cloud of dust and gas. This is the **big bang theory,** the most widely accepted theory today of how the universe began.

The big bang theory rests on a key assumption, namely that the universe is expanding. Before the twentieth century, astronomers assumed that the universe had existed as it was, forever. It wasn't until the 1920s that there was evidence that the universe was changing. Einstein's theory of relativity, published in 1915, first led other scientists to explore this idea.

In 1919, Dutch astronomer Willem de Sitter showed how Einstein's calculations could be used to describe an expanding universe. A second important contributor was Georges-Henri Lemaître, a Belgian astronomer and Jesuit priest, who came to be known as the "Father of the Big Bang." In the late 1920s, Lemaître deduced that if the universe was expanding, then by going back in time one would find that everything started from one point. He suggested that the universe had originated as a great "cosmic egg," which exploded and expanded outward.

Opposite page: Diagram depicting crucial periods in the development of the universe. The top oval represents the big bang, the next oval shoes the COBE sky map measuring background radiation, and the final oval shows galaxies and stars beginning to form.

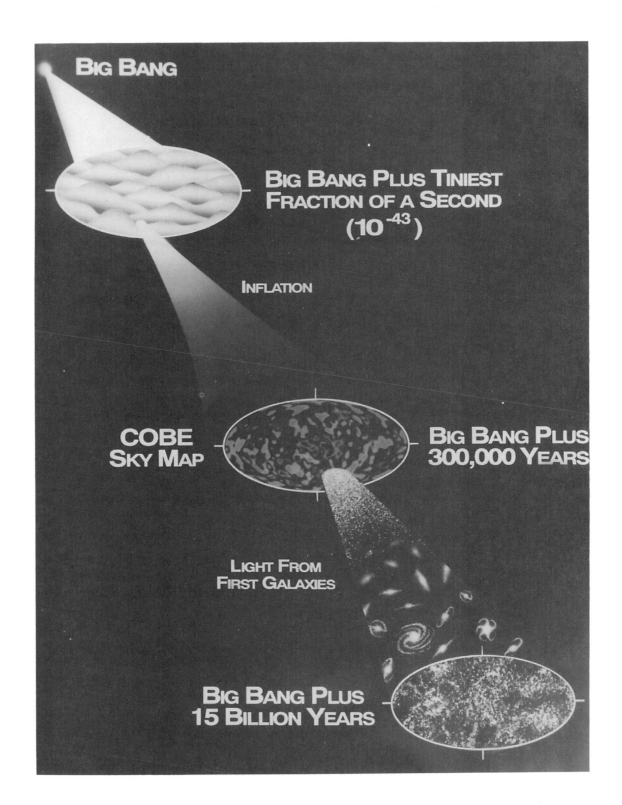

BIG BANG

BIG BANG PLUS TINIEST
FRACTION OF A SECOND
(10^{-43})

INFLATION

COBE
SKY MAP

BIG BANG PLUS
300,000 YEARS

LIGHT FROM
FIRST GALAXIES

BIG BANG PLUS
15 BILLION YEARS

Evidence of the Big Bang

In 1929, American astronomer Edwin Hubble made what has been called the most significant astronomical discovery of the twentieth century. He found observable proof that stars exist in huge groups called galaxies. By tracing the light of those stars, he also found that all matter in space is moving away from each other. Milton Humason, Hubble's colleague, photographed the distant galaxies and determined that some galaxies were moving at about one-seventh the **speed of light.**

The implications of this discovery were enormous. Here was proof that the universe was expanding, and it made the big bang theory seem much more likely to be true.

In 1948, astronomer George Gamow furthered the argument in favor of the big bang theory. If a bang had occurred, he stated, it would have left traces of background radiation that could persist even after many billions of years. He calculated that the radiation would have cooled to just a few degrees above **absolute zero.** He was later proven correct when radio engineers Arno Penzias and Robert Wilson detected faint background radiation coming from all over the sky that matched Gamow's calculation.

By the mid-1960s, the big bang theory had become the most widely accepted explanation of how the universe began, but problems remained. For instance, measurements of background radiation produced by the big bang implied that the early universe was evenly distributed and that it evolved at a constant rate following the big bang. In this case one would expect to find **homogeneity,** or evenness of distribution of objects in the universe. Instead, what exists are clumps of matter, such as star clusters and galaxies.

The explanation for this inconsistency came in two steps. First, Massachusetts Institute of Technology professor Alan Guth proposed an **"inflationary theory."** This theory states that the early universe underwent a rapid expansion—at a rate much faster than the speed of light —and then slowed down.

The second part of the explanation came in 1992, when NASA's *Cosmic Background Explorer* (*COBE*) looked fifteen billion **light-year**s into space (the same as looking fifteen billion years into the past). It detected tiny temperature changes in the cosmic background radiation, which may be evidence of gravitational disturbances in the early universe. These ripples, which were as long as ten billion light-years, could have eventually come together to form the lumpy mixture that is our universe. This last piece of evidence has caused all other theories of how the universe began to be all but discarded—at least for now.

See also **Cosmic Background Explorer**; **Gamow, George**; **Hubble, Edwin**; **Inflationary theory**; and **Steady-state theory**

Big Bear Solar Observatory

The southern California Big Bear Solar Observatory is one of the best facilities in the world for observing the sun. It's located outside of Big Bear City, 100 miles (160 kilometers) east of Pasadena, at 6,700 feet (2,040 meters) above sea level. At that height, the air is clear and interference from water molecules and turbulence in the Earth's atmosphere is minimal. The skies above the observatory are nearly cloudless, meaning the sun can be observed virtually every day. The most interesting feature of this observatory is that it is situated in the middle of a lake, on an artificial island. The purpose of this arrangement is to avoid the disturbance of images that results when solar heat is re-radiated up from the ground.

Big Bear was built in 1969 and is owned and operated by the California Institute of Technology (CalTech). The observatory is best known for its imaging of solar activity, in particular **sunspot**s and solar **flare**s. A sunspot is the sun's version of a "storm." It is actually a cool area of magnetic disturbance (about 2,700 degrees Fahrenheit, or 1,480 degrees Celsius, cooler than the rest of the surface) that appears as a dark blemish on the sun's surface. Eventually the sunspot erupts in a solar flare, a temporary bright spot. From the flare, a stream of subatomic particles is ejected into space.

Big Bear consists of one large dome, painted white to keep it cool, within which is a cluster of three telescopes. These include a 26-inch (66-centimeter) **reflector,** a 10-inch (25-centimeter) **refractor,** and a 6-inch (15 centimeter) refractor. The smallest telescope is used to monitor the entire sun. The two larger telescopes have higher magnification and can study only limited regions of the sun at a given time.

One consideration in designing a **solar telescope** is that the sunlight entering the telescope is very hot, and must be cooled or it will destroy the instruments. For the two large telescopes, the cooling mechanism is a vacuum system. In a vacuum system the telescopes are set in a structure that is completely devoid of air. Hence there are no gas molecules to absorb the heat. The small telescope is kept sufficiently cool by the dome's huge fans.

The Big Bear telescopes analyze the **spectra** of sunlight, as well as magnetic activity and visible solar phenomena. Each telescope is equipped with special filters to observe sunlight only within certain wavelength ranges. Filtering out the other parts of the **spectrum** allows for easier observation of individual elements (such as hydrogen, helium, and calcium) present within the sun.

The 10-inch (25-centimeter) telescope is equipped with a magnetograph, which measures the magnetic forces associated with solar activity and records them on magnetic tape. Time-exposure images of the sun are recorded on videotape, which is displayed on monitors so that observers can keep track of solar activity.

The final instrument at Big Bear is a **helioseismograph.** This instrument juts out of an opening beneath the three telescopes. It measures oscillations of sound waves within the sun, similar to the way in which a seismograph measures earthquakes. Helioseismograph readings provide the best clues we have as to the sun's rotation and interior structure.

See also **National Solar Observatory** and **Solar telescope**

Big crunch theory

How did it all begin and how will it end? These are two questions about the universe to which we have no answers, just theories. Three main theories have been developed to answer these questions. The future of our universe (which is presently expanding) is undoubtedly written in one of these scenarios: the **big crunch,** the "big bore," and the "plateau" theories.

The big crunch is a catastrophic prediction: it foresees a point, very far in the future, where matter will reverse directions and crunch back into the single point from which it began. The second (known as the "big bore" because it has nothing exciting to describe) claims that all matter will continue to move away from all other matter and the universe will expand forever. The third is almost as boring as the second. It predicts the expansion will slow and at some point nearly cease, after which the universe will reach a "plateau" and remain essentially the same.

The three major theories put forth to describe the birth of the universe are: the **big bang theory,** the **steady-state theory** and the **plasma theory.** The big bang theory is currently the most commonly accepted explanation. It states that around fifteen to twenty billion years ago an infinitely dense, single point underwent a tremendous explosion, spewing forth particles that eventually came together to form planets, stars, and all other forms of matter. The steady-state theory claims that matter is created continuously and that the universe looks the same, not only in all places, but at all times. The plasma theory proposes that the universe was born out of the interaction of electrical and magnetic currents in **plasma,** which caused matter to clump together into planets, stars, and other celestial objects.

Astronomers believe that the fate of the universe is in the hands of a mysterious substance called **dark matter.** Although by its nature dark matter is virtually undetectable, it is thought to account for 90 percent of the **mass** in the universe. Dark matter is considered the "cosmic glue" that holds **galaxies** and clusters of galaxies together, thereby controlling the rate of universal expansion.

While the composition of dark matter is still not completely understood, recent studies have found that **white dwarf**s account for about half of its mass. The rest may be a combination of large and small objects, such as the remains of massive stars called **black hole**s; the burnt-out embers of white dwarfs called **black dwarf**s; and objects that never quite became stars called **brown dwarf**s. Other candidates include the alphabet soup of subatomic particles.

The reason that dark matter was first presumed to exist is that galaxies alone do not contain enough mass to hold together individually, or in clusters. Mass is what creates **gravity,** the force that keeps objects from spinning wildly away from one another. Dark matter is credited with providing the extra mass that creates enough gravity to control the rate at which stars and galaxies move apart.

Scientists have calculated, as a theoretical limit, that dark matter cannot account for more than 99 percent of the mass of the universe. If it were to exceed this amount, there would be so much gravity that matter would begin to move back together. Then it would only be a matter of time before everything ended with a big crunch.

See also **Big bang theory**; **Dark matter**; **Plasma theory**; and **Steady-state theory**

Binary star

A **binary star** is a star system in which two stars orbit each other around a central point of **gravity.**

Before the nineteenth century, astronomers thought that binary stars were an optical illusion. An observer might see two stars that appeared to be side by side, but assumed that one was actually behind the other, and that they just appeared in the same line of sight.

William Herschel made the first discovery of a true binary system in the 1700s. At the time, he was studying the **parallax** of stars, the apparent change in their position due to the Earth's motion around the sun. Herschel observed the motion of a pair of stars and concluded that they were in orbit around each other. Herschel's discovery provided the first evidence that gravity exists outside our **solar system.**

Herschel never was able to measure parallax (that was achieved by Friedrich Bessel in 1848), but he did discover over eight hundred double stars. He called these star systems binary stars. His son, John Herschel, continued the search for binaries and catalogued over ten thousand systems of two or more stars.

Types of Binary Systems

Several kinds of binary stars exist. A **visual binary** is a pair in which each star can be seen distinctly, either through a telescope or with the

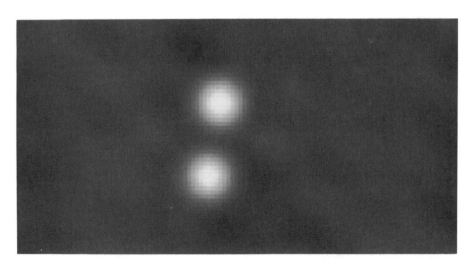

Capella, a binary star system. Just 45 light-years from Earth, the stars are so close together that conventional telescopes view them as a single star (also called Alpha Aurigae), the seventh brightest in the sky.

naked eye. In an **astrometric binary,** only one star can be seen, but the wobble of its orbit implies the existence of another star in orbit around it.

When the plane of a binary's orbit is nearly edgewise to our line of sight, each star is partially or totally hidden by the other as they revolve. This system is called an **eclipsing binary.**

Sometimes a binary system can be detected only by using a **spectroscope** (a device for breaking light into its component frequencies). If a star that appears to be a single star gives two different **spectra,** it is actually a pair of stars, called a **spectroscopic binary.**

These classes of binaries are not mutually exclusive. That is, a binary may be a member of one or more classes. For instance, an eclipsing binary may also be a spectroscopic binary if it is bright enough that its light **spectrum** can be photographed.

The only accurate way to determine a star's **mass** is by studying its gravitational effect on another object. Binary stars have proven invaluable for this purpose. The masses of the two stars can be determined from the size of their orbit and the length of time it takes them to revolve around each other.

As it turns out, binary stars are quite common. A recent survey of 123 nearby sun-like stars showed that 57 percent had one or more companions.

See also **Bessel, Friedrich**; **Herschel, William**; and **Spectroscopy**

Black hole

Black holes may well be the strangest and most mysterious elements in the **cosmos.** In addition to being a favorite subject for science fiction writers, a black hole is a place where space and time meet and stretch out for infinity. Black holes are impossible to see, yet may account for 90 percent of the content of the universe.

Simply put, a black hole is all that remains of a massive star that has used up its nuclear fuel and collapsed under tremendous gravitational force into a single point. At this point, called the **singularity,** pressure and density are infinite. When anything (any object, or even light) gets too close to a black hole, it gets pulled in, stretched to infinity, and remains forever trapped.

Black hole

The idea of black holes was first developed in the late eighteenth century by English geologist John Michell and French astronomer Pierre-Simon Laplace. They surmised that if an object were big enough and dense enough, it would exhibit so much **gravity** that nothing could escape.

This concept can be better understood by looking at the effects of gravity on known objects. In order to break free of Earth's gravitational forces, a spaceship has to travel at a speed of at least 7 miles (11 kilometers) per second. It would have to travel much faster—at least 37 miles (60 kilometers) per second—to leave Jupiter, and 380 miles (611 kilometers) per second to break free of the sun. Thus, if an object were big and dense enough, a spaceship would have to go faster than the **speed of light** to escape from its gravitational attraction. But that is impossible, because nothing travels faster than the speed of light. A black hole is an object of this kind.

Scientists once called black holes "gravitationally collapsed objects,"

Artist's conception of a black hole.

a rather sterile sounding name for such an exciting concept. Russian scientists suggested the name "collapsar," which was a little better, but still not very catchy. Then in 1969, physicist John A. Wheeler of Princeton University coined the term "black hole," which became instantly popular.

Formation of a Black Hole

To end up as a black hole, a star must be at least two or three times the **mass** of our sun. Any star will collapse once its nuclear fuel is all used up. The reason is that the force of the **nuclear fusion** process pushing outward from the star's core balances its immense gravity. An average-sized star, like the sun, will shrink and end up as a **white dwarf** star. A star one-and-a-half times the size of the sun will explode to produce a **supernova,** shedding much of its mass, and end up as a densely packed **neutron star.** However, if the original star is more than double the sun's mass, the gravitational collapse is so complete that, after the supernova, only a black hole remains.

As a giant star collapses, its mass gets so concentrated that the force of gravity becomes completely overpowering. The collapsed star's surface, called the **event horizon,** becomes the point of no return. Anything crossing the event horizon gets drawn in and cannot escape.

Stephen Hawking, professor of mathematics at Cambridge University and noted researcher of black holes, added a new twist to the theory of black holes. Hawking does not believe that a black hole is the final stage of a massive star's life. Rather, he proposes that a black hole continues to evolve by "evaporating" and giving off radiation (called Hawking radiation) in the form of heat.

The theory goes like this: space, instead of being empty, is actually filled with virtual particles. Virtual particles cannot themselves be detected, but their presence is only known by their effect on other objects. These particles have two halves and when approaching a black hole, one half gets sucked in while the other half evaporates, or radiates outward. Through the evaporation process, the black hole loses mass until, many billions of years later, there is nothing left.

Evidence for Black Holes

In 1963, the discovery of **quasars** lent support to the theory of black holes. Quasars are small and extremely distant objects that emit tremendous quantities of radiation, including visible light and **X-ray**s. Mathematician Roy Kerr concluded, in the mid-1960s, that black holes could be the source of the quasars. The radiation emission could be the result of huge quantities of matter crossing the event horizon and disappearing into a black hole.

In 1972, an X-ray telescope aboard the satellite *Uhuru* detected what may be a black hole in our **galaxy.** A star called Cygnus X-1, emitting intense amounts of X-rays, is believed to be a **binary star** whose companion is a black hole. The unseen companion, which may have ten times the mass of the sun, seems to be pulling in stellar material from Cygnus.

A second black hole candidate in our galaxy was discovered in 1975. This star in the **constellation** Monoceros came to the attention of astronomers because of the enormous amount of X-rays it produces. A third star, in the constellation Aquila the Eagle, may also be a black hole. The star appears to be a binary system containing one big star and a dense invisible unknown object. As the two objects orbit around each other, the possible black hole sucks in matter from its companion and spews out radiation.

The only way to detect a black hole is by seeing its effect on visible objects, such as adjoining stars. The problem is like trying to find an invisible person. You might not be able to see the person, but you would know the person was in the room if you saw the door open and close and a dent form upon the couch cushions.

A great debate continues over black holes. As of yet, no solid proof for their existence has been obtained.

See also **Hawking, Stephen**

Bluford, Guion (1942–)

American astronaut

On August 30, 1983, Guion "Guy" Bluford, Jr. became the first Black American in space. He served as a mission specialist (a crew member responsible for the equipment and controls) on the **space shuttle** *Challenger.* That flight was the first shuttle mission to both take off and land at night. It was also international in flavor. The crew set an Indian communications satellite in orbit and conducted experiments with a Canadian-built manipulator arm. This piece of equipment, operated by remote control, is used to repair satellites in space or to pull them into the spacecraft's cargo bay.

Bluford was born in Philadelphia, Pennsylvania. He was the oldest of three boys. His father was a mechanical engineer who designed machines and his mother taught special education classes in the public schools. From an early age, Bluford had an interest in model airplanes. And he preferred learning about how things work on his own to what he was taught in school.

Bluford decided as a youngster that he wanted to be a pilot, but more, that he wanted to design airplanes. These goals did not seem very realistic for a young Black man, since there were very few Black pilots in America at that time, and Black aerospace engineers were even more scarce. Only through his parents' encouragement and his own willpower did Bluford succeed.

Bluford graduated from Overbrook High School in Philadelphia in 1960. He then enrolled in Pennsylvania State University. Four years later he graduated with a bachelor of science degree in aerospace engineering.

While at Penn State, Bluford was a member of the Reserve Officer Training Corps (ROTC). Upon graduation, he entered the U.S. Air Force and learned to fly. Between 1965 and 1967, he flew 144 combat missions, many of them over North Vietnam. On his return to the United States, Bluford became an instructor pilot at Sheppard Air Force Base in Texas.

In 1972, Bluford entered the Air Force Institute of Technology at the Wright-Patterson Air Force Base in Ohio. He earned his master's degree there in 1974 and four years later completed a Ph.D. in aerospace engineering, with a minor in laser physics. Bluford then stayed on as a staff engineer.

Bluford Becomes an Astronaut

In 1978, Bluford was selected by the National Aeronautics and Space Administration (NASA) to undergo astronaut training. A year later, having completed the training, he was working on Spacelab experiments, systems to be used on board the space shuttles, and other assignments. In April 1982, he was chosen for the mission that would make him the first Black American in space.

Bluford made his second space flight in late October 1985. This time he was part of an eight-member crew on a scientific mission called Challenger/Spacelab, which carried the German Spacelab into orbit. Since then, Bluford has flown in space twice more, both times on the space shuttle *Discovery*. The first flight took place in April 1991 and the second in December of the following year. Each of his last two flights were missions for the U.S. Department of Defense.

Guion Bluford has been promoted several times over the years and now holds the rank of colonel. Also among his many accomplishments has been the publication of several scientific papers. Bluford lives with his wife, Linda, an accountant, in Clear Lake, Texas. They have two sons.

Bode, Johann Elert (1747–1826)

German astronomer

Johann Elert Bode, born in Hamburg, Germany, was a self-taught astronomer. He became director of the Berlin Observatory in 1786 and fifteen years later published an enormous catalogue of the positions of stars. Bode is best known, however, for his development of **Bode's Law,** a simple yet flawed mathematical formula describing the distances of the planets from the sun.

Bode's Law is really misnamed because it was not Bode, but German physicist and mathematician Johann Titius, who devised the formula. Titius published the information as a footnote in a book he had translated in 1766, which did not receive much attention. By the time Bode restated the formula in 1772, Titius had been all but forgotten, and Bode got the credit.

Johann Elert Bode.

Titius found that the distances from all the known planets at the time (Mercury, Venus, Earth, Mars, Jupiter, and Saturn) to the sun followed a mathematical progression. The progression has the following form: call the distance from the sun to the closest planet, Mercury, four units. Then the distance from the sun to the next closest, Venus, can be found by adding three. The distance from the sun to the next farthest planet, then, can be found by doubling the second number in the equation each time. Thus, the distance from the sun to the Earth is 4+6=10 and to Mars is 4+12=16. The distance from the sun to the next planet, Jupiter, however, is 4+48=52 instead of 4+24=28, implying that a missing planet was to be found between Mars and Jupiter.

In 1781, Uranus was discovered in the place Bode's Law predicted the next planet after Saturn should be. At that point, previously skeptical astronomers started taking the law more seriously.

However, Bode's Law breaks down entirely past Uranus. The locations of Neptune and Pluto are not at all where the law says they should be. As a result, most scientists today regard the fact that Bode's Law successfully describes the locations of some planets as pure coincidence.

One of the greatest ironies of this law is that it inspired important discoveries. The perceived gap between Mars and Jupiter drove astronomers on a frenzied search for the "missing planet." In the year 1800, six German astronomers formed an international society jokingly called the Celestial Police to hunt down the elusive object. They never found such a planet, but other scientists in the same time period who observed that region of the sky discovered an entire **asteroid** belt.

Bradley, James (1693–1762)

English astronomer

James Bradley.

James Bradley was born in Gloucestershire, England. In 1717, he earned a master's degree from Oxford University. Believing he could not make a living at astronomy, Bradley became a vicar in the Church of England. But in 1721, Bradley was able to return to Oxford as a professor of astronomy. He was named England's Astronomer Royal in 1742, an office he held until his death twenty years later. Bradley was the first to provide proof of the Earth's rotation and calculate the **speed of light.**

Bradley never actually set out to determine the speed of light. Instead he was trying to measure **parallax,** the observed change in a star's position due to the motion of the Earth around the sun. Bradley attached a 212-foot-long (65-meter-long) telescope to his chimney in an effort to see stars pass through its field of view. He did not find a shift due to parallax, but instead observed that all stars shifted by exactly the same amount throughout the year, in the same direction that the Earth moved.

In 1728, it became clear to Bradley that the apparent movement of the stars he observed was due to the Earth's motion forward into the starlight (called the **aberration of light**). This concept is similar to the sensation that makes it seem like raindrops are falling slightly towards you as you walk through the rain and causes you to angle your umbrella forward. Thus, to observe stars from a moving Earth, Bradley had to angle his telescope very slightly.

The amount he angled his telescope allowed Bradley to determine the ratio between the speed of light and the speed at which the Earth moves. He calculated first that light moves ten thousand times faster than the Earth, then that the Earth travels at 18.5 miles (11.5 kilometers) per second. Thus he put the speed of light at 185,000 miles (114,700 kilometers) per second. His calculations came very close to the actual speed of light, which we now know to be about 186,000 miles (115,320 kilometers) per second.

Bradley made several other important discoveries during his lifetime. In 1733, he succeeded in measuring Jupiter's diameter, shocking the scientific community with the news of the planet's immense size. He also found that the Earth's axis shifted slightly due to the gravitational tug of the moon as it orbits the Earth. He studied this phenomenon, which he called **nutation,** for nineteen years before publishing his results in 1748.

Using what he had learned about star shifts due to the aberration of light, Bradley prepared an accurate chart of the positions of over sixty thousand stars that is still useful today. He never did measure parallax though. That accomplishment had to wait another century for Friedrich Bessel.

See also **Bessel, Friedrich** and **Speed of light**

Brahe, Tycho (1546–1601)

Danish astronomer

Tycho Brahe was born in Denmark to a family of great social standing. When he was a child he was kidnapped by his uncle, who had no children of his own and wanted an heir. Brahe entered the University of Copenhagen at age thirteen to study rhetoric and philosophy. He was then sent to the University of Leipzig in Germany. His uncle decided Brahe should become a lawyer and hired a private tutor, but law was not Brahe's interest. Ever since Brahe had witnessed an eclipse of the sun in 1560, he had been fascinated by astronomy. He took courses in mathematics and astronomy, went out at night to observe the skies, and spent his allowance on astronomy books.

Brahe also had an interest in **astrology,** which is the way he earned his living for a time. He gave lectures on astrology in Copenhagen and cast horoscopes for his friends and colleagues.

In November 1572, Brahe noticed a new star (which he called a **nova**) in the **constellation** Cassiopeia. This star was so bright, it could be seen even in the daytime. We now know that what Brahe saw was a **supernova,** not a new star at all, but the explosive death of a massive star.

Viewing a new star led Brahe to conclude that the universe is not perfect and unchanging, as Aristotle had claimed. But he needed to prove that this object was indeed a star, and not a planet or a **comet.** At the time, comets were believed to be phenomena in the Earth's atmosphere, like lightning. When observed from different points, the positions of comets, planets, and the moon all appeared to shift, but the position of stars remained constant.

Tycho Brahe.

Brahe traveled all over Europe to make observations of the star he had discovered. Since its position did not shift relative to the other stars in the constellation, he concluded that it must be even farther from Earth than the moon, not a planet, and certainly not within the Earth's atmosphere. He had demonstrated that change does occur in the universe. Brahe published his finding in a book, *De nova stella* (*Concerning a New Star*), which, by its premise that the heavens are not perfect, caused quite an uproar within the religious community.

Brahe's Observatory at Hveen

Word of Brahe's discovery reached King Frederick II of Denmark, who decided to provide the astronomer with his own observatory on his own island. Brahe—consistent with his roots as a nobleman—turned the island, called Hveen, into an empire. Provided with vast sums of money, Brahe oversaw the construction of a castle called Uraniborg ("Castle of the Heavens") and the first modern research observatory, which he called Stjerneborg ("Castle of the Stars").

Brahe designed and built elaborate research equipment and hired a staff of assistants. He also had constructed on the island a paper mill, a printing press (to publish his observations along with some poetry), a chemical laboratory, elaborate gardens, fish ponds, and even a prison where he sent people who annoyed him.

In 1577, Brahe observed the elongated path of a bright comet. This observation caused him to question the two current models of the **solar system** and to devise a new one. The **Ptolemaic,** or **geocentric, model** placed the Earth at the center of the solar system, with the sun and other planets revolving around it. The **Copernican,** or **heliocentric, model** placed the sun at the center, with the planets revolving around it. Both models claimed that the planets and sun were carried around the sky by "spheres," which Brahe felt could not exist, since the comet had crossed several planetary paths.

In Brahe's model, the sun and moon revolve around the Earth and all the other planets revolve around the sun. He did away with the planetary spheres. In this way he kept the Earth at the center of the solar system, which was not just a scientific theory, but a belief held by the church.

Brahe's Observations of Astronomical Phenomena

Brahe did not have the advantage of using a telescope or other modern equipment, but he did have the finest instruments that were available in that day. He crafted his own **sextant,** a **quadrant** with a radius of 6 feet (2 meters), a two-piece arc, an **astrolabe**, and various **armillary sphere**s.

Between 1576 and 1596, Brahe made daily observations and recorded the positions of the sun, moon, and planets. He published very accurate solar tables, as well as the most precise and complete record of the positions of the planets at that point in history. He also determined the length of the year to within one second.

Brahe was as much characterized by his arrogance as he was by his intellect. In fact, at age twenty, his nose was sliced off in a duel over a mathematical point, and he wore a metal nosepiece as a reminder for the rest of his life. He managed to anger just about everyone with whom he came in contact, including King Frederick II's son, Christian IV. When Christian became king in 1596, Brahe's royal support ended. Christian evicted Brahe from Hveen, and made it a gift to one of his own mistresses. Brahe then moved to Prague to work for the Holy Roman Emperor, Rudolph II of Bohemia.

There Brahe took on Johannes Kepler as an assistant. Kepler's accomplishments in astronomy eventually became at least as important as those of his superior. Brahe, worried about being excelled by his younger colleague, kept most of his findings to himself. Nonetheless, Kepler obtained enough of Brahe's records after Brahe's death to devise the laws of planetary motion.

It was Brahe's extravagances and stubbornness that led to his death in 1601. He drank too much wine at a party and did not want to appear rude by leaving to relieve himself. This decision resulted in a urinary tract infection, from which Brahe never recovered.

Braun, Wernher von (1912–1977)
German engineer

Wernher von Braun, born in Wirsitz, Germany, had a lifelong interest in rocketry and space travel. Unfortunately, like so many other scientists and engineers during wartime, his intellect was put to use creating weapons. Only later in his life was he able to work for peaceful purposes including playing a key role in developing the technology to put a man on the moon.

Born into a wealthy family, von Braun became an amateur astronomer at an early age. Upon graduating from high school, he joined the Society for Space Travel, a group that built several experimental **rocket**s that reached heights of up to 1 mile (1.6 kilometers). When Adolf Hitler came to power in the early 1930s, the German military took over the group. They banned further private research in rocket technology.

Von Braun studied physics at the University of Berlin and earned his doctorate in 1934. At the same time, he worked at a small testing facility near Berlin, where he was in charge of research and development of rockets as military weapons for the German army.

*Wernher von Braun
holds a model of the
Jupiter-C rocket
while James van
Allen looks on.*

Throughout World War II, von Braun worked as the technical director at an army research center on the Baltic coast, developing long-range missiles. There, von Braun and his colleagues developed the A-4, the forerunner of all later rockets and ballistic missiles. It weighed 29,000 pounds (13,158 kilograms), carried 2,000 pounds (907 kilograms) of high explosives, and traveled at a speed of 3,000 miles (4,827 kilometers) per hour at a height of about 50 miles (80 kilometers). It was first launched successfully in 1942.

The rocket was later renamed the V-2 (Vengeance Weapon 2) by the German Propaganda Ministry, and thousands were ordered built by concentration camp prisoners. The V-2 was one of the war's most terrifying weapons. Over one thousand V-2s carrying 2,500 pounds (1,134 kilograms) of explosives were fired on London, England, alone. They killed 2,500 people, seriously injured 6,000, and destroyed numerous buildings and infrastructure. When von Braun learned what his missiles had accomplished, he later recounted, "it was the darkest hour of my life."

In 1944, the Gestapo (Hitler's secret police force) accused von Braun and two of his colleagues of working on exploratory space flight instead of using all of their energies to develop weapons. They were arrested and jailed, but von Braun was freed after two weeks because the Germans needed his leadership in the weapons development program.

Near the end of the war, von Braun moved to Bavaria where he and a group of other scientists hid in small villages. With the Nazis defeated, they feared for their lives. When the American troops arrived, the scientists turned themselves in.

Von Braun Joins the U.S. Space Program

Von Braun and 126 other German scientists were hired by the U.S. government and brought to the United States under the code name Project Paperclip. Using captured V-2s, the German scientists taught the Americans about their rocketry. They also continued their rocket research and test flights at the White Sands Proving Grounds in New Mexico and at Fort Bliss in Texas.

Several years later, the German scientists were transferred to the National Aeronautics and Space Administration (NASA) George C. Marshall Space Flight Center in Huntsville, Alabama. Von Braun was named the center's first director and presided over the construction of a new long-range ballistic missile called the Redstone. The missile was 70 feet (21 meters) tall, twice the size of the V-2.

Von Braun was also busy writing articles and exploring future space travel. He provided the inspiration for many of NASA's space endeavors. Anxious to develop a rocket that could launch a satellite into orbit, von Braun led the design of the Jupiter-C, a three-stage rocket capable of flying at a height of 680 miles (1,095 kilometers) and covering a distance of 3,300 miles (5,310 kilometers).

When the Russians launched the first Sputnik satellite in 1957, the U.S. space program shifted into high gear. The following January, von Braun's Juno 1 (a modified Jupiter-C) was used to launch the *Explorer 1* satellite into orbit.

Von Braun's next project was to develop a booster for a space capsule that would carry humans. His Redstone was used for two short flights: Alan Shepard, Jr. traveled in a suborbital flight for fifteen minutes in May 1961 and Gus Grissom made a similar flight the following July.

Soon thereafter von Braun worked on the giant Saturn rocket **launch vehicle.** At 150 feet (47 meters) tall and 21 feet (6.4 meters) thick at the base, this rocket was remarkably efficient and safe. In 1968, a variation of this rocket, the Saturn V, was used to launch *Apollo 8,* the first manned mission to the moon. When this goal had finally been achieved, von Braun stated: "I think it is equal in importance to that moment in evolution when aquatic life came crawling up on the land."

Von Braun continued working on Saturn rockets while directing the Marshall Space Flight Center. In 1970, he was transferred to the NASA planning office in Washington, D.C. He remained there, helping with the early stages of the **space shuttle** program, until his retirement in 1972. President Gerald Ford awarded von Braun the National Medal of Science shortly before his death in 1977.

Brown dwarfs

A **brown dwarf**—if it exists at all—is a small, dark, cool, star-like object. It is thought to be a ball of matter, formed out of a small amount of dust and gas, that never quite completes the process of becoming a star. This object never gets large enough to produce the tremendous pressure it takes to begin **nuclear fusion,** the process that makes stars bright and hot. In theory, an object with less than 8 percent of the **mass** of the sun cannot become a star. A brown dwarf could be about the size of Jupiter.

Brown dwarfs are too dark to be seen through ordinary telescopes. Their existence was first suggested in the 1930s, when observers at Swarthmore College in Pennsylvania noticed visible stars that bounced in their paths across the sky. This kind of motion is typical of a star that is being tugged at by the gravitational pull of a companion star. The name "brown dwarfs" was given to these invisible companion stars by American astronomer Jill Tarter in 1975.

Since the 1970s, David McCarthy, an astronomer at the University of Arizona, has used **infrared astronomy** to search for brown dwarfs. He is operating on the theory that these objects may emit enough infrared energy and light to be detectable using infrared telescopes and detectors. He and his colleagues have discovered several objects that may be brown dwarfs, but their existence has yet to be proven.

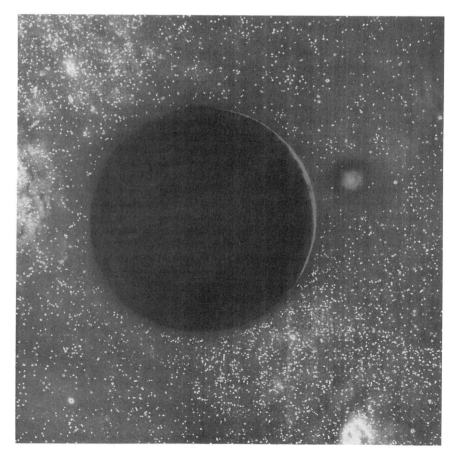

What a brown dwarf might look like if it were visible. In spite of the lack of evidence of their existence, many astronomers believe that there are millions of brown dwarfs throughout space, and that this accounts for some of the missing dark matter that is thought to make up 90 percent of the universe.

Calendar

The existence of ancient stone **calendar**s, preserved from as far back as 2500 B.C., shows that civilizations throughout the centuries have felt a need to organize time into days, months, and years. Without calendars it would have been impossible to record historic events or to set dates for annual holidays (such as religious observances). In our daily lives we use calendars to keep track of birthdays, to set up appointments, to make summer vacation plans, and for many other purposes.

Units of time are defined by three different types of motion: a day is one rotation of the Earth about its axis; a month is one revolution of the moon around the Earth; and a year is one trip of the Earth around the sun. Making a yearly calendar, however, is no simple task because these periods of time do not divide evenly into one another. For instance, it takes the moon 29.5 days to orbit the Earth, and it takes the Earth 365.242199 days to orbit the sun. The calendar we use currently has rules to account for the extra fraction of a day in each year.

Our calendar is the latest in a series that have been developed, improved upon, and standardized over time. The original model for our calendar was created by the ancient Romans and Greeks as far back as the eighth century B.C. The first big improvement to that 365-day calendar that we know of was made by Julius Caesar in the year 46 B.C. With the help of astronomer Sosigenes, Caesar developed a system that gave 365.25 days to each year. In this new Julian calendar (named after Caesar) an extra day, or leap day, was added to every fourth year.

The Julian calendar, however, was still off by eleven minutes and fourteen seconds each year. That amount of time might not sound like much, but over four centuries it added up to just over three days. One consequence of this change was that the vernal **equinox** (the first day of spring) slipped back from March 25 to March 21. By the mid-1500s the calendar was another ten days ahead of the Earth's natural yearly cycle.

The Gregorian Calendar

By 1582, the beginning of spring had moved back to March 11, and it was once again necessary to adjust the date so it would line up with the seasons. Pope Gregory XIII introduced another change in the calendar in an attempt to narrow the gap between the Julian calendar of 365.25 days per year and the natural year consisting of 365.242199 days per year.

First, Gregory declared that the current date would be set ahead ten days in order to bring the start of spring back to March 21. Then he pro-

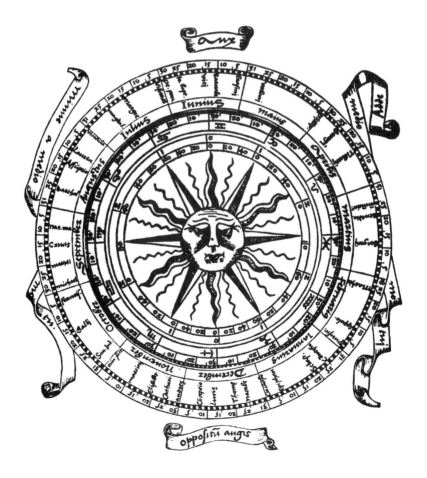

Undated Latin calendar.

ceeded to eliminate three days from every four centuries in the future. This was accomplished by modifying the leap-year rule, so that only one of every four century-years would be a leap year. Under the Julian calendar, every century-year (200, 300, 400, etc.), divisible by four, was designated as a leap year. Gregory ruled that only those century-years divisible by four hundred (400, 800, 1200, etc.) would be a leap year. The new calendar was named the Gregorian calendar and is the still in use today in most of the Western world.

The Gregorian calendar, although not perfect, is accurate to within .000301 days (or 26 seconds) per year. At this rate, it will be off by one day every thirty-three hundred years. As we approach the year 2000, we still have nearly two millennia before the extra day catches up with us. This should be ample time for calendar-makers to find a solution.

See also **Time**

Cannon, Annie Jump (1863–1941)
American astronomer

Annie Jump Cannon developed a fascination with astronomy at an early age when she was a child in Dover, Delaware. Cannon's mother improvised an observatory in their attic where she and her daughters would study the sky.

In 1880, Cannon entered Wellesley College in Massachusetts to study astronomy. She became especially interested in stellar **spectroscopy,** the process in which starlight is broken apart into its component colors so that the various elements of the star can be identified.

After graduating from Wellesley in 1884, Cannon returned home for a brief period before coming down with scarlet fever. The illness left her hard of hearing. After her mother died, Cannon returned to Wellesley in 1893 to earn her master's degree. She then continued her studies at Radcliffe College in Massachusetts.

During her second year at Radcliffe, Cannon became an assistant at the Harvard College Observatory, the first observatory to include women as staff members. There she put to use her knowledge of spectroscopy to make a detailed study of starlight.

At first, it took Cannon a month to study five thousand stars. Later she could record observations of three hundred stars an hour with great accuracy. In total, Cannon observed, classified, and analyzed the **spectra** of two hundred-fifty thousand stars. She worked with astronomer Edward C. Pickering to compose the nine-volume star index called the "Henry Draper Catalogue" of the stars (named for its benefactor Henry Draper), which is still in use today. She also gave lectures and published reports.

In 1911, Cannon almost was offered a faculty appointment at Harvard. But some university officials refused to promote a woman to such a high status. Instead she became curator of astronomical photographs, with a salary of twelve hundred dollars a year.

In 1936, when Cannon was seventy-three years old, she began a study of ten thousand very faint stars. Harvard finally hired her as a permanent faculty member two years later.

*Annie Jump Cannon
looks at one of the
three hundred
thousand
photographic plates
of stars in the
Harvard University
collection, April 30,
1930.*

Not until 1956 did Harvard hire its first woman as a full professor. Her name was Cecilia Payne-Gaposchkin, and she was Cannon's colleague. "When I think of her as a person I am at a loss for words," said Gaposchkin about Cannon. "She wore her hearing aid with an air, and made a virtue of necessity by unshipping it [turning it off] when she wanted to be undisturbed or to do concentrated work. She was warm, cheerful, enthusiastic, hospitable."

Cannon became known as the world's expert in the classification of stars. The information she collected has proven invaluable to later studies, and she laid the groundwork for modern stellar spectroscopy. Cannon received many honors and awards during her forty-four-year career. She retired from Harvard in 1940 and died the following year at the age of seventy-eight.

Cassini, Gian Domenico (1625–1712)
Italian-born French astronomer

Cassini was born in Perinaldo, Italy, near Nice, France. He was educated by Jesuit priests and astronomers Giovanni Riccioli and Francesco Grimaldi. At the age of twenty-five, he was hired as a professor of astronomy at the University of Bologna.

While at Bologna, Cassini tracked the orbits of Jupiter's moons over a long period of time and published a table of his results. Other astronomers who subsequently used Cassini's data noticed that when the Earth and Jupiter were farthest apart, the moons appeared to take longer to pass in front of Jupiter than Cassini's table indicated. Some scientists realized that the table was not in error, but that the discrepancy occurred only because the light of the moons took longer to travel the greater distance between Earth and Jupiter. In 1676, Olaus Roemer, working from this theory, used Cassini's table to calculate the **speed of light.**

In 1669, King Louis XIV of France offered Cassini a job as director of the new Paris Observatory. Cassini accepted. In his new post he discovered four more moons orbiting Saturn. (The first moon discovered had been Titan, observed by Christiaan Huygens in 1656.)

A s t r o n o m y   &   S p a c e

Cassini also made detailed observations of Mars, the only planet whose surface can be seen clearly from Earth. He discovered that Mars has polar caps that spread during the Martian winter and shrink in the summer. These seasonal variations caused him to consider the possibility of life on Mars.

Cassini was the first person to detect the dark gap that divides Saturn's ring into two sections. The gap is now known as "Cassini's Division." Although Cassini had theorized that the gap was empty space, the Voyager missions of 1980 and 1981 have shown that the gap is filled with at least a hundred tiny ringlets, each composed of countless particles.

Cassini is best known for a measurement that shed light on the immense size of the **solar system.** He first found the **parallax** of Mars, based on two sets of observations: his own, made in Paris; and those of his colleague Jean Richer, made in French Guiana in South America. With this information he was able to calculate the distance from Earth to Mars, and then from Earth to the sun.

In 1672, Cassini defined the **astronomical unit,** the distance from Earth to the sun, as 87 million miles (140 million kilometers). While this estimate was low (we now place the value of one astronomical unit at 93 million miles, or 150 million kilometers), it was much more accurate than earlier estimates. In the previous decades, Tycho Brahe had put the distance at 5 million miles (8 million kilometers) and his successor, Johannes Kepler, had estimated 15 million miles (24 million kilometers).

Cassini retired from the Paris Observatory in 1710 after going blind and died two years later. The position of director passed next to his son, and later to his grandson.

Cepheid variables

Variable stars are stars that vary in brightness over time. In most cases, these changes occur very slowly, over a period of months or even years. However, one class of variables changes in brightness much more quickly, on a regular cycle lasting three to fifty days. These stars are called **cepheid variable**s.

Cepheids are blinking yellow **supergiant** stars, the pulsation of which seems to be caused by the expansion and contraction of their sur-

Opposite page: *Gian Domenico Cassini.*

face layers. The time it takes a cepheid to complete one pulsation is related to its brightness at a constant distance from Earth. For this reason, these stars have been given the name "astronomical yardsticks."

Cepheid variables were discovered by American astronomer Henrietta Swan Leavitt in 1904. Leavitt realized that the longer it took one of these stars to complete a cycle, the brighter it was. She was unable, however, to observe this relationship between time and brightness, for stars in our **galaxy.** The reason is that a relatively close star may appear bright or dim due to its nearness or farness from us, or our view of it may be partially blocked by dust. A star's true brightness, or **absolute magnitude,** can only be observed at great distances (in galaxies beyond the **Milky Way**), so far away that all the stars are roughly the same distance from us.

Thus Leavitt traveled to Harvard University's observatory in Peru and studied cepheids in a nearby galaxy called the Small Magellanic Cloud. She timed how long it took each cepheid to complete its bright-dim cycle and measured its absolute magnitude. Based on the relationship of these two figures, Leavitt was able to roughly estimate their distance (and consequently, the distance of the entire galaxy) from Earth.

Harlow Shapley, an astronomer at Mount Wilson Observatory in Pasadena, California, then used Leavitt's findings to measure the size of the Milky Way. He discovered many new cepheid variables within **globular cluster**s of stars and attempted to calculate the distance to those clusters.

In this way, Shapley concluded that our galaxy was three hundred thousand **light-year**s across. This size was so drastically different from previous estimates of fifteen to twenty thousand light-years, that Shapley's colleagues had difficulty believing it. Shapley further changed our concept of the galaxy by estimating that the sun was fifty thousand light-years from the center, whereas before it had been assumed that the sun was at the galactic center.

It turns out that Shapley's estimate of the size of the Milky Way was about three times too large. The reason for Shapley's error is that the variable stars he used as "astronomical yardsticks" were really smaller and dimmer than he had thought and hence not as far away. Accordingly, he positioned the sun too far from the center of the galaxy, but only by about twenty-thousand light-years.

About ten years later, in 1924, another Mount Wilson astronomer named Edwin Hubble undertook a study of **nebula**e, clouds of gas and dust. He was most interested in whether they were part of our galaxy, as was commonly believed, or whether they were extragalactic objects. At that time it was thought that the Milky Way was the only galaxy in the universe.

To answer this question, Hubble identified twelve cepheid variables in one nebula in a region of space called Andromeda. Hubble, like Leavitt and Shapley before him, used the cepheids as distance markers and learned that the nebula was at least eight hundred thousand light-years away. This distance was much greater than the farthest reaches of the Milky Way, meaning that the Andromeda was a separate galaxy.

Cepheid variables are still the best indicator of distance in the skies. Originally their usefulness was limited to the thirty or so galaxies in which they could be detected. Now with the Hubble Space Telescope astronomers are able to locate cepheids in galaxies up to sixteen million light-years away.

See also **Variable stars**

Cerro Tololo Interamerican Observatory

The best place for astronomers to observe the universe is on a satellite, such as the Hubble Space Telescope. The next best place is high on a mountaintop. The reason for this fact is that the source of major interference in ground-based observations of space is the Earth's atmosphere. Atmospheric gas molecules tend to scatter light from celestial objects, distorting their image. The higher up one goes on the Earth, however, the thinner the atmosphere. The peak of Cerro Tololo, a mountain in Chile, extends beyond the bottom quarter of the atmosphere. Thus the air there is considerably thinner than at sea level.

This consideration was an important factor in convincing scientists to select Cerro Tololo as the site for a major observatory in the Southern Hemisphere. The mountaintop also features clear, dark skies; low humidity; and reasonable accessibility, all important characteristics for an astronomical observatory.

The Cerro Tololo Interamerican Observatory (CTIO) is one of a handful of Southern Hemisphere observatories, most of them located in

The 158-inch (401-centimeter) reflector telescope, currently the largest in the Southern Hemisphere, at the Cerro Tololo Interamerican Observatory in Chile.

South America or Australia. The major South American observatories were begun by Northern Hemisphere scientific organizations and universities in order to observe the portion of the sky that cannot be seen at northern **latitudes.** For instance, the Large and Small Magellanic Clouds, the **galaxies** nearest to the **Milky Way,** can be seen only from southern skies. The Southern Hemisphere is also the best place from which to view the center of our own galaxy.

Astronomers wishing to use CTIO must submit a detailed proposal describing their work, at least six months in advance. A committee selects those applicants whose projects they deem worthy, about one-quarter of all applicants. Viewing time is given out in two-to-six night stretches. And if it happens to be overcast during an astronomer's precious time at CTIO, he or she is just plain out of luck.

The journey to CTIO is not an easy one. From Miami, Florida, it is about a seven and one-half hour flight to Santiago, the capital of Chile. Next comes a seven-hour bus ride to the mountain town of La Serena. The observatory is 35 miles (56 kilometers) east of La Serena, at an altitude of 7,200 feet (2,200 meters). In addition to the long journey, astronomers must contend with a twelve-hour jet lag and chilly temperatures.

CTIO has been operating since 1976. It is one of the National Optical Astronomy Observatories, the others being Kitt Peak National Observatory in Tucson, Arizona, and the National Solar Observatory at Sacramento Peak, California. CTIO is operated by the Association of Universities for Research in Astronomy in conjunction with the University of Chile and is funded by the National Science Foundation.

The observatory has a mystical appearance. It sits atop a mountain, the peak of which has been bulldozed and covered with an acre of concrete. On this concrete slab sit seven white domes, packed closely together. Huge birds called condors circle overhead, casting shadows on the domes. Each dome has, in addition to a telescope, a control room with several computer monitors. The monitors display information about the telescope, the object or objects under observation, and updated weather reports.

CTIO is home to six optical telescopes, including a 158-inch (401-centimeter) **reflector** which is currently the largest in the Southern Hemisphere, and a **radio telescope.** Plans are underway to add a 315-inch (800-centimeter) telescope capable of observing ultraviolet light by the end of the 1990s.

See also **European Southern Observatory**

Challenger

In 1982, *Challenger* became the second member of the fleet of **space shuttle** orbiters. An orbiter is a winged space plane designed to transport astronauts and equipment into space and back. Together with solid **rocket** boosters and an external tank, it constitutes a space shuttle (officially called the Space Transportation System).

Because of its tragic ending, the name *Challenger* is probably recognized by more people worldwide than any other shuttle orbiter. *Challenger* completed nine flights, the first in April 1983, before its demise in 1986.

On its first flight, *Challenger* carried a tracking and data relay satellite into space. Two months later, *Challenger* flew again. On the crew of this flight was Sally Ride, the first U.S. female astronaut in space. On board the *Challenger*'s third flight was Guion Bluford, the first Black American astronaut in space. On its various missions, *Challenger* placed into orbit the European Spacelab as well as a number of military and scientific satellites.

Challenger's next flight was to be on January 28, 1986. The launch had already been delayed four times before that cold, fateful morning at Cape Canaveral. Despite the presence of icicles on the launch tower, flight officials decided the weather conditions posed no threat and that the launch should proceed. Seventy-three seconds after lift-off *Challenger* exploded, killing all seven people on board.

This flight would have been the twenty-fifth of the four-shuttle fleet (made-up of *Challenger, Atlantis, Columbia,* and *Discovery*) the first twenty-four having returned safely. This flight had been highly publicized because it carried the first schoolteacher into space, Christa McAuliffe. McAuliffe had been chosen from a pool of eleven thousand applicants. She had been scheduled to broadcast a number of lessons while in orbit directly into schools. The other six astronauts reflected a cross-section of the American populace in terms of race, gender, home state, and religion. Millions of people around the world who tuned in to watch the televised lift-off became witnesses to the tragedy.

The *Challenger* disaster led to the grounding of the entire space shuttle fleet for the next two years and eight months, while the National Aeronautics and Space Administration (NASA) investigated the cause of the explosion. NASA officials found that the accident had been caused by a

A Lockheed employee at the Kennedy Space Center watches as the space shuttle Challenger *explodes, January 28, 1986.*

leak in one of the two solid rocket boosters that ignite the main fuel tank, the result of a faulty rubberized seal called an "O-ring." The probe into the accident also turned up other flaws in the shuttle construction, such as weaknesses in the braking system used for landing. The three remaining shuttles were carefully inspected and upgraded before flights resumed.

The space shuttle orbiter is a vessel that acts like a spacecraft but looks like an airplane. It contains engines, astronaut living and work quarters, and a cargo bay large enough to hold a bus. The orbiter is launched vertically using its own engines, aided by two attached rocket boosters. The boosters fall away from the orbiter about two minutes after launch and parachute into the ocean, where they are captured for re-use.

When the orbiter is ready to come back to Earth it brakes with its engines. Its delta-shaped wings facilitate its re-entry into the Earth's atmosphere and it glides in for a landing on a specially designed, 3-mile-long (5-kilometer-long) runway.

Of the four original space shuttle orbiters, all but *Challenger* are still in use. The newest shuttle, *Endeavour,* was completed in 1991 to replace *Challenger.*

See also **Space shuttle**

Chandrasekhar, Subrahmanyan
(1910–1995)
Indian-born American astronomer

Subrahmanyan Chandrasekhar was born in Lahore, a part of India that is now in Pakistan. He attended Madras University in India, where he wrote an award-winning essay on quantum physics. For his prize, he selected Sir Arthur Eddington's book *Internal Constitution of the Stars,* which furthered his interest in astronomy. In 1930, Chandrasekhar won a Government of India scholarship and entered a Ph.D. program at Cambridge University in England.

On his sea voyage to Great Britain, Chandrasekhar thought a lot about the death of stars. Using theories from Eddington's book as well as Albert Einstein's theory of relativity, he calculated that a star greater than a certain size would not undergo the evolution that astronomers had predicted for it. That is, it would not become a **white dwarf,** but would just keep on collapsing.

After he completed his degree in 1934, Chandrasekhar returned to his work on white dwarfs. He theorized that any star with a **mass** more than one-and-a-half times that of the sun (now known as **Chandrasekhar's limit**) could not become a white dwarf because it would be crushed by its own **gravity,** becoming either a **neutron star** or a **black hole.**

Some years later, Chandrasekhar abandoned this topic, after being harshly criticized by Eddington, who was not happy that a much younger colleague made major modifications to his work. Eddington, whom Chandrasekhar had long admired, publicly ridiculed him in a 1936 speech at Harvard University, saying that Chandrasekhar "seemed to like the stars to behave that way, and believes that this is what really happens." He called Chandrasekhar's theory "stellar buffoonery." Eddington's words un-

Subrahmanyan Chandrasekhar, left, receives the 1983 Nobel Prize in physics from King Carl Gustaf of Sweden.

dermined Chandrasekhar's standing within the scientific community and lost him any chance of obtaining a position at Cambridge.

The same year, Chandrasekhar came to the United States He was hired to teach at the University of Chicago and to conduct research at the Yerkes Observatory in Wisconsin. He became a naturalized citizen in 1953.

Chandrasekhar's calculations about white dwarfs were finally accepted by astronomers. He went on to make several advances in the field of **astrophysics,** most significantly regarding the transfer of energy in the atmosphere of stars. He has won several awards over the years, including the Nobel Prize in physics in 1983. Chandrasekhar did of heart failure in Chicago at age eighty-four.

See also **Eddington, Arthur**

Columbia

April 12, 1981, was the date of the first piloted flight of the Space Transportation System, better known as the **space shuttle.** The program had opened with an experimental phase using the test shuttle *Enterprise* in 1977. In early 1981, after ten years in development, *Columbia* was completed. It was the first shuttle designed to ferry astronauts and equipment into space and back.

On its first flight, *Columbia*'s only mission was to test its orbital flight and landing capabilities. After spending fifty-four hours in space and completing thirty-six Earth orbits, it landed safely. *Columbia* made four more voyages before the next shuttle, *Challenger,* was completed. *Columbia* has logged nineteen flights as of April 1996.

Columbia is an orbiter, which together with solid **rocket** boosters and external tank, constitute a space shuttle. An orbiter is a winged space plane. It contains engines, astronaut living and work quarters, and a cargo bay large enough to hold a bus. It is launched vertically using its own engines, aided by two attached rocket boosters. The boosters fall away from the orbiter about two minutes after launch and parachute into the ocean, from which they are retrieved and used again.

Opposite page: A camera mounted on the service structure produced this bird's-eye view of the space shuttle Columbia *lifting off on November 11, 1982.*

Once in orbit, the vessel can use its own rocket motors to change direction. When it is ready to come back to Earth, the orbiter brakes with its engines. Its delta-shaped wings facilitate its re-entry into the Earth's at-

mosphere and it glides in for a landing on a specially designed 3-mile-long (5-kilometer-long) runway.

Columbia was named for the first American ocean vessel to circle the globe in the late 1700s. It has completed numerous assignments over the last fifteen years. In 1983, on its sixth flight, it carried the first European-built Spacelab on a ten-day research mission. On its seventh flight in 1986 its passengers included Franklin Chang-Diaz, the first Hispanic astronaut and Bill Nelson, the first U.S. Congressman in space. *Columbia*'s accomplishments also include the delivery into space of a number of civilian and military satellites, the retrieval of satellites in need of repair, and the operation of further Spacelab experiments.

Of the four original space shuttle orbiters, three are still in use. Besides *Columbia,* these include *Atlantis* and *Discovery.* The fourth, *Challenger,* was destroyed in a tragic accident in 1986. It has since been replaced with the newest shuttle, *Endeavour.*

See also **Space shuttle** and **Spacelab**

Comet Hyakutake

Comet Hyakutake (hi-yah-koo-tah-kay), visible to Earthlings in the spring of 1996, was the brightest and closest **comet** to come our way in two decades. It was brilliant enough to have been witnessed even by naked-eye viewers in light-polluted cities. This comet came much closer to Earth than Halley's comet ever did in its greatly anticipated (and quite disappointing) 1985 fly-by. The closest Halley came on that trip was 39 million miles (63 million kilometers) from Earth. Hyakutake, on the other hand, approached within 9.3 million miles (15 million kilometers), just forty times the distance to the moon.

Comet Hyakutake took the world by surprise. It had been discovered only two months before its arrival by an amateur astronomer in Japan named Yuji Hyakutake. Hyakutake was his second comet discovery in two months. He had given the same name to the first, a much fainter comet.

Comet Hyakutake was first visible in the Northern Hemisphere in mid-March and reached its closest point to Earth on March 25. At the end of April, the comet looped around the sun, and in May it passed by the

Earth again. This time it was visible to people in the Southern Hemisphere. It then traveled off into space, continuing its long orbit around the sun.

While astronomers usually have years to prepare for the arrival of a comet, Hyakutake posed a different problem. They had relatively little time to set up ground-based cameras and had to divert telescopes from other projects. They also prepared the Hubble Space Telescope to capture detailed images of the comet. What they discovered was an icy nucleus surrounded by jets of dust. It appeared that gas and dust were escaping through holes in the comet's surface.

This description fits the general view of comets as being "dirty snowballs," nothing more than clumps of rocky material, dust, and ice made of frozen methane, ammonia, and water. And, as comets are known to do, Hyakutake had an ion tail (made mostly of electrically charged hydrogen compounds) that pointed away from the sun. This tail is formed when some of the comet melts as it nears the sun and the gas is swept back by the **solar wind.** Hyakutake was unusual, however, in that it also had a second, smaller tail made of dirt particles.

Hyakutake was estimated to be about 10 miles (16 kilometers) across, about the same size as Halley's comet. It traveled at about 93,000 miles (150,000 kilometers) per hour—forty-five times faster than a speeding bullet. At 9.3 million miles (15 million kilometers) away, however, it appeared to stand still in the sky. The comet's change in position could only be detected from night to night, as it showed up in progressively westward locations.

Comet Hyakutake.

The 1996 visit of Hyakutake was the only chance humans alive today will have to see the comet. It will not pass this way again for another ten thousand to twenty thousand years.

See also **Comets**

Comets

Comets are best described as "dirty snowballs." Clumps of rocky material, dust, and frozen methane, ammonia, and water, they streak across the sky on long, elliptical (oval-shaped) orbits around the sun. A comet is star-like in appearance and consists of a nucleus, a head, and a gaseous tail. The tail (which always points away from the sun) is formed when some of the comet melts as it nears the sun and is swept back by the **solar wind** (electrically charged subatomic particles that flow out from the sun).

Throughout the ages, a great deal of mythology has been associated with the presence of comets. Because of their unusual shape and sudden appearance, comets were commonly viewed as omens, both good and bad. A comet appearing in 44 B.C. shortly after Julius Caesar was killed was thought to be his soul returning. In A.D. 451, the Romans felt that a comet's appearance was responsible for the defeat of Attila the Hun, and in A.D. 684 a comet was blamed for an outbreak of the plague. People used to print and distribute pamphlets every time a comet was coming, some with titles such as "News of the Terrible and Fearsome Comet."

Aristotle, the famous Greek philosopher and scientist from the third century B.C., mistakenly believed that comets were atmospheric phenomena and that they were a sign of coming weather. Once astronomers finally determined that comets occur in space, beyond the Earth's atmosphere, they tried to determine where a comet's journey begins and ends.

Johannes Kepler, who observed the comet of 1607, concluded that comets follow straight lines, coming from and disappearing into infinity. Somewhat later, German astronomer Johannes Hevelius suggested that comets followed slightly curved lines. Then in the latter half of the 1600s, Georg Samuel Dörffel suggested that comets follow a parabolic course.

Shortly thereafter, English astronomer Edmond Halley calculated the paths traveled by twenty-four comets. Among these, he found three—those of 1531, 1607, and one he viewed himself in 1682—with nearly identical paths. This discovery led him to the conclusion that comets follow an orbit around the sun, and thus reappear periodically. In 1695, Halley wrote in a letter to Isaac Newton, "I am more and more confirmed that we have seen that Comett now three times, since ye yeare 1531."

Halley predicted that this same comet would return in 1758. Although he did not live to see it, his prediction was correct, and the comet was named Halley's comet.

We now know that Halley's comet and other comets orbit the sun on elliptical paths. (Since they orbit the sun, they are members of the **solar system.**) Early astronomers believed that a second group of comets also exist, those that appeared only once and have parabolic paths. Further study showed that all comets follow elliptical paths, but that some paths are so elongated, even taking millions of years to complete, that they appear to be parabolic.

The most commonly accepted theory about where comets originate was suggested by Dutch astronomer Jan Oort in 1950. Oort's theory states that trillions of inactive comets lie on the outskirts of the solar system, about one **light-year** from the sun. They remain there in what is called an **Oort cloud,** until a passing gas cloud or star jolts a comet into orbit around the sun. The Oort cloud lies somewhere between 50,000 and 150,000 **astronomical unit**s from the sun.

In 1951, another Dutch astronomer, Gerard Kuiper, suggested that there is a second cometary reservoir located just beyond the edge of our solar system, around one thousand times closer to the sun than the Oort cloud. His hypothetical **Kuiper belt** is located somewhere between 35 and 1,000 astronomical units from the sun. It contains an estimated ten-million-to-one-billion comets, far fewer than the Oort cloud.

There are many theories as to what happens at the end of a comet's life. The most common is that the comet's nucleus either splits or explodes, which may produce a **meteor shower.** It has also been proposed that comets eventually become inactive and end up as **asteroid**s. Yet another theory is that **gravity** or some other disturbance causes a comet to exit the solar system and travel out into the **interstellar medium.**

In 1986, when Halley's comet was scheduled to pass near the sun, over one thousand scientists from forty countries coordinated the International Halley Watch. Soviet, Japanese, and European **space probe**s were sent to get a close look at the comet, while other spacecraft and telescopes were used for observation. The European Space Agency's probe, *Giotto,* flew in toward the comet's center and took pictures. These photographs showed the nucleus to be a 9.3 mile-long, 6 mile-wide, (15-kilometer long, 9.7-kilometer wide) coal-black, potato-shaped object marked by hills and valleys. Two bright jets of gas and dust, each 9 miles (14.5 kilometers) long, exit from of the nucleus. Halley's comet will next pass by Earth in the year 2061.

See also **Comet Hyakutake**; **Halley, Edmond**; **Halley's comet**; and **Oort, Jan**

Command module

A **command module** (CM) is the area of a spacecraft that houses astronauts and the controls needed to operate the spacecraft. The command module was originally created for use in the Apollo space program of the years 1967–1972. Fifteen Apollo spacecraft in all were constructed with the goal of landing astronauts on and exploring the moon. A command module provides the crew and the instruments with protection against extreme changes in temperature, collisions with **meteorite**s, and the force of splashdown. The other elements of an Apollo spacecraft were the **service module** (SM), which contained supplies and equipment; and the **lunar module** (LM), which detached to land on the moon.

The CM is a cone-shaped unit that perched at the top of the ship. At 127 inches (323 centimeters) tall and 154 inches (391 centimeters) in diameter, it was just big enough to accommodate three astronauts. Tucked away in its front end was a 33-foot-long (10-meter-long) **rocket** capable of guiding the CM away from the rest of the structure in case of an emergency during launch. That end also contained two small thrusters for reentry into the Earth's atmosphere and parachutes for use during the fall to Earth. Beyond all that equipment was a tunnel with an airtight hatch, used for linking up with the LM.

Three couches, on which the astronauts could sleep or sit and operate the control panels, took up most of the space in the CM. The control panels consisted of 24 display instruments, 111 lights, and over 560 switches. The center couch folded up to save space. Storage bins lined the walls of the CM, which held food, clothing, and water. The pressure and temperature (75 degrees Fahrenheit, or 24 degrees Celsius) within the cabin were kept constant, allowing the astronauts to move about without their spacesuits (except during takeoff and re-entry).

Five windows were built into the cabin at the insistence of astronauts who wanted to view their surroundings. Two of the windows faced forward so they could watch the docking procedure with the LM. The other three faced out to the sides, for general sightseeing.

For most of the voyage to the moon and back, the CM remained linked with the SM. The CM, however, was the only unit capable of returning safely to Earth. Thus, just before re-entry, the CM and the SM (together called the CSM) separated. The large flat end of the CM was covered with a special heat shield made of a 2-inch-thick (5-centimeter-thick) reinforced plastic capable of withstanding temperatures of up to 5,000 degrees Fahrenheit (2,760 degrees Celsius). The plastic charred and peeled

The Apollo 11 *command and service module (CSM).*

off, carrying the heat away with it. After its scorching re-entry, the CM un-furled parachutes to slow its descent before splashing down in the ocean.

See also **Apollo program**; **Lunar module**; and **Spacecraft design**

Communications satellite

The age of communications satellites has brought about worldwide tele-phone and television connections, the pictures we see on nightly weather reports, electronic international banking, and the transfer of huge amounts of scientific data. One satellite can carry more than one hundred thousand phone calls and several television signals at one time. Almost any infor-mation that relies on cables, lines, or antennas can now be communicated by satellite.

A communications satellite is a relay station equipped with receivers (which receive a signal), amplifiers (which enlarge a signal) and transmit-ters (which send a signal back). Most of these satellites circle Earth in a **geosynchronous orbit,** a path that takes twenty-four hours to complete, like one rotation of the Earth. If a satellite is launched over the equator, it may attain a **geostationary orbit,** a special kind of geosynchronous orbit. This means that the satellite always travels in the same plane as the Earth's equator and maintains constant contact with relay stations on the ground below it. A network of satellites connects all parts of the globe.

Before 1956, the potential for trans-Atlantic communication did not look very promising. People could speak to each other by radiotelephone, but this was subject to atmospheric conditions. During a storm, the con-nection would be poor. In 1956, the first trans-Atlantic cables were in place on the ocean floor, but there were not enough of them to handle the increasing volume of phone calls. Scientists looked up, rather than down, for the next phase of communications technology.

The concept of communications satellites was first introduced by British science fiction writer Arthur C. Clarke in 1945. He proposed con-structing an international communication system using three orbiting satel-lites. To make this a reality, scientists had to overcome many obstacles. They had to design a machine that could withstand extreme heat and cold and have a power supply that would last years. They also had to figure out how to launch it into orbit.

Opposite page: Early Bird communications satellite getting ready for a test of its antenna. The satellite was launched into a synchronous orbit for two-day phone channels between Europe and North America in 1965.

Scientists in the former **Soviet Union** (now Russia and its surrounding countries) were the first to accomplish this. In 1957, the Soviets
launched the first satellite into orbit, called *Sputnik 1.*

The first U.S. communications satellite, named *Echo,* was launched
in 1960. Developed by John Pierce of Bell Telephone Laboratories, *Echo*
was an aluminum-coated, gas-filled plastic balloon, 100 feet (30 meters)
in diameter. It was placed in a low orbit and functioned until 1968 as the
world's first passive reflector communication satellite (meaning that it
bounced signals back to Earth, rather than actively transmitting them). The
next satellite, *Echo II,* was in service from 1964 to 1969.

AT&T developed *Telstar,* the first active-transmitting communications satellite. It was launched in 1962, and transmitted telephone calls and
television broadcasts between locations in Maine, England, and France. At
the same time, the National Aeronautics and Space Administration
(NASA) was building a similar satellite called *Relay.* Together, *Telstar* and
Relay demonstrated the potential of multi-satellite communications systems for telephone and television transmissions. Telstar satellites are still
in use—one was launched as recently as 1993.

Also in 1962, the United States formed the Communications Satellite Corporation (Comsat), to develop a worldwide communications satellite network. Two years later, eleven countries of the international community came together and formed the International Telecommunications
Satellite Organization (Intelsat), to create a jointly owned communications
system and to conduct scientific research. There are now more than 130
member nations of Intelsat.

The problem with the early satellites is that they did not have geosynchronous orbits. They shifted position relative to the Earth and moved
in and out of range of the ground stations from which the signals originated. *Telstar* could communicate with a ground station for only one to
four hours per day.

That problem was solved in 1963, with the launching of *Syncom*—a
geostationary satellite developed by Hughes Aircraft and NASA. *Syncom*'s
high altitude and twenty-four-hour orbit allowed it to stay in constant contact with stations on the ground. A second Syncom-class satellite was
launched in 1964 and several more have been launched since 1984 during
space shuttle missions. In 1965, the Soviets put the *Molniya* into orbit, a
geosynchronous satellite that provided television, telephone, and telegraph

links all over that huge nation, as well as a platform for scientific observation. In 1971, the Soviet Union, together with other Communist bloc nations, formed an international communications organization called Intersputnik.

Other classes of communications satellites include: Marisat, Westar, and Oscar. Marisat satellites provide communication links between ships and stations on shore; Westar satellites, operated by the Western Union Telegraph Company, provide video, data, and voice transmissions throughout the United States, Puerto Rico, and the Virgin Islands; and Oscar satellites are used by amateur radio operators in over sixteen countries.

One problem that has emerged recently is that there are so many satellites out there, it's hard to find room for new ones. Satellites can't be too close together on the geosynchronous orbit or they will interfere with each other's signals. Recent improvements in fiber optics (the use of fine, flexible glass rods to reflect light), however, may mean a shift back toward the use of ocean-bottom cable for many types of communications in the future.

See also **Intelsat**

Compton Gamma Ray Observatory

In 1991, the Compton Gamma Ray Observatory (CGRO) was sent into space by the National Aeronautics and Space Administration (NASA). Named for Nobel-prize-winning physicist Arthur Holly Compton, its mission has been to provide a detailed picture of cosmic **gamma ray**s.

Gamma rays are the shortest-wavelength radiation in the **electromagnetic spectrum.** The type of **electromagnetic radiation** with which we are most familiar is visible light, which includes all the colors of the rainbow. The entire electromagnetic spectrum, however, is much larger than the visible region we can see. Some objects in space do not shine with any visible light, but their presence can be detected because of **radio waves**, **X-ray**s, or gamma rays they give off.

Gamma rays are high-energy subatomic particles formed either by the decay of radioactive elements or by nuclear reactions. Terrestrial gamma rays—those produced on Earth—are the only gamma rays we can observe here. A second class of gamma rays, called cosmic gamma rays, are unable to penetrate the Earth's protective **ozone layer.** The only way to detect cosmic gamma rays, which are created by **nuclear fusion** that takes place on the surface of stars, is by sending a satellite-observatory, like the CGRO, into space.

The CGRO had many predecessors. The first satellites to detect gamma radiation in space, launched in 1967, were called Velas. In the early 1970s, NASA launched other small, gamma-ray-detecting satellites, leading up to the High Energy Astrophysical Observatories of the late 1970s. In all, these satellites revealed thousands of previously unknown stars and several possible **black hole**s. They found that the entire **Milky Way** shines with gamma rays.

The 1991 Launch of the CGRO

The CGRO was transported into space by the **space shuttle** *Atlantis* on April 5, 1991, and continues to orbit the Earth and send back information. This 16-ton (14.5-metric ton) observatory has provided scientists with an all-sky map of cosmic gamma ray emissions, as well as with new information about **supernova**s; young star clusters; **pulsar**s; black holes; **quasar**s; solar **flare**s; **nova**s; and gamma-ray bursts. Gamma-ray bursts are intense flashes of gamma rays that occur uniformly across the sky and are of unknown origin.

A major discovery of the CGRO has been the class of objects called gamma-ray blazars, quasars that emit most of their energy as gamma rays and vary in brightness over a period of days. Scientists have also found evidence for the existence of anti-matter based on the presence of gamma rays given off by the mutual destruction of electrons and positrons in the **interstellar medium.**

Four gamma-ray telescopes function on board the CGRO, each of which detects gamma rays at a distinct range of wavelengths. These instruments are ten times more sensitive than those of any previous gamma-ray satellite.

The CGRO has enough fuel to function for seven to ten years, until sometime between 1997 and 2001. When the satellite's fuel runs low, NASA will have to decide whether to send up a space shuttle for refueling or to guide the CGRO back to Earth.

See also **Anti-matter** and **Gamma ray astronomy**

Conrad, Charles (1930–)

American astronaut

Charles "Pete" Conrad, Jr. had one of the most extraordinary careers of any astronaut. He made four space flights between the years 1965 and 1973, including the Apollo mission on which he became the third person ever to set foot on the moon. He also traveled twice on Gemini spacecraft and participated in the first mission to the *Skylab* **space station.**

Born in 1930 in Philadelphia, Pennsylvania, Conrad grew up in the nearby suburb of Haverford. He attended high school in New Lebanon, New York, after which he entered Princeton University. He graduated from Princeton in 1953 with a bachelor's degree in aeronautical engineering.

Conrad then enlisted in the Navy and trained to be a pilot in Pensacola, Florida. Beginning in 1957, he spent several years at Patuxent River, Maryland. He first went through the Navy Test Pilot School there and then stayed on as a flight instructor and engineer.

While stationed at the Naval Air Station at Miramar, California, in 1962, Conrad was selected by the National Aeronautics and Space Administration (NASA) to be among the second group of astronauts. Conrad had been a candidate for the original Mercury group of astronauts, but had been expelled when he objected to the extensive medical tests.

Conrad made his first space flight in August 1965, when he piloted *Gemini 5*. He and his crew-mate Gordon Cooper circled the Earth 120 times and set a new endurance record of 191 hours, almost eight days, in space.

Conrad's next flight came a year later on *Gemini 11*. On the first orbit of their three-day mission, Conrad and pilot Richard Gordon docked with an Agena spacecraft. Agena was an unmanned **rocket** modified specifically for use as a rendezvous and docking vehicle for the Gemini program. (In the past it had been used as an upper stage for larger rockets that put a number of satellites into space). Agena was chosen for the Gemini program because of its accuracy and ability to be controlled in space. They then conducted a **gravity** experiment by connecting the two vessels with a tether, allowing each vessel to rotate around the other. That flight, which rose to a height of 853 miles (1,372 kilometers) over the Earth, set a new record for altitude.

Conrad Lands On the Moon

Conrad's greatest achievement came in November 1969, when he commanded *Apollo 12,* the second piloted mission to the moon. Conrad and his crew-mate Alan Bean arrived at the lunar surface in the **lunar module.** They spent seven hours and forty-five minutes crossing the moon's surface, installing equipment for scientific experiments, and gathering samples of the lunar surface for later analysis. They also inspected the *Surveyor III* spacecraft, an unmanned **probe** that had landed on the moon three years earlier.

Conrad's fourth and final space flight was in May 1973, when he was among the first group of visitors to the *Skylab* space station. On that mission, called *Skylab 2,* the crew first repaired the damage that had been done to *Skylab* during launch and then spent the next twenty-eight days conducting scientific experiments on board the station.

In December 1973, Conrad retired from the U.S. Navy, ending a twenty-year career, eleven years of which were with NASA. He then began serving as an executive for various private industries, including American Television and Communications Corporation, the Douglas Aircraft Company, and others. Conrad is currently the Staff Vice President for McDonnell Douglas Corporation in St. Louis, Missouri.

See also **Apollo program**; **Gemini program**; and *Skylab* space station

Constellations

A **constellation** is one of eighty-eight groups of stars in the sky, named for mythological beings. Although some constellations may resemble the animals or people they are named for, others were merely named in honor of those figures. The constellations encompass the entire **celestial sphere,** the imaginary sphere that surrounds the Earth. The celestial sphere provides a visual surface on which scientists can plot the stars and other objects in space and chart their apparent movement caused by the Earth's rotation.

You can see constellations on any clear night. The particular constellations that are visible depends on where in the world you are, what time of year it is, and what time of night it is. As the Earth makes its daily rotation about its axis and its yearly revolution around the sun, the celestial sphere appears to shift, and different constellations come into view.

Originally the constellations had no fixed boundaries. It was not until 1930 that the International Astronomical Union defined limits for the constellations that are still accepted today. These boundaries are imaginary lines, running north-south and east-west across the entire celestial sphere, so that every point in the sky belongs to some constellation or another

A constellation does not represent a scientific grouping of objects. Two objects in the same constellation may or may not have anything in common or any influence on one another. They may even be separated by a greater distance than objects in different constellations. To say that a particular star, planet, or **nebula** (cloud of gas and dust) is located "within" a given constellation does not take into account the actual distance of that

Stellar constellations in the night sky over Providence, Rhode Island. The very bright object is Saturn.

Make Your Own Planetarium

Large planetariums, often located at observatories or in museums, consist of a simulated night sky on a domed ceiling. They do this by projecting light through tiny holes, arranged in the pattern of the stars. You can create your own planetarium, one constellation at a time, with a modified flashlight, cardboard, black paper, and a star map.

First you have to turn your flashlight into a projector. To do this, unscrew the flashlight and take out the lens. Then paint the reflector (the concave surface behind the bulb) black and put the flashlight back together. Next, remove the top and bottom of a can and paint the inside black. Cut out a piece of dark cardboard to fit in one end of the can. Then cut a hole in that piece of cardboard, through which the end of the flashlight can fit. Use dark tape to secure the cardboard to the can and flashlight—be sure to cover any cracks so no light gets in.

The next step is to create your constellation disks. Cut several circles from cardboard to fit in the open end of the can. Take a pushpin and poke holes in the cardboard circles, creating a different constellation on each one. (Consult your star map to learn the patterns of constellations.)

Now, it's showtime! Tape a constellation disk on the open end of the can, turn off all the lights in the room, and shine the light from your flashlight projector onto a wall. Show all of your constellations and see how many your family can recognize.

object from Earth or from any other object in the constellation—it merely means that it can be found by looking in one general area in the sky, in relation to Earth.

The naming of constellations dates back to ancient civilizations. Of the original forty-eight constellations indexed by Alexandrian astronomer Ptolemy in A.D. 140, all but one are still included in present-day catalogs. Argo Naris (the Argonaut's Ship), the one constellation no longer included in catalogs, was subdivided into four separate constellations in the 1750s. Several new ones were named in later centuries, mostly in previously unexplored parts of the sky in the Southern Hemisphere, some of which were later discarded.

Many of the constellations were originally given Greek names. These names were later replaced by their Latin equivalents, names by which they are still known today. Some of these include Aquila (the Eagle); Cancer (the Crab); Cygnus (the Swan); Hercules; and Ursa Major (the Great Bear).

Among the constellations that are no longer recognized (most of which were re-classified as parts of other constellations) is a series of constellations proposed in the late 1700s by German astronomer Johann Elert Bode. Bode named these constellations for technological devices, such as the telescope and the printing press. Another system consisted of the so-called "Christian Constellations," named for saints and biblical figures, proposed by Catholic astronomer Julius Schiller shortly before his death in 1627.

Copernicus, Nicholas (1473–1543)
Polish mathematician and astronomer

Nicholas Copernicus (Mikolaj Kopernik in Polish) was born into a wealthy family. His father died when he was ten years old, so he was raised by his uncle, who was a prince and a bishop.

Nicholas Copernicus.

Young Nicholas had an excellent education. At the age of eighteen, he went to the University of Cracow, in his native Poland, where he studied mathematics and painting. Five years later, in 1496, he went to Italy. There he studied astronomy in Bologna, medicine at the University of Padua, and religious law in Ferrara.

In 1506, Copernicus' uncle was named the bishop of Ermeland, in East Prussia (a former country in north-central Europe). He appointed Copernicus as his assistant and personal physician.

A year later, Copernicus announced a revolutionary theory for the structure of the **solar system.** It had long been assumed that the Earth was the center of the solar system, and that the other planets and the sun revolved around it. Copernicus proposed that the sun was at the center. He also suggested that the Earth was a relatively small and unimportant component of the universe.

Actually, Greek astronomer Aristarchus had come up with the sun-centered theory as early as 260 B.C. But in A.D. 100, another Greek astronomer named Ptolemy had convinced the scholars that the Earth was at the center of the solar system. His theory was accepted as truth for over fourteen hundred years.

Basing his calculations on a **heliocentric** (sun-centered) **model,** Copernicus developed a much simpler table of planetary positions than had existed previously. According to the **geocentric** (Earth-centered) **model,** the other planets had to move in strange ways to account for their positions relative to the Earth. For instance, Mars, Jupiter, and Saturn—but not Mercury and Venus—were said to move in a reverse direction from time to time. Copernicus explained that this backward motion was merely an illusion that occurs because of the different lengths of the planets' orbits. Since Mars, Jupiter, and Saturn were farther from the sun, their orbits were longer than the Earth's orbit. Thus Copernicus said, the Earth "overtook" the other planets as it circled the sun on its shorter path. By the same token, Mercury and Venus, closer to the sun than Earth, have shorter orbits and race around the sun several times during an Earth year.

Copernicus mistakenly assumed, however, that planetary orbits are perfectly circular. It was only determined a century later by Johannes Kepler that the orbits are elliptical (oval-shaped).

De Revolutionibus Orbium Coelestium

In 1512, after the death of his uncle, Copernicus moved to the region of Frauenburg, where he served as a priest. From his quarters overlooking a lake near the Baltic Sea, Copernicus wrote *De Revolutionibus Orbium Coelestium* (*Revolution of the Heavenly Spheres*), a book explaining his theory.

Copernicus realized that his theory would not be readily accepted and was hesitant to make his ideas public. The religious community placed a great importance on the Earth's role as the center of the heavens. Therefore, he would be contradicting not just the scientific establishment, but also the teachings of the church.

Copernicus waited until 1530 to present his ideas to other scholars. He waited another thirteen years—until just before his death—to have his work published.

A Lutheran minister named Andreas Osiander was in charge of publishing the book. His job was made more difficult by the fact that Martin Luther, the founder of his denomination, disagreed with Copernicus. "This Fool wants to turn the whole Art of Astronomy upside down," Luther said.

So Osiander wrote a preface to the book, which he did not sign so it would look as though Copernicus had written it. The preface stated that the heliocentric model was merely a concept used to calculate planetary positions. "These hypotheses need not be true nor even probable; if they provide a calculus consistent with the observations, that alone is sufficient," wrote Osiander. This preface made it appear that Copernicus was not proposing that the solar system was sun-centered.

It is said that Copernicus died just hours after seeing the first copy of his book. This false impression of Copernicus and his work continued until 1609, when Kepler discovered the truth and cleared up the matter.

De Revolutionibus Orbium Coelestium did not receive much attention for several reasons. First, Copernicus' reputation suffered as a result of the preface, in which he seemed to contradict his own findings. Second, the book was written in such a technical language that only a mathematician could understand it. Third, not many copies were printed, and those available were very expensive. Finally, the book was placed on the Roman Catholic Church's list of banned books where it remained until 1835.

See also **Kepler, Johannes**; **Planetary motion**; and **Ptolemy**

Cosmic Background Explorer

In 1992, the *Cosmic Background Explorer* (*COBE*) looked fifteen billion **light-year**s into space (the same as looking fifteen billion years into the past) and turned up the most convincing evidence to date in support of the **big bang theory.** The big bang theory states that the universe was born about fifteen to twenty billion years ago when an infinitely dense, single point underwent a tremendous explosion (the "big bang"). Sub-atomic particles formed shortly after the explosion and then hurled outward into space. Eventually, the particles were brought together by gravitational sources, forming atoms. Atoms, in turn, then combined to produce planets, stars, **galaxies** and other objects in space.

One important assignment for *COBE,* a satellite-laboratory of the National Aeronautics and Space Administration (NASA), was to measure the **microwave** background radiation that was presumably left behind by the big bang. When first constructed, *COBE* was relatively large. It was 15 feet (4.5 meters) in diameter and weighed 10,000 pounds (5,800 kilograms). *COBE* was originally scheduled for launch aboard a **space shuttle,** but that plan was changed following the *Challenger* explosion in 1986. A Delta **rocket** was selected as the alternative **launch vehicle.** Thus, *COBE* had to be rebuilt to smaller dimensions to fit on the rocket. It was reduced to half its original size and weight. It was finally sent into space in the fall of 1989 where it operated until 1994.

COBE contained three instruments: the Differential Microwave Radiometer, the Far-Infrared Absolute Spectrometer, and the Diffuse Infrared Background Experiment. The first two instruments mapped the entire sky, looking for differences in the brightness of the background radiation. The third sought out infrared light from primitive galaxies.

Evidence for the Big Bang Theory

Various theories as to how the universe began have been proposed over the decades. By the mid-1960s, however, evidence pointed to the big bang theory as the most likely. The first important piece of supporting evidence was Edwin Powell Hubble's discovery in the 1920s that galaxies are moving away from one another and, therefore, that the universe is expanding.

In 1948, astronomer George Gamow suggested that if a big bang had occurred, it would have left traces of background radiation that could persist even after many billions of years. He felt that by the present century the radiation would have cooled to just a few degrees above **absolute zero.** This theory was shown to be correct in 1964 by radio engineers Arno Penzias and Robert Wilson, who detected microwave radiation in space at the temperature predicted by Gamow.

While this discovery convinced most people that the big bang theory was true, some questions still remained. For instance, Penzias and Wilson's measurements of background radiation imply that the early universe was very evenly distributed and that it evolved at a constant rate following the big bang. In this case one would expect to find matter evenly distributed in the universe. Instead, astronomers have found clumps of matter, such as star clusters and galaxies.

Part of the answer was provided by *COBE*. Looking out fifteen billion light-years into space, it detected tiny temperature changes in the cosmic background radiation. These ripples, up to ten billion light-years across, are considered evidence of early gravitational disturbances. They could have eventually come together to form the lumpy mixture that is our universe.

Since this remarkable discovery almost every astronomer has become convinced that the big bang is the best available theory for the creation of the universe.

See also **Big bang theory**

Cosmic rays

Cosmic rays are invisible, high-energy particles that constantly bombard Earth from all directions. Most cosmic rays are high-speed protons (hydrogen atoms that have lost an electron) although they also include the nuclei of all known elements. They enter Earth's atmosphere at a rate of 90 percent the **speed of light,** or about 167,654 miles (269,755 kilometers) per second.

Cosmic rays were first discovered in 1912 by Austrian-American physicist Victor Hess during a hot-air balloon flight. He used an **electroscope** to measure the background radiation that seemed to come from everywhere on the ground. But the higher he went in the balloon, the more radiation he found.

Then in 1925, American physicist Robert A. Millikan lowered an electroscope deep into a lake and detected powerful radiation down there as well. He was the first to call these energy particles cosmic rays, but did not know what they were made of.

In 1932, American physicist Arthur Holly Compton measured radiation at many points on the Earth's surface and found that it was more intense at higher than at lower **latitude**s. He concluded that the Earth's **magnetic field** was affecting the rays, deflecting them away from the equator and toward the Earth's magnetic poles. Since magnetism was shown to affect the rays, they had to be electrically charged.

More was learned about cosmic rays in 1958, from information gathered by the *Explorer 1* satellite. The satellite detected regions of charged particles encircling the Earth. These regions, named **Van Allen belts** (after James Van Allen, the leader of the team of scientists analyzing *Explorer*'s information) contained trapped cosmic rays that spiral down to the Earth's magnetic poles.

The Source of Cosmic Rays

Scientists have not been able to completely explain the origin of cosmic rays. One possible source is **supernova** explosions. These explosions produce tremendous amounts of energy, and there are enough of them to produce the quantity of cosmic rays striking Earth. It's just not understood exactly how the energy produced by a supernova can accelerate protons and other atomic nuclei to the speed of cosmic rays.

Scientists believe that the sun is one source of low-energy cosmic rays. The sun produces a **solar wind**—a flow of charged particles—that breaks free of the sun's gravitational field. When these particles reach the

Cosmic rays research. View of one of the four telescopes used to study the Cherenkov radiation produced by the interaction between high-energy particles in the cosmic rays and atoms in the upper atmosphere.

Earth's atmosphere, they ionize (create an electric charge within) the oxygen and nitrogen gas, causing it to glow. These phenomena are known as the **aurora borealis** and **aurora australis,** the northern and southern lights.

See also **Aurorae**; **Solar wind**; and **Van Allen belts**

Cosmic string

In one episode of the popular science fiction television show *Star Trek: The Next Generation,* the starship *Enterprise* rescues two-dimensional people who have wandered too far from their home on a **cosmic string.** The Star-Trekkian cosmic string is described as a long strand of matter in space with a tremendous gravitational pull. This description is similar to one that astronomers would give for cosmic strings, with two exceptions. First, they would point out that cosmic strings are still a theoretical concept. Second, they would explain that cosmic strings, if they exist, are unable to support life.

According to current theories, a cosmic string is a giant vibrating strand or closed loop of material that was created at an early stage in the history of the universe. Cosmic strings are believed to have been produced by gravitational shifts in the early universe, immediately following the **big bang.** They are thought to be the "creases" left in an otherwise smooth transition from the initial phases of universal evolution. They have also been described as "wrinkles" in the configuration of matter, radiation, and empty space.

Although calculated to be just a tiny fraction of an inch thick, much thinner than even a single hair, these strands or rings are believed to contain the **mass** of thousands of **galaxies.** They are also thought to carry an extremely strong electrical current.

Whereas the universe may have at one time contained a large number of cosmic strings, most of them have probably decayed by now, leaving only a few of the longest ones. In today's universe it's possible that a cosmic string acts as a sort of barrier between different regions of **space-time.** For instance, one clue to the existence of a cosmic string would be the discovery of a galaxy that ended abruptly in a straight edge—signalling that the other part of the galaxy had been sucked in by the cosmic string or existed in another time and place.

If the **Milky Way** galaxy were to get too close to a cosmic string, the galaxy (including our entire **solar system**) would probably get pulled into the string. No one should worry too seriously about that problem, however, until the existence of cosmic strings has actually been proved.

The evidence needed to prove the existence of cosmic strings may actually be close at hand. Astronomers are currently analyzing photos taken by the Hubble Space Telescope (HST) for signs of these mysterious lines in space. If cosmic strings do indeed exist, there is a good chance the HST will find them.

Cosmology

Cosmology is the study of the origin, evolution, and structure of the universe. This science grew out of mythology, religion, and simple observations, and is now grounded in mathematical theories, technological advances, and space exploration.

The earliest notions of our universe were put forward by ancient astronomers over a period of thirty-five hundred years (from about 2200 B.C. to about A.D. 1200). The astronomers who recorded observations were in Babylon, China, Greece, Italy, India, and Egypt.

Early astronomers made observations without the assistance of sophisticated instruments. One of their first quests was to determine the Earth's place in the universe. Two competing theories were developed regarding this question. Most people believed in the **geocentric model,** that the Earth is at the center of the universe with the other planets, the moon, and the sun revolving around it. The other theory, the **heliocentric model,** held that the sun is at the center of the **solar system,** with the Earth and other planets in orbit around it.

One of the earliest astronomers to propose the heliocentric theory was Aristarchus in 260 B.C. In contrast, an early proponent of the geocentric theory was Alexandrian astronomer Ptolemy, who suggested in A.D. 100 that everything in the solar system revolved around the Earth. People at the time (and the Christian Church in particular) liked the idea of being at the center of the universe and accepted Ptolemy's theory more readily. His theory remained largely unchallenged for thirteen hundred years.

The Structure of the Solar System

Not until the publication of *De Revolutionibus Orbium Coelestium* (*Revolution of the Heavenly Spheres*) in 1543 by Polish astronomer Nicholas Copernicus did the heliocentric model receive widespread attention. A generation later, Danish astronomer Tycho Brahe, and his successor, Johannes Kepler, offered proof supporting the **Copernican model.** This proof consisted of careful calculations of the positions of planets. In the early 1600s, Kepler developed the laws of planetary motion, showing that the planets follow oval-shaped paths around the sun. He also pointed out that the universe was bigger than previously thought, although he still had no idea of its truly massive size.

The first astronomer to work with a telescope was Italian Galileo Galilei. Beginning in 1609, he revealed never-before-known details about the surface of the sun and moon, saw Jupiter's moons and Saturn's rings, and discovered many stars too faint to be seen with the naked eye. His observations of the solar system led him to support the heliocentric concept of the universe. This position made Galileo unpopular with church officials, who placed him under house arrest for the last nine years of his life.

The next significant discovery was made by Isaac Newton, an English scientist born in 1642 (the same year Galileo died). Newton introduced the theories of **gravity** and **mass,** and explained how they are responsible both for an apple's falling to the ground and for the motion of the planets around the sun.

In 1781, English astronomer William Herschel discovered a new planet (Uranus), many multiple star systems (groups of two or more stars orbiting each other), and interstellar clouds called **nebula**e. He also studied our **galaxy,** the **Milky Way,** and suggested that the universe contained other galaxies and other solar systems.

The early 1800s brought the discovery of **asteroid**s, small, rocky members of our solar system. The first one, Ceres, was discovered by Father Giuseppe Piazzi. He was one of many observers searching for a planet between Mars and Jupiter. What astronomers discovered, instead, was an asteroid belt.

In the mid-1800s, Gustav Kirchhoff and Christian Johann Doppler developed **spectroscopy,** a method of breaking down light into its components. The technique made it possible for astronomers to determine the chemical composition of the sun and other stars and to show that the stars are moving. Around this time, English astronomer John Couch Adams and

French astronomer Urbain Leverrier, working independently, accurately predicted the location of the planet Neptune beyond Uranus.

The Origins of Modern Cosmology

In 1914, Albert Einstein developed the theory of relativity, which states that the **speed of light** is a constant and that the curvature of space and the passage of time are linked to **gravity.**

Einstein believed the universe was unchanging. He inserted a mathematical device known as a "cosmological constant" into his calculations to make them fit the concept of an unchanging universe. A few years later Dutch astronomer Willem de Sitter did away with the cosmological constant and used the theory of relativity to show that the universe is always expanding.

In about 1920, American astronomer Harlow Shapley calculated the size of the Milky Way galaxy and determined that a nucleus of stars is at the center, rather than the sun as was previously believed. Dutch astronomer Jan Oort then showed that the galaxy is rotating about its center.

Our view of the universe was revolutionized in the 1920s when American astronomer Edwin Hubble discovered other galaxies. At about the same time, Vesto Melvin Slipher discovered that the galaxies were expanding outward, away from each other. Thus the universe was shown to be much larger than previously thought, and growing, confirming de Sitter's theory.

Creation of the Universe

Astronomers have also long been interested in the question of how the universe was created. The two most popular modern theories are the **big bang theory** and the **steady-state theory.** The big bang theory was first elaborated by Belgian astronomer and Jesuit priest Georges-Henri Lemaître in the late 1920s. Lemaître suggested that fifteen to twenty billion years ago, the universe came into being with a big explosion. Almost immediately, gravity came into being, followed by atoms, stars, and galaxies. The solar system formed four and one-half billion years ago from a cloud of dust and gas.

The steady-state theory, in contrast, claims that all matter in the universe has been created continuously, a little at a time, at a constant rate, from the beginning of time. The theory also says that the universe is structurally the same all over, and has been forever. In other words, the universe is infinite, unchanging, and will last forever. This theory, first elaborated by Thomas Gold and Hermann Bondi in 1948, was largely discredited in 1963 with the discovery of **quasar**s, very distant, bright, starlike objects. The steady-state theory would have them distributed evenly throughout the universe, but quasars exist only in places very far from Earth. Recent discoveries pointing to changes in the universe that have occurred throughout time have lent support to the big bang theory.

Discoveries made in this decade have caused astronomers to revise their notion as to the size of the universe. They continue to discover that it is larger than they thought. In 1991, astronomers making maps of the universe discovered that great "sheets" of galaxies in clusters and super-clusters fill areas hundreds of millions of **light-year**s in diameter. They are separated by huge empty spaces of darkness, up to four hundred million light-years across.

The question as to whether extraterrestrial life exists continues to remain unanswered by scientists—but they keep looking. As recently as late 1995 and early 1996, three new planets were discovered, each orbiting different stars in the Milky Way galaxy. In one mission in early 1996, the Hubble Space Telescope photographed at least fifteen hundred new galaxies in various stages of formation. As more and more pieces of the universe are discovered, the possibility increases that intelligent life exists in places other than Earth.

Dark matter

Until very recently, the composition of **dark matter** was a cosmological secret, frustrating to even the most brilliant astronomers. While you cannot touch it, taste it, and for the most part cannot see it, dark matter is thought to make up at least 90 percent of the **mass** of the universe. The principal way dark matter can be detected is by observing its gravitational effect on nearby objects.

Astronomers believe that dark matter is a "cosmic glue," holding together rapidly spinning **galaxies** and controlling the rate at which the universe expands.

Many theories have been proposed about the composition of dark matter. Among the candidates that have been suggested are the cooling shrunken cores left when stars die called **white dwarf**s, and the bodies left when white dwarfs cease to glow called **black dwarf**s. There are also the barely detectable objects that never quite become stars called **brown dwarf**s. Another possible source of dark matter is **black hole**s—the remains of massive stars with infinite gravitational fields.

Astronomers are also considering that dark matter could be made of objects as large as **dwarf galaxies** (small, faint galaxies), which number in the billions, and objects as small as subatomic particles. Also on the list are MACHOs and WIMPs. MACHOs stands for "massive compact halo objects" and includes black holes, large planets, and brown dwarfs.

WIMPs stands for "weakly interacting massive particles" and includes particles of elements that have very little effect on ordinary matter.

In early 1996, after decades of hunting, astronomers announced that they had discovered the composition of about half of the mysterious dark matter: white dwarfs. A team of astronomers, headed by David Bennett of the Lawrence Livermore National Laboratory in California, detected objects the size of white dwarfs (ranging from one-tenth the mass of the sun to the mass of the sun) around the edges of the **Milky Way.** They deduced that since ours is a typical galaxy, that white dwarfs similarly encircle other galaxies.

Swiss astronomer Fritz Zwicky, known for his work on **supernovae** and galaxies, first pointed out in the 1930s that dark matter must exist. The reason for this, he claimed, was that the mass of known matter in galaxies is not great enough to hold a cluster of galaxies together. Each indepen-

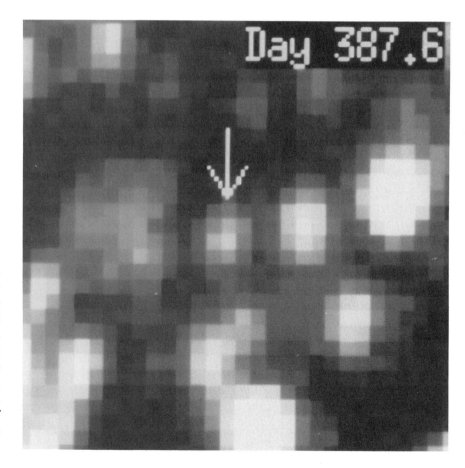

The arrow points to a brown dwarf star in the Large Magellanic Cloud which could help account for the missing dark matter, which should make up about 90 percent of the mass of the universe.

dent galaxy moves at too great a speed for the galaxies to remain in a cluster. Yet the galaxies were not spinning away from each other. They had to be held together by a gravitational field created by undetected mass.

Over forty years later, astronomer Vera Rubin found that the same principle is true within a single galaxy. The mass of the stars alone do not exert enough gravitational force to hold the galaxy together. She discovered that stars in the far reaches of a galaxy rotate about the galactic center at the same speed as stars that are close-in. Rubin concluded, therefore, that some invisible, massive substance surrounds a galaxy, exerting gravitational force on all the stars.

Scientists have calculated that dark matter can occupy no more than 99 percent of the universe. Beyond this amount, matter would reverse directions, and the universe would collapse in upon itself, in what is known as the **big crunch.** Short of that, the universe will slowly expand forever.

See also **Big crunch theory** and **Zwicky, Fritz**

Discovery

The **space shuttle** *Discovery* was named after the eighteenth-century ship of British explorer James Cook, in which he sailed the South Pacific and became the first non-native to set foot on the Hawaiian Islands. *Discovery* was the third shuttle orbiter constructed, after *Columbia* and *Challenger.* It has flown twenty-one times, more than any other shuttle in the fleet. Its first mission was in August 1984, and its most recent was in July 1995. It is slated to fly again in February 1997.

Discovery is one of the original four reusable winged space planes. These vehicles each contain engines, astronaut living and work quarters, and a cargo bay large enough to hold a bus. The orbiter is the main component of the Space Transportation System, better known as the space shuttle. The other parts of a shuttle include solid **rocket** boosters and an external tank.

The orbiter is launched vertically using its own engines, aided by two attached rocket boosters. The boosters fall away from the orbiter about two minutes after lift-off and parachute into the ocean, where they are captured and used again. When an orbiter returns to earth, it brakes with its

Launch of the space shuttle Discovery, *July 13, 1995.*

engines and lands like an airplane on a specially designed 3-mile-long (5-kilometer-long) runway.

Space shuttles are used to carry satellites into space; to retrieve and/or repair damaged equipment in space; to conduct scientific research; and to deliver or bring home astronauts and equipment from the Russian *Mir* **space station.**

The first mission of the space shuttle *Discovery* lasted six days, during which time it launched three communications satellites and tested solar panels, located on a "solar wing" that extended from the cargo bay of the shuttle. Among the crew for that flight was the second U.S. woman astronaut in space, Judith Resnik. On board for the next *Discovery* mission was Ellison Onizuka, the first Asian-American astronaut in space. Onizuka and Resnik were later killed in the 1986 explosion of the *Challenger* spacecraft.

On December 29, 1988, thirty-five months after the *Challenger* disaster, *Discovery* was the first shuttle to resume flight. Its successful mission was an important factor in restoring the faith of the American public in the space shuttle program.

Of all its missions, *Discovery* is probably best known for its deployment of the Hubble Space Telescope in 1990. *Discovery* also made headlines in 1995 when, guided by the first female pilot, Eileen M. Collins, it flew by the *Mir* space station. Over the years, *Discovery* has also deployed several satellites for military and scientific uses (including satellites owned by other countries), rescued stranded satellites, and transported the first U.S. Senator into space, Jake Garn of Utah.

Following its twenty-first flight in July 1995, *Discovery* was grounded for maintenance and upgrading. It is presently being outfitted for the special task of transporting into space components of the International Space Station, slated for construction early next century.

Of the four original space shuttle orbiters, three are still in use. Besides *Discovery,* these include *Atlantis* and *Columbia.* The fourth, *Challenger,* was destroyed in a tragic accident in 1986. It has since been replaced with the newest shuttle, *Endeavour.*

See also **Hubble Space Telescope** and **Space shuttle**

Drake, Frank (1930–)

American astronomer

Frank Drake is driven by a singular passion to discover extraterrestrial civilizations. Since 1959, the professor of astronomy and **astrophysics** at the University of California, Santa Cruz, has been involved in a series of projects associated with the search for extraterrestrial intelligence (SETI). Currently head of the SETI Institute in Mountain View, California, Drake has also done much throughout his career to generate public enthusiasm over the possibility that intelligent extraterrestrial life exists.

Drake grew up in Chicago, Illinois, in a fundamentalist Baptist home. He continually rebelled against his religious upbringing, particularly at Sunday school, where he felt that the teachings were probably untrue and certainly irrelevant to his life in twentieth-century Chicago. Drake was much more interested in visiting the Museum of Science and Industry, where he spent so much time at that he claims to have learned every square inch of the institution. Drake credits his time at the museum, as well as his exposure to religion (and his rejection of it), with spawning his interest in science. He also credits his natural childhood curiosity. Since the age of eight, he recalls, he has wondered whether intelligent beings exist elsewhere in the universe.

During his teenage years, Drake built three telescopes. For the first instrument he used a lens from an old slide projector. The other two were larger, **reflector telescope**s, for which he ground his own mirrors. In high school, however, his interest in astronomy waned. Drake blames his lack of interest on his high school's curriculum, which did not include astronomy.

His old passion for astronomy was rekindled as a sophomore at Cornell University, when he took an astronomy class as an elective. In a published interview, Drake described one class session in which students made observations of Jupiter through a small telescope. "I remember looking at Jupiter and being just thrilled to see there really was an object with four satellites going around it," he said. "You could see the cloud belts on it and all. It made the whole business seem very real. It hit me and I was hooked from that time on." Drake graduated from Cornell with a bachelor's degree in engineering physics in 1952.

Drake's Work On the Ozma Project

Drake then entered the Navy, after which he went to Harvard University for graduate school. He completed a master of arts degree in 1956 and a Ph.D. in astronomy in 1958.

Drake's first job was at the National Radio Astronomy Observatory in Green Bank, West Virginia. There he conducted the first large-scale SETI experiment, called Project Ozma. The project was named for Princess Ozma in L. Frank Baum's science fiction story *Ozma of Oz*. Drake spent over 150 hours working at an 85-foot-diameter (26-meter-diameter) **radio telescope** dish, poised to receive signals from Epsilon Eridani and Tau Ceti, two nearby stars that are similar to our sun. His project detected one signal he initially thought was from a distant star in the Pleiades cluster, but it turned out to be coming from a secret military experiment here on Earth. Drake's time at Green Bank, however, was not all spent in vain. It was there that he discovered **Van Allen belts** around Jupiter.

After leaving Green Bank in 1963, Drake spent a year as director of the Lunar and Planetary Sciences Section at the Jet Propulsion Laboratory,

Frank Drake, the father of the search for extraterrestrial life in space.

a branch of the National Aeronautics and Space Administration (NASA) that is operated by the California Institute of Technology in Pasadena, California. Following that, he became a professor of astronomy at Cornell University as well as director of the National Astronomy and Ionosphere Center. In 1984 he moved back West, to assume his present post as Dean of Natural Sciences at the University of California, Santa Cruz.

In the mid-1970s, Drake joined forces with astronomer Carl Sagan for another SETI experiment. They used the 1,000-foot-diameter (304-meter-diameter) radio telescope dish (the largest in the world) at Arecibo Observatory in Puerto Rico to listen for signals from nearby **galaxies.** In addition, they broadcast a radio message of their own to a **globular cluster** twenty-five thousand **light-year**s away, just in case anyone was listening. Again, they found no sign of extraterrestrial civilizations.

In addition to his many technical publications, Drake has written numerous articles and two books about SETI for the general public. His first book, *Intelligent Life in Space,* was published in 1967 and his second, *Is Anyone Out There? The Scientific Search for Extraterrestrial Intelligence,* came out in 1992. He has served as advisor for numerous observatories and projects including the National Radio Astronomy Observatory, Very Large Array, Kitt Peak National Observatory, and Cerro Tololo Interamerican Observatory. Drake also serves on the SETI Advisory Committee of NASA's Office of Aeronautics and Space Technology.

While SETI experiments have yet to yield positive results, Drake and other seekers of extraterrestrial life feel they are closer than ever before. In recent years, with the discoveries of new planets circling nearby stars, the possibility that extraterrestrial life exists seems greater than ever. Drake continues to scan the skies in the hope of making that first contact.

When asked what motivates his search, Drake answered, ". . . I'm just curious. I like to explore and find out what things exist. And as far as I know, the most fascinating, interesting thing you could find in the universe is not another kind of star or galaxy or something, but another kind of life."

See also **Extraterrestrial life** and **Van Allen belts**

Dynamical system

A dynamical system is any grouping that has moving parts. Dynamics is the study of dynamical systems, or the effect of certain forces on the movement of objects. These systems include sets of objects on Earth as well as in space, the **solar system** in particular.

One can follow the time line of great astronomers and mathematicians to see how theories about dynamical systems have progressed throughout history. That time line begins with Greek philosopher Aristotle in the fourth century B.C., who described different types of motion and attempted to explain how they controlled the behavior of objects in the solar system. He claimed that the sun and planets revolved around the Earth in perfectly circular orbits. This **geocentric** (Earth-centered) **model** of the solar system was strengthened by the calculations of Alexandrian astronomer Ptolemy around A.D. 140. Although we now know that the geocentric model is wrong, people believed it until the mid-1500s.

Polish astronomer Nicholas Copernicus then described a solar system in which the planets, including Earth, revolved around the sun. But Copernicus still believed the orbits were circular. His claims of a **heliocentric** (sun-centered) solar system were supported by German astronomer Johannes Kepler in 1618, but Kepler differed with earlier astronomers over the shape of the orbits. Kepler developed the laws of planetary motion which explained that the orbits were elliptical (oval-shaped) and that each planet traveled at its own rate around the sun.

The law of **inertia** was introduced by French mathematician and philosopher René Descartes in 1644. This law states that an object will continue in motion at the same speed, in the same direction, forever, unless it is slowed or stopped by another force.

Later that century English scientist Isaac Newton theorized that the same force responsible for an apple falling from a tree on Earth is also responsible for the motion of the planets around the sun. In other words, the same rules apply to both dynamical systems. This force is **gravity.**

Newton also expanded upon the law of inertia with his three famous laws of motion. He proposed that 1) an object at rest tends to remain at rest, and an object in motion tends to remain in motion; 2) any change in the motion of an object will be in proportion to the strength and direction of the force acting on it; and 3) for every action there is an equal and opposite reaction. Newton published his discoveries in 1687 in *Philosophiae Naturalis Principia Mathematica* (*Mathematical Principles of Natural Philosophy*).

See also **Newton's laws of motion**

Earth survey satellite

Literally thousands of human-made satellites can now be found in space. The ones we tend to hear about in the news are very far away, exploring other planets. But there are also satellites providing us with very important information about our own planet.

Earth survey satellites tell us about soil conditions, the flow of ice in arctic regions, and the location of minerals and oil beneath the Earth's surface. Using satellite photographs, cartographers (map makers) learn about areas that are hard to reach by land; environmentalists monitor air pollution and oil spills; farmers get advance warning of droughts; and hydroelectric engineers (people who design water-power systems) see where snow is melting in mountain ranges and identify sites for dams.

In 1966, the U.S. Department of the Interior requested that the National Aeronautics and Space Administration (NASA) construct a satellite that would gather information about the nation's natural resources. NASA hired General Electric to develop a satellite for topographical and geological exploration. Topography deals with the physical features of the Earth's surface, while geology concerns the structure of the Earth, on and below the surface. This satellite, originally named *Earth Resources Technology Satellite* (*ERTS*), was first launched in 1972.

Landsat 4 and *Landstat 5* are still in operation and orbit the Earth about fifteen times every day at an altitude of 438 miles (705 kilometers). One Landsat satellite is capable of observing almost every place on the globe in an eighteen-day period. It can bring into focus areas as small as about ten football fields. *Landsat 7* is scheduled to be launched in the late 1990s.

There are also two satellites studying the **ozone layer.** One is called *Earth Radiation Budget Satellite* (*ERBS*). It was launched from the **space shuttle** *Challenger* in 1984. In addition to measuring ozone, *ERBS* measures other elements in the atmosphere and provides information about worldwide climate changes.

The other ozone-measuring satellite is called *Total Ozone Mapping Spectrometer* (*TOMS*). The first *TOMS* was sent into orbit in 1978. The second one, in 1991, was a joint U.S.-Soviet project called *TOMS-Meteor 3*. This satellite consisted of a *TOMS* carried by a Soviet Meteor-3 meteorological (weather-studying) satellite. This satellite pair studies the ozone hole that forms over Antarctica every fall.

Two Earth survey satellites are dedicated to surveying the oceans. These satellites have provided useful information to fisherman and shipping companies. The first satellite, called *Seasat,* was launched in June 1978. After just one hundred days in operation, it stopped operating because of a power failure. While in orbit, *Seasat* used radar-**microwave** techniques as well as visual and infrared sensors to determine water surface temperature, wind speed, wind direction, wave height, and weather conditions on the seas.

The data collected by *Seasat* was used in the creation of the next oceanographic (ocean-studying) satellite, called the *Ocean Topography Experiment* (*TOPEX*). The *TOPEX* was combined with France's *Poseidon* satellite and launched in 1992. In cooperation with the World Ocean Circulation Experiment, the *TOPEX/Poseidon* creates near-perfect maps of ocean topography, complete with ice floes (chunks of floating ice), wind, and waves.

Earth's atmosphere

The Earth's atmosphere is unique within the **solar system.** In particular, it stands out as the only planetary atmosphere capable of sustaining life. By way of comparison, Mercury and the moon have essentially no atmosphere. The atmospheres of Jupiter, Saturn, and Neptune, on the other hand, are each more massive than the entire Earth. And while our atmosphere is mainly made of nitrogen, those of Mars and Venus are dominated by carbon dioxide.

A planet's ability to retain an atmosphere is determined by its gravitational field. A gravitational field, in turn, depends on a planet's **mass.** In the case of our planet, Earth's mass is great enough to keep most gases (except for very light gases like hydrogen and helium) from escaping.

The Earth's atmosphere is made of 78 percent nitrogen, 21 percent oxygen, and 1 percent argon, with minute quantities of water vapor, carbon dioxide, and other gases. Various theories have been proposed as to the origin of these gases. One theory states that when the Earth was formed, the gases were trapped in layers of rock beneath the surface. They eventually escaped, primarily through volcanic eruptions, to form the atmosphere.

Water vapor was the most plentiful substance to spew out, which condensed to form the oceans. Carbon dioxide was second in terms of quantity, but most of it dissolved in the water or was altered chemically through reactions with other substances in the rocks. Nitrogen came out in smaller amounts, but has always remained in its present form because it never underwent reactions or condensation. For that reason, it is the most abundant gas in the atmosphere today.

Oxygen only became part of our atmosphere when green plants came into being. Green plants, through photosynthesis, produce oxygen by converting carbon dioxide. The other gases in the atmosphere were probably released from underground by volcanic activity—a process that began

Image of the Earth's atmosphere from space.

long before green plants came into being. Oxygen is also removed from the atmosphere when green plants, as well as animals, die. As they decay, they oxidize—a process that uses up oxygen.

Another more recent theory is that the elements found in the Earth's atmosphere were deposited here by **comet**s. Debris from comets is shown to have carbon and nitrogen in roughly the same proportion as found in our atmosphere. And there are numerous impact craters on Earth from past collisions with comets.

Characteristics of the Atmosphere

The Earth's atmosphere changes in pressure and density with altitude. Its density is greatest near the Earth's surface and thins out at higher altitudes. The atmosphere extends above the surface of the Earth to a distance of about 600 miles, but 50 percent of its total mass is found within 4 miles (6 kilometers) of the surface.

The bottom layer of atmosphere is called the **troposphere.** This level contains clouds and all weather patterns. At higher altitudes in the troposphere, the temperature drops rapidly. About 9 miles (14 kilometers) above ground, one reaches the **stratosphere.** There the temperature is about -58 degrees Fahrenheit (-50 degrees Celsius), except for a warm area between an altitude of 25 and 40 miles (40 and 65 kilometers).

That warm zone in the stratosphere is the **ozone layer.** Ozone is a form of oxygen that has three atoms per molecule instead of the usual two. It absorbs ultraviolet rays, heating up the space around it. The ozone layer has been mentioned frequently in the news in recent years. The reason is that the ozone layer, which protects us from the sun's harmful rays, is being damaged by chemical substances. Fortunately, governments around the world have begun to ban most of these dangerous substances, giving the protective shield another chance.

The region of stratosphere above the ozone layer is the **mesosphere.** This belt exists from about 40 to 50 miles (65 to 80 kilometers) above Earth. Here the temperature is the same as it was below the ozone layer. The atmosphere becomes warmer at altitudes above 50 miles (80 kilometers). In the next zone, called the **thermosphere,** temperatures rise to a peak of about 1,800 degrees Fahrenheit (1,000 degrees Celsius).

The highest layer of the atmosphere is the **exosphere,** whose lower boundary line lies at an altitude of about 200 miles (320 kilometers). Within this layer, molecules of gas break down into atoms. Many of the atoms become ionized (electrically charged) by the sun's rays. For this reason, the upper atmosphere is also called the **ionosphere.**

Earth's magnetic field

Magnetism radiates from the entire Earth, almost as though there were a giant magnet buried deep inside. This **magnetic field** is probably a result of heat and motion in the Earth's core, which contains liquid metal. The movement of the Earth's rotation causes the core to act like a giant electrical generator, creating electricity and magnetism.

Magnetic force exits from the south magnetic pole (in the Southern Hemisphere) and returns through the north magnetic pole (in the Northern Hemisphere). The **magnetic axis**—the imaginary line connecting the magnetic poles—lies at an angle of about 12 degrees to the axis around which the Earth rotates.

Travelers have long used the Earth's magnetic field to determine the direction in which they are headed. The magnetized needle of a compass lines up almost parallel to the Earth's magnetic field and points just slightly away from the north and south magnetic fields. In a compass shaped like a ball, the needle also tilts vertically depending on where the observer is located on the Earth. This effect is known as the magnetic dip. As one approaches the north magnetic pole, the needle points downward and approaching the south magnetic pole, it points upward. Standing directly on the north magnetic pole, the needle would point straight down.

The influence of the magnetic field does not stop at the Earth's surface. In fact, it extends for many tens of Earth radii into space, an area known as the **magnetosphere.**

Some Effects of the Magnetosphere

Charged particles originating from the sun in **cosmic rays** are swept outward toward Earth by **solar wind** and solar **flare**s. When these particles reach the magnetosphere, they become trapped and spiral around the lines of the Earth's magnetic field.

Some particles become trapped in one of two radiation-filled regions encircling the Earth known as **Van Allen belts.** The *Explorer 1* satellite mapped out the shape of these regions and found that it was like a fat doughnut, widest above the Earth's equator and curving toward the Earth's surface near the polar regions. The doughnut's "hole" was at the Earth's axis, the line connecting the poles.

Scientists in this century have discovered a very interesting fact about the Earth's magnetic field: it reverses direction from time to time. In 1906, French physicist Bernard Brunhes found rocks with magnetic fields oriented opposite that of the Earth's magnetic field. He proposed that those rocks had been laid down at a time when the Earth's magnetic field was opposite that of the time.

This proposal sparked a debate that lasted more than fifty years. Brunhes' theory received support from the research of Japanese geophysicist Motonori Matuyama who, in 1929, studied ancient rocks and determined that the Earth's magnetic field had reversed several times in history. A detailed study made in the 1960s offered further proof, counting nine reversals in the past 3.6 million years. Today, scientists have accepted the proposition that the Earth's magnetic field can exist in two opposite states, with changes taking from two thousand to ten thousand years to complete.

How does a reversal occur? One theory states that a period of intense solar flare activity could erase the Earth's magnetic field. When the field is restored, it would be reversed (north would be south, and vice versa). Scientists have found a 6 percent reduction in the strength of the Earth's magnetic field in the last century. This trend could be a sign that the Earth is in the process of going through another reversal.

See also **Solar wind** and **Van Allen belts**

Earth's rotation

The Earth turns so slowly that we are not even aware of it. In ancient times, people assumed that the Earth was at the center of the **solar system** because it appeared that the Earth stood still and the sun and planets changed their positions in the sky. Beginning in the 1500s with Nicholas Copernicus, the **heliocentric** (sun-centered) **model** of the solar system began to replace the **geocentric** (Earth-centered) **model** as the more likely scenario. In order to explain the movement of the sun and planets in the sky, scientists determined that our planet must be rotating. This idea was first demonstrated by Jean Bernard Léon Foucault in 1852, when his pendulum offered the first proof that the Earth, not the sun and stars, was moving.

The Earth rotates about an imaginary line called its axis connecting the North and South poles. It takes about one day (just slightly less than twenty-four hours) to complete one rotation.

The distance to travel in one rotation is greatest at the equator. An observer on the equator travels at a greater speed—about 1,038 miles (1,670 kilometers) per hour—than at any other point on Earth. At a point halfway between the equator and either pole, the observer travels at half the speed, about 519 miles (835 kilometers) per hour. And at either pole, the observer's speed is 0 miles per hour.

Early astronomers wondered why, if the Earth were rotating, did people, buildings, and other objects not fly off it? The answer to this question came in 1664 when Isaac Newton introduced the concept of **gravity.**

See also **Foucault, Jean Bernard Léon**; **Gravity**; and **Newton's laws of motion**

This 1978 experiment is a reconstruction of the first earth rotation experiment conducted in Paris in 1852. The spike on the pendulum cuts through the sand showing that the line it creates changes with the rotation of the Earth.

Eddington, Arthur (1882–1944)
English astronomer

Arthur Stanley Eddington was born in Westmoreland, England, the son of a school headmaster. Eddington had a brilliant mind for mathematics from an early age. He began teaching astronomy at Cambridge University in 1913 and was named the director of the Cambridge Observatory one year later. Eddington soon distinguished himself as the most highly respected astronomer of his time.

Eddington's main field of research concerned the structure and life cycle of stars. He was the first scientist to propose that the tremendous heat production at a star's core is what keeps a star from collapsing under its own **gravity.** The temperature at a star's core, Eddington said, reaches millions of degrees, creating an outward pressure to balance the inward pull of gravity. He outlined these concepts in a book, *Internal Constitution of the Stars*, that was later used by German-born American physicist Hans Bethe in his description of **nuclear fusion.**

Eddington also proposed a theory that every star ends its life by collapsing to a small, dense, glowing object known as a **white dwarf.** A star the size of the sun would thus end up as a white dwarf the size of the Earth, yet so dense that a teaspoonful would weigh at least 5.5 tons (5 metric tons).

This theory was later amended by Indian-born American astronomer Subrahmanyan Chandrasekhar, who determined that Eddington's calculations did not hold true for stars with a **mass** greater than one and one-half times that of the sun. Chandrasekhar showed that a more massive star would be crushed by its own gravity and become either a **neutron star** or a **black hole.**

Eddington's research into the structure of stars also disproved a popular theory about how the **solar system** was formed. Some scientists at the time believed that the solar system had to been created when another star had passed by the sun millions of years ago. The star's gravitational field had pulled material away from the sun, and this material then formed into the planets. Eddington showed that any material pulled from a star's core would explode into a thin gas when it was removed from the star's balance of energy production and gravity.

Another of Eddington's achievements was his development of the **mass-luminosity law.** Introduced in 1924, this law describes the relation-

Arthur Eddington.

ship between a star's mass and brightness: the more massive a star, the greater the interior pressure and temperature, and therefore the greater its brightness. The law also set an upper limit for the mass of a star: fifty times the mass of the sun. A star more massive than that would be blown apart by the force of its own energy output.

Eddington was a Quaker and a pacifist who refused to fight in World War I. He was a kind man who loved a vigorous scientific debate. He was a bachelor known for his long, solitary bicycle trips that criss-crossed England. Eddington wrote several non-technical books on astronomy that captured the imagination of many non-scientists.

See also **Bethe, Hans**; **Big bang theory**; and **Chandrasekhar, Subrahmanyan**

Einstein, Albert (1879–1955)
German-born Swiss American physicist

Albert Einstein in a playful moment.

Despite his difficulty in school as a youngster, Albert Einstein distinguished himself as one of the world's most brilliant thinkers. He is best known for his theory of relativity, which provided a new way of looking at the universe; for proving the relationship between energy and **mass,** represented by the famous equation: $E=mc^2$; and for clearly explaining the concept of **gravity.**

Einstein was born in Ulm, Germany, to a tightly knit Jewish family. When he was sixteen, his father's business failed, and his family moved to Milan, Italy. The family left Einstein behind to finish school in Munich, but he soon dropped out and joined his family in Milan. Einstein did so poorly in school at the time that one teacher told him, "You will never amount to anything."

What that teacher did not realize was that Einstein was a free thinker who did not learn well in a formal classroom setting. In Milan,

Einstein began studying the one subject that interested him—mathematics. He soon taught himself advanced math, including calculus.

In 1895, Einstein went to Zürich, Switzerland, to take the entrance examination at the Swiss Polytechnique Institute. He failed it on his first attempt. After studying for another year, however, he re-took the exam and passed it. Again, Einstein did not do particularly well in the classroom. It is said that he graduated only with help from his fellow students.

Two years after graduation, in 1902, Einstein finally found a job at the Swiss Patent Office. Later that year, his father died, and the next year Einstein married Mileva Maric, who was a classmate from the Polytechnique Institute. The Einsteins eventually had two sons, one who became a professor of engineering at the University of California in Berkeley and one who died in 1965 in a psychiatric hospital. Einstein and Maric also had a daughter one year before they were married, a child whom they gave up for adoption.

Einstein's job at the patent office was easy and gave him plenty of time for his own studies. He worked there for seven years, during which time he completed a Ph.D. program at the University of Zürich and published five of the most important reports in the history of science.

Einstein's Earliest Research

Two of those reports dealt with Brownian movement, the way particles move when suspended in water. Einstein derived mathematical equations describing the process by which water molecules bombard the particles, causing the particles to move.

A third paper focused on the photoelectric effect, the discharge of electrons from metal that has been exposed to light. Einstein explained that the electrons in the metal absorb energy from the light. If there is enough energy absorbed, electrons can escape the metal. If the light consists of low-frequency wavelengths, like red light, then there may not be enough energy to cause the ejection of electrons. Thus the energy of electrons emitted during the photoelectric effect depends on the frequency of the light, and not its intensity, as was previously thought. This work won him the Nobel Prize in physics in 1921.

The Special Theory of Relativity

The final two papers represented the work for which Einstein is most famous, the **special theory of relativity** and the relationship of energy to mass. The special theory is so-named because it applies only to situations in which motion is constant, that is, in which no speeding up or slowing down takes place. The special theory of relativity was so revolutionary that even Einstein had trouble accepting it. "I must confess," he later stated, "that at the very beginning when the special theory of relativity began to germinate in me, I was visited by all sorts of nervous conflicts."

According to the special theory of relativity, time and space are not fixed. They change depending on the position of the observer. Einstein explained that four dimensions are required to describe the universe, three dimensions in space plus time. Although this concept plays an insignificant role in a place the size of Earth, it gains importance when applied to an area as vast as the universe. This theory introduced the idea of a **space-time** continuum.

Einstein started from the assumption that measurements of time and space depend on how fast and in what direction the observer is moving. For instance, if you are standing still and observe a clock pass by at the **speed of light,** the clock's hands would not appear to move. That is, time would be standing still. But if you are also moving at the speed of light, you would observe the clock's hands moving normally. Another way to imagine this idea is if you were standing alongside a road with a friend, you cannot help but notice the cars speeding by. But if you were with your friend inside a car traveling at a constant speed, you can talk to your friend and not even be aware the car is moving.

Einstein also demonstrated that in any reaction in which an object gives off energy, the object loses mass. The lost mass is turned into energy. In other words, matter and energy are basically the same, although they exist in different forms. Einstein described this concept in his famous equation: $E=mc^2$ (E=energy, m=mass, and c=the speed of light). The equation means that when an object is not moving, its total kinetic energy (energy of motion) is equal to its mass times the speed of light squared.

In 1909, Einstein left his job at the patent office and began working at universities in Switzerland, Germany, and Czechoslovakia. As Einstein's scientific achievements became known, job offers started coming in. In 1911, he was appointed to the chair of physics at the German University in Prague, Czechoslovakia. The next year he returned to Zürich to teach. Then, in 1914, Einstein went to work at the Kaiser Wilhelm Physical Institute in Berlin. At this point, his marriage fell apart, and his wife and sons returned to Zürich. Einstein remained in Berlin for eighteen years.

In 1916, Einstein published the expanded version of his special theory of relativity, called the **general theory of relativity.** While the special theory deals only with objects in constant motion, the general theory includes cases in which objects are accelerating (speeding up) or decelerating (slowing down). The general theory also explains the concept of gravity.

One of the main findings of the general theory is that the mass of an object causes space to curve around it. As a lighter object (like a planet) approaches a heavier object in space (like the sun), the lighter object follows the lines of curved space, which draw it near to the heavier object and into orbit. This, according to Einstein, is how gravity works.

Einstein predicted that even light bends as it passes through a strong gravitational field. In 1919—the same year that Einstein married his cousin Elsa—he was proven correct. Scientists studying stars during a **solar eclipse** found that the positions of the stars appeared to change during the eclipse, meaning that the light from the stars was influenced by the sun's gravitational field. This discovery made news headlines, and Einstein became an international celebrity.

Einstein Comes to the United States

During the years he worked in Berlin, Einstein also came to the United States as a visiting professor at the California Institute of Technology (CalTech). In 1933, during his third visit to CalTech, Hitler came to power in Germany. The Nazis ransacked Einstein's home and took over his bank account. Einstein never returned to Germany.

Soon thereafter, Einstein took a faculty position at Princeton University in New Jersey, where he remained for the rest of his life. He became a U.S. citizen in 1940.

Einstein was a lifelong pacifist who had managed to avoid military service and all war-related research. In 1939, however, he became afraid that Hitler's army would develop a terribly destructive weapon and win World War II. Einstein agreed to support the U.S. effort to build an atomic bomb, but after he saw the destruction caused by the bombs dropped on Hiroshima and Nagasaki, Japan, Einstein was heartbroken. "Had I known that the Germans would not succeed in producing an atomic bomb," he said, "I would not have lifted a finger."

Einstein's last years were spent trying to devise, unsuccessfully, a single theory to explain all gravitational and electromagnetic phenomena. To this day, no scientist has succeeded at this task.

In 1952, Einstein, a longtime supporter of the concept of a Jewish nation, was asked to be president of the newly created state of Israel. He declined, saying, "Politics is for the present, but an equation is for eternity." He died in New Jersey on April 8, 1955.

See also **Bethe, Hans** and **Chandrasekhar, Subrahmanyan**

Electromagnetic waves

Electromagnetic waves transmit energy through the interaction of electricity and magnetism. This process occurs naturally both on Earth and throughout the universe (the radiation put out by the sun and other stars is electromagnetic in nature). Electromagnetic waves have different properties, depending on their wavelength. The **electromagnetic spectrum** includes **radio wave**s, light waves, **microwave**s, infrared, ultraviolet, **X-ray**s, and **gamma ray**s.

Scientists first discovered the link between electricity and magnetism in the nineteenth century. In 1820, Danish physicist Hans Christian Oersted discovered that an electric current running through a conductor creates a **magnetic field.** Soon thereafter, British physicist Michael Fara-

The spectrum of electromagnetic radiation.

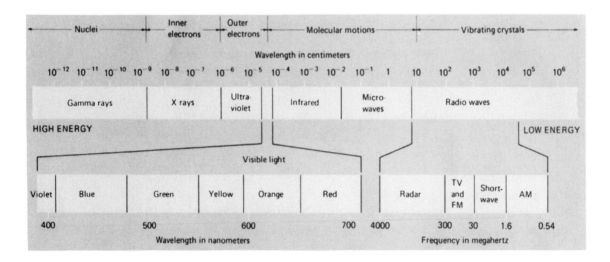

day found that a changing magnetic field can cause an electric current to flow through a conductor.

But the real proof of the close workings of electricity and magnetism was offered by Scottish mathematician James Clerk Maxwell. Between 1864 and 1873, Maxwell showed that a changing electric charge creates an electromagnetic field that radiates outward at a constant speed, the **speed of light.** Maxwell found that light itself is a form of **electromagnetic radiation,** and that light waves represent just one small part of the electromagnetic spectrum. His equations are still used today.

Electromagnetic waves also have different frequencies. Frequency is the number of waves that pass by a given point in a given time period. That number is determined by the number of times per second the electrical charge vibrates. The frequency is measured in hertz (cycles per second), a unit named for German physicist Rudolf Heinrich Hertz. Frequency is inversely proportional to wavelength. That is, the shorter the wavelength, the greater the frequency, and vice versa.

Hertz used a spark gap to create electromagnetic waves with very long wavelengths (2 feet, or 0.6 meters, long each). Such waves are known as radio waves. The longest radio waves in use today are 6 miles (10 kilometers) long. A subset of radio waves, those less than 3 feet (0.9 meters) across, are called microwaves.

The next longest electromagnetic waves are infrared waves, which are invisible but can be felt as heat. Infrared waves can be detected by special devices, many of which are made of material with moderate electrical conductivity. These conductors work by generating an electrical signal when they are struck by infrared waves.

Occupying a small space in the middle of the electromagnetic spectrum is visible light. The spectrum of light waves is subdivided into colors, red having the longest wavelengths and violet having the shortest wavelengths.

Ultraviolet waves have wavelengths even shorter than those of visible light, followed by X-rays, which have a high frequency but short wavelengths.

The shortest waves on the spectrum are gamma rays, which have wavelengths smaller than the diameter of an atom.

Elliptical galaxy

A **galaxy** is a huge region of space that contains hundreds of billions of stars, planets, glowing **nebula**e, gas, dust, and empty space. Galaxies may also have a **black hole,** a single point of infinite **mass** and **gravity** at their center. The fifty billion or so existing galaxies are believed to contain most of the detectable mass in the universe; this does not include invisible **dark matter,** which may make up as much as 90 percent of the mass in the universe.

Galaxies come primarily in three shapes: elliptical, spiral, and irregular. **Elliptical galaxies,** which are the most plentiful in the universe, appear in photographs as fuzzy patches of light. They vary in shape from circles to narrow, ovals and may be spherical or flat. The stars at the center of an elliptical galaxy are the brightest, those at the edges are dimmest, and the stars in between fade out in a smooth progression. An elliptical galaxy becomes more and more sparse at the edges until it merges gradually into space. This fact makes it nearly impossible to define precisely the boundaries of an elliptical galaxy.

Recent studies using **X-ray** and **radio telescopes** show that elliptical galaxies have a complex **interstellar medium** (the space between stars). Gas in these areas, which is sprinkled with hydrogen clouds, may be as hot as 180 million degrees Fahrenheit (100 million degrees Celsius). This fact contradicts prior theories that indicated that the interstellar space of these galaxies was virtually empty.

Elliptical galaxy.

Elliptical galaxies are comprised mostly of old stars. They come in a huge range of sizes, mass, and brightness. If one were to take a sample of one thousand of the brightest galaxies, about 20 percent of them would be elliptical, 75 percent spiral, and 5 percent irregular. However, if smaller, dimmer galaxies, such as **dwarf galaxies** were included in the survey, then the majority would fall in the elliptical category. Furthermore, the very brightest known galaxies are giant ellipticals.

Scientists regard it as possible that elliptical galaxies eventually form arms and become **spiral galaxies.** And it may happen that spiral galaxies lose their arms over time and become elliptical. However, most experts now believe that the two kinds of galaxies are basically different from each other and that one type will not evolve into the other type.

See also **Galaxy** and **Spiral galaxy**

Endeavour

Endeavour is the newest addition to the National Aeronautics and Space Administration's fleet of **space shuttle** orbiters. It was built in 1991 to replace *Challenger,* which was destroyed in an explosion in 1986. *Endeavour* was named after the research vessel of eighteenth-century British explorer James Cook.

Endeavour stands 122 feet (36.6 meters) tall and 78 feet (23.4 meters) wide, weighs 78 tons (71 metric tons), and cost more than two billion dollars to build. It was the fifth shuttle orbiter constructed and is one of four still in operation. The others include *Columbia, Discovery,* and *Atlantis.* It appears that *Endeavour* will be the last orbiter, as NASA has no plans to build more.

Endeavour, like the orbiters before it, is a reusable, winged space plane. It contains engines, astronaut living and work quarters, and a cargo bay large enough to hold a bus. An orbiter is the main component of the Space Transportation System, better known as the space shuttle. The other parts of a shuttle include solid **rocket** boosters and an external tank.

An orbiter is launched vertically using its own engines, aided by two attached rocket boosters. The boosters fall away from the orbiter about two minutes after lift-off and parachute into the ocean, where they are captured and used again. When an orbiter returns to earth it brakes with its engines

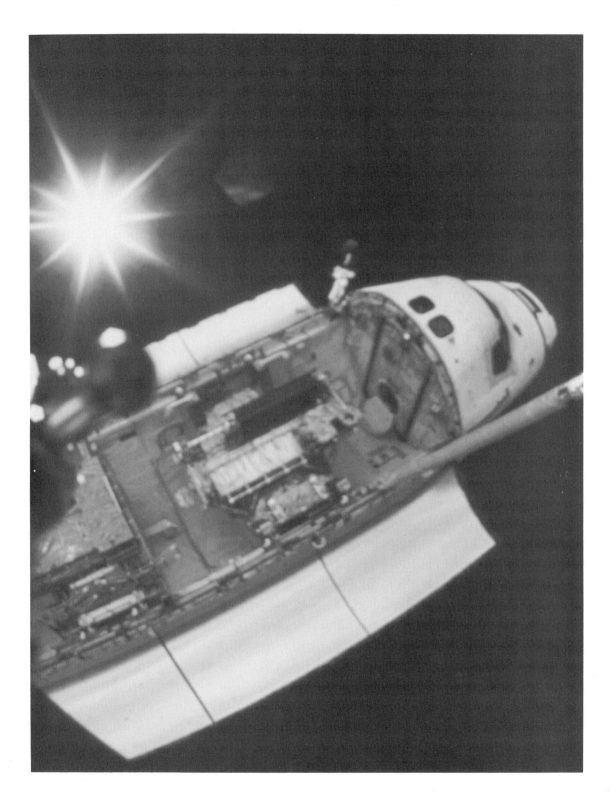

and lands like an airplane on a specially designed 3-mile-long (5-kilometer-long) runway. *Endeavour,* in addition to having improved electronics, also has a new tail parachute that shortens the distance it travels on the runway after touchdown.

May 7, 1992, was the date of *Endeavour's* maiden voyage. It was an adventurous mission involving the rescue of a damaged Intelsat communications satellite. The mission required several dangerous and complex **space walk**s to attach a motor to the satellite, that could be used to move it to a correct orbit. *Endeavour's* second flight, in September 1992, stands out because it included among its crew Mae Jemison, the first African-American woman astronaut in space.

Endeavour's most memorable mission took place from December 2–12, 1993, when it repaired the faulty Hubble Space Telescope (HST). The *Endeavour* flight crew joined up with the HST and brought it into the orbiter's cargo bay. Crew members then replaced some instruments, fixed others, and performed routine maintenance on the orbiting observatory. The HST was then returned to orbit. Since that time, the HST has been fully operational.

The most recent *Endeavour* flight, in January 1996, was geared toward both scientific research and preparation for the future construction of the International Space Station. Among the crew was Japanese astronaut Koichi Wakata. During the mission a research satellite was released for two days and then retrieved. The crew then picked up a Japanese satellite that had been deployed ten months earlier. Crew members also took two space walks to practice construction techniques in space and to try out new tools.

See also **Hubble Space Telescope** and **Space shuttle**

Equinox

Every year, beginning about June 22 (the summer **solstice**), the days grow shorter and the nights longer. On about December 22 (the winter solstice), this situation reverses and the number of hours of daylight increases until June 22, after which the cycle starts all over. This pattern hold true for the Northern Hemisphere. The cycle is reversed for the Southern Hemisphere.

On just two days a year, all points on Earth experience the same length of day and night, twelve hours of each. These days are called the

Opposite page: While on a space walk, one of the space shuttle Endeavour's crew members captured this view of the shuttle with the sun displaying a rayed effect.

equinoxes. The word equinox means "equal night." The vernal equinox occurs about March 21 and ushers in spring. Fall begins about September 23 with the autumnal equinox.

The equinoxes are the two opposite points on the Earth's orbit around the sun—and the only two days of the year—at which both of the Earth's hemispheres are bathed in equal amounts of sunlight. The rest of the time, the combination of the tilt of the Earth's axis and the angle of Earth's path around the sun means that sometimes the Earth is slightly above the sun and sometimes slightly below it. As a result, each hemisphere receives different amounts of sunlight. For half the year it's the Northern Hemisphere's turn to be sunnier and for the other half the year, it's the Southern Hemisphere's turn. Only twice each year, on the equinoxes, does the Earth's orbit reach a point where the equator faces the sun directly, exposing equal amounts of each hemisphere to the sun.

The term equinox also refers to the two locations on the **celestial sphere**—the imaginary sphere which surrounds Earth, on which we can plot celestial objects and chart their apparent movement due to the Earth's rotation. These points can be found by first drawing a straight line connecting the positions of the Earth and sun on the days of equinox. By extending this line until it intersects with the celestial sphere, you can locate the equinox.

This means that every thirteen thousand years the Earth tilts in the opposite direction and the seasons during which each hemisphere receives the greatest amount of sunlight are reversed.

See also **Seasons** and **Solstice**

European Southern Observatory

The European Southern Observatory (ESO), located in mountainous La Silla, Chile, is run by a group of eight European nations based in Garching, Germany. The La Silla center is one of three astronomical observatories within a 100-mile (161-kilometer) radius in north-central Chile. The other two are Cerro Tololo Interamerican Observatory, funded by the National Science Foundation, and Las Campanas, a private observatory financed by the Washington D.C.-based Carnegie Institution.

The popularity of this region among astronomers is based on the fact that the quality of viewing here is unsurpassed. This region of the Chilean Andes sits above the Atacama Desert and contains the second driest air in the world after Antarctica. As a result, the skies here are generally clear. About three quarters of the nights are completely cloudless. And at this elevation (about 7,500 feet, or 2,300 meters) the Earth's atmosphere is thin. This factor is important because molecules in the atmosphere tend to scatter light from celestial objects, distorting their image. The higher up one goes in the atmosphere, the less interference is encountered.

Construction at La Silla began in 1965. The site now consists of a guest house for visiting astronomers and several domed buildings containing the observatory's fifteen telescopes. The first telescope, a 59-inch-diameter (150-centimeter-diameter) **reflector,** went into operation in 1976. The telescopes subsequently installed include reflectors ranging from 20 to 150 inches (50 to 380 centimeters) across, a 40-inch (100-centimeter) **Schmidt telescope,** and a **radio telescope** with a 49-foot-wide (15-meter-wide) dish. In comparison, the largest reflector in the world is the 393-inch (1,000-centimeter) Keck Telescope at the Mauna Kea Observatory in Hawaii.

The ESO employs about 270 people in total, about 120 of them at La Silla and the rest at its headquarters in Europe. About one-third of the staff works as technicians, overseeing the operation of the equipment. Another 35 employees are staff astronomers. They use the equipment about one-third of the time, while the rest of the observing time is divided among visiting astronomers who come for short stays.

The astronomers' day at La Silla begins at about 5 P.M. with a meal and an equipment check. By 9 P.M. it is usually dark enough to get to work. This means observing the skies while sipping coffee all night long, seated in front of a wall of computer monitors in a tube-shaped control room. For much of the year, nighttime is around eleven hours long, a good chunk of observing time, especially in clear weather conditions.

See also **Cerro Tololo Interamerican Observatory**

European Space Agency

The European Space Agency (ESA) is an organization of fourteen European countries, founded in 1975 for peaceful scientific purposes. The agency's mission includes the development and launch of communication

The European
Space Agency's
Ariane 5 satellite
launcher is wheeled
out of its final
assembly building to
the launch pad in
Kourou, French
Guiana, on July 30,
1995.

and weather satellites, scientific spacecraft, and space transportation systems. ESA member nations jointly fund and decide upon projects for the agency.

ESA is a combination of two earlier space organizations in Europe, the European Space Research Organization (ESRO) and the European Launcher Development Organization (ELDO). The member nations of ESA are Austria, Belgium, Denmark, Finland, France, Germany, Ireland, Italy, the Netherlands, Norway, Spain, Sweden, Switzerland, and the United Kingdom.

ESA has an operating budget of two billion dollars a year and employs a two thousand-person staff. While each member nation must contribute to the general operating fund, contributions to individual projects are optional. ESA headquarters are located in Paris, France. The organization also has offices in the Netherlands, Germany, and Italy and is planning to open an astronaut training center in Germany in the near future.

One of the most noted accomplishments of the ESA has been the Ariane **rocket** series. These liquid-**propellant** rockets have launched European scientific and communications satellites into space and have been made available for use by other nations. The first successful Ariane launch was in 1979. Since then, the rocket has been used many times. One famous mission involving Ariane was the 1985 launch of the ESA's *Giotto*, a **probe** that flew very close to the center of Halley's **comet.**

The Ariane 2 rocket was introduced in 1983. Six years later it was used to launch the Swedish Tele-X satellite. The latest version of the rocket is Ariane 5.

Another major project of ESA has been the Earth observation program, called SPOT (Satellite Pour l'Observation de la Terre). Developed by France, Sweden, and Belgium, SPOT was first launched in 1986 by an Ariane rocket. Three SPOTS currently orbit the Earth about 517 miles (832 kilometers) above ground. Together they produce images of the whole Earth every twenty-six days.

Recently, ESA has fallen on difficult economic times and has had to cancel a number of planned projects, primarily the development of its own **space shuttle.**

ESA has worked in cooperation with the National Aeronautics and Space Administration (NASA) on several projects over the years, including the Hubble Space Telescope and the Spacelab science experiments carried on board various U.S. space shuttles. The two agencies are presently working toward the construction of an International Space Station, slated to begin early in the next century.

See also **International Space Station** and **Spacelab**

Explorer 1

In late 1957, the pressure was on the United States to get a satellite into orbit around the Earth. The former **Soviet Union** had just launched the *Sputnik 1* satellite and was winning the **space race,** the contest between the United States and the former Soviet Union for superiority in space exploration. U.S. officials put their own space program in high gear.

The first U.S. attempts at launching a satellite were failures. In December 1957—just two months after *Sputnik*'s launch—the National Advisory Committee for Aeronautics (NACA) attempted to launch a satellite with a Vanguard **rocket.** Just a few feet off the ground the rocket burst into flames. After other disasters with the Vanguard, NASA turned the project over to Wernher von Braun, a German engineer who had come to the United States after World War II.

Von Braun was a rocket specialist who had developed some of the Nazis' most destructive long-range missiles. These explosive-carrying rockets could travel hundreds of miles. Once in the United States, von Braun turned his efforts to space flight. He had been developing the Jupiter-C rocket, which was capable of flying at a height of 680 miles (1,094 kilometers). On January 31, 1958, just one month after the first Vanguard rocket had failed and four months after the launch of *Sputnik,* von Braun's modified Jupiter-C, called the Juno-1, successfully propelled the *Explorer 1* satellite into orbit.

Explorer 1 was a bullet-shaped satellite, designed by a team of scientists at the University of Iowa, led by James Van Allen. *Explorer 1* was much smaller than *Sputnik.* It was about 6.5 feet (2 meters) long and weighed only 31 pounds (14 kilograms). It contained instruments to measure the temperature and density of Earth's upper atmosphere. It also had a radiation detector that found rings of radiation surrounding the Earth. These areas were later named **Van Allen belts,** after James Van Allen. These belts contain protons and electrons given off by the sun.

Explorer 1 remained in orbit until 1967. It represented a tremendous

America's first satellite, Explorer 1, leaves Earth on the nose of a Jupiter-C rocket on January 30, 1968.

achievement for the U.S. space program and showed how valuable satellites can be for scientific research.

Sixty-four more Explorer satellites were launched between 1958 and 1984. They provided us with detailed pictures of our planet, and provided data on a range of space phenomena, including **solar wind, magnetic fields**, and **ultraviolet radiation.**

See also **Braun, Wernher von**; **Space race**; and **Van Allen, James**

A software engineer holds one of the boards of the new Multichannel Spectrum Analyser (MSA), part of the Microwave Observing Project set up by the SETI Institute. In this project, several radio antennas across the world will perform an all-sky survey looking for an extraterrestrial signal.

Extraterrestrial life

Life has never been found anywhere in the universe except on Earth, but that does not dampen the enthusiasm of astronomers who are searching for it elsewhere. While visions of extraterrestrial creatures used to be limited to the pages of science fiction novels and people's imaginations, the search for extraterrestrial intelligence (or SETI, as it is called) has in recent years become a scientific venture with widespread respectability. With the discoveries over the last few years of new planets circling nearby stars, the possibility that extraterrestrial life exists seems greater than ever. And astronomers believe that, if life exists on other planets, our generation possesses the technological capability of finding it and perhaps even communicating with it.

The first known scientific attempt to locate extraterrestrial life was undertaken by the turn-of-the-century astronomer Percival Lowell. Lowell, who was independently wealthy, built his own observatory in Arizona. He searched intently for signs of life on Mars, but came up empty handed.

Modern search missions have most commonly employed **radio telescope**s tuned to nearby stars, listening for signals that may have been sent by alien civilizations. The success of these missions depends not only on the existence of extraterrestrial life, but on a species intelligent enough to figure out how to send us signals across the huge expanse of space. Needless to say, none of these experiments produced positive results as of yet.

The first large-scale SETI experiment, called Project Ozma, was begun by astronomer Frank Drake in 1960. The project was named for Princess Ozma in L. Frank Baum's science fiction story, *Ozma of Oz*. Drake spent countless hours at the National Radio Astronomy Observatory in Green Bank, West Virginia, with a radio telescope poised to receive signals from outer space. His project detected one signal he initially thought was from a distant star, but it turned out to be coming from Earth.

SETI Research in the 1990s

In October 1992, the National Aeronautics and Space Administration (NASA) began a large, sophisticated study of its own. The plans called for a ten-year search of one thousand nearby stars similar to our sun, as well as a scan of the entire sky, for signals. A year later, however, due to budget restraints, Congress canceled funding for the experiment.

One current SETI project is being conducted 30 miles (48 kilometers) outside of Boston, at the Harvard-Smithsonian radio telescope. The project is called BETA, the Billion-channel Extra-Terrestrial Assay, and consists of an 84-foot-diameter (25-meter-diameter) antenna dish that rotates on its stand and sweeps the sky for signals. Signals from the antenna are converted into digitized signals and fed into a supercomputer. If the antenna picks up a strange signal, the computer is programmed to alert the project coordinators.

Other SETI research is being carried out by two private groups, the SETI Institute in Mountain View, California, headed by Frank Drake, and the Planetary Society, an organization of amateur astronomers, led by astronomer Carl Sagan.

The search for extraterrestrial life received a huge boost in late 1995 and early 1996, when three new planets were found in our **galaxy.** The planets orbit nearby stars, ranging between thirty-five and forty **light-years** from the Earth. The first planet, discovered by Swiss astronomers Michel Mayor and Didier Queloz of the Geneva Observatory, orbits a star in the **constellation** Pegasus. The next two planets were discovered by Americans Geoffrey Marcy and Paul Butler. One is in the constellation Virgo and the other is in the Big Dipper.

These discoveries are significant to SETI for at least two reasons. First, they show that our planet may not be unique, as we had previously believed. The discovery of three planets, in a star system containing one hundred billion stars, indicates that many more planets remain to be discovered. Second, the two most recently discovered planets seem to be at a temperature at which water can remain in its liquid state, a necessary component for life as we know it.

New Plans for SETI at NASA

These discoveries prompted NASA to step up its own efforts to find new planets, particularly those with the potential to support living beings. NASA officials now rank the search for extraterrestrial life as one of their highest priority scientific undertakings for the next twenty-five years. In concrete terms, NASA has announced a new program, called the Origins Project, which will use space-based telescopes to search for extraterrestrial life. As NASA administrator Daniel Goldin said in a 1996 interview, "We are restructuring the agency to focus on our customer, the American people." Goldin's comment is in response to the SETI enthusiasts who for decades have lobbied NASA to find answers.

In addition, plans are underway to fit the Hubble Space Telescope with a new infrared camera by the year 1997. This modification would give astronomers their first pictures of the newly discovered worlds. And by the year 2010, NASA hopes to deploy a new tool in the search for other worlds: Project Pathfinder, an interferometer in space. Pathfinder will be able to identify Earth-like planets and to study their atmospheres for the presence of life-sustaining substances like oxygen.

For those interested in extraterrestrial life who have long been subjected to ridicule by their colleagues in the scientific community, things have never looked brighter. This positive outlook was expressed in a 1996 interview with SETI leader and Harvard physicist Paul Horowitz. "Intelligent life in the universe?" asked Horowitz. "Guaranteed. Intelligent life in our galaxy? So overwhelmingly likely that I'd give you almost any odds you'd like."

See also **Drake, Frank** and **Sagan, Carl**

Faget, Maxime (1921–)
American engineer

Maxime Faget is a pioneer of the U.S. space program. He designed the Mercury capsule (used in the first American piloted space flights), the Apollo **command** and **service modules** (used in the first voyages to the moon), and the **space shuttle** orbiter (the first reusable spacecraft). Although most of his ideas were warmly welcomed by the National Aeronautics and Space Administration (NASA), the organization probably should have listened to him even more closely. If Faget's design for a one-piece solid-**rocket** booster had been used, it might have prevented the tragic explosion of the space shuttle *Challenger* in 1986.

Originally from Honduras, Faget occupied himself building model airplanes as a child. He went to college at Louisiana State University and graduated with a bachelor of science degree in 1943. Three years later, he went to work for the National Advisory Committee for Aeronautics (NACA), which later became the National Aeronautics and Space Administration.

At NASA's Langley Aeronautical Laboratory in Hampton, Virginia, Faget designed high-speed jets. As part of the propulsion-and-performance team, he helped design the X-15, the experimental plane that flew six times the speed of sound.

Faget also worked on developing the first spacecraft in which humans could travel. Such a spacecraft would have to protect its passengers from the forces of **gravity** and heat upon re-entry to the Earth's atmosphere. Faget's model, which was used for the Mercury capsule, was designed to decrease speed high in the atmosphere, where the effects of re-entry would not be as intense.

Faget Works On Apollo and Space Shuttle Programs

From 1961 to 1981, Faget worked in Houston, Texas, as the director of engineering and development at the Manned Spacecraft Center (later renamed the Johnson Space Center). At the center, Faget and his colleague Caldwell Johnson designed the Apollo command module and service module. The command module is the front section of the spacecraft, containing astronauts' living quarters and control panels; the service module is the section of the spacecraft behind the command module, containing the main engine and fuel, water, and other supplies.

Faget and Johnson originally planned to have the entire command-and-service module land on the moon and return to Earth. But it soon became apparent that this design would require too large a rocket for launching and landing on the moon. So they modified their design to include a small **lunar module,** a shuttle that would take astronauts from the orbiting main spacecraft down to the moon's surface and back.

Faget's next project was to help design the space shuttle orbiter. The space shuttle program was necessary to NASA for creating a permanent station in space. A reusable craft that could shuttle astronauts into space and back would be critical to the construction and use of a **space station.** The central component of the shuttle is the orbiter, a winged space aircraft that contains engines, rocket boosters, astronaut living quarters and command center, and a cargo bay large enough to hold a bus.

Maxime Faget.

The first space shuttle, *Columbia,* was put into use in 1981. Five space shuttles have now been built, four of which are still in use. One shuttle, the *Challenger,* was destroyed in an explosion in 1986.

In 1981, Faget left NASA to work in the private aerospace industry. In 1983, he founded Space Industries, Inc., and began work on an industrial space facility, a permanent storage shed in space to hold research equipment.

See also **Apollo program**; **Mercury program**; and **Space shuttle**

Foucault, Jean Bernard Léon
(1819–1868)
French physicist

In 1852, a crowd gathered at the Pantheon monument in Paris, France, to watch a large, swinging, iron ball suspended from the dome ceiling by a 200-foot-long (60-meter-long) wire scratch its path with a pointer in the sand below. Over the course of the day, while the path of the ball remained constant, the line etched out by the pointer slowly and continually shifted to the right, eventually coming full circle. This ball was Foucault's pendulum, and it offered the first proof that the Earth's rotation was real, and not an optical illusion caused by the sun and stars revolving around it.

Jean Bernard Léon Foucault was born in Paris. Sickly as a child, he was educated at home. He first studied to be a doctor, but found he could not stand the sight of blood. Therefore, he moved on to other areas of science and math. Foucault was also a writer, producing textbooks on arithmetic, geometry, and chemistry, as well as a science column for a newspaper.

Together with physicist Armand Fizeau, Foucault was the first person to use an old-fashioned camera to photograph the sun. This camera, called a daguerreotype, took pictures on a light-sensitive, silver-coated plate. To take their photos, Fizeau and Foucault had to leave the camera focused on the sun for so long that the sun's position relative to the Earth would change.

This problem inspired Foucault to invent a pendulum-driven device to keep the camera in line with the sun. He noticed that the pendulum tended to keep swinging in the direction in which it was first released. If he tried to turn the pendulum, it always returned to its original path.

This observation led to Foucault's method for demonstrating that the Earth is rotating. When he released the giant ball before the crowd in Paris, it scratched a straight line in the sand. But over the course of one day, that line shifted

Jean Bernard Léon Foucault.

to the right again and again until it came full circle. Since the pendulum did not change course, it had to be the Earth that was rotating beneath it.

Foucault applied the same principle in his invention of the **gyroscope.** This device has a wheel spinning around a rod through its center. The wheel continues spinning in the same direction, even when you change the direction that the instrument is pointed.

Foucault's Research On Light

Foucault's other claim to fame was to his accurate measurement of the **speed of light.** His results were within 1 percent of the value currently accepted. To determine the speed of light he used two mirrors, one rotating and one stationary. The moving mirror reflected light to the still mirror, which bounced the light back. The light again struck the moving mirror, and reflected off to another point. Using geometry, Foucault was able to calculate the angle of rotation of the moving mirror, the distance the light had traveled, and the time it took to get there.

He also realized that light slowed down slightly as it passes through water. At the time, a debate within the scientific community focused on the question as to whether light was made up of waves or particles. Foucault's findings seemed to support the wave theory. Today we know light acts as both.

Foucault next turned his efforts to improving telescopes. He started with the **reflecting telescope,** developed by Isaac Newton. This design uses a mirror to reflect light through an eyepiece. Foucault developed a mirror that was lighter and would not tarnish easily. When placed in a telescope, it gave a brighter, clearer image than before.

Foucault, who dedicated his life to his work, accomplished much before an early death at the age of forty-eight from a brain disease.

See also **Earth's rotation** and **Speed of light**

Gagarin, Yuri (1934–1968)

Soviet cosmonaut

On April 12, 1961, Yuri Gagarin became the first person to travel in space. His country, the former **Soviet Union** had been developing a space program over the previous decade, in part spurred on by the desire to best its rival, the United States. The two countries were in the midst of the **cold war** and space flight had become an important symbol of national superiority.

Gagarin's historic flight was made on a Vostok spacecraft, which orbited Earth one time, in just one hour and forty-eight minutes. While in space, Gagarin communicated by radio. He described his view of Earth as follows: "It has a very beautiful sort of halo, a rainbow." *Vostok 1* then reentered the atmosphere and two miles above ground Gagarin parachuted safely into a field.

The Soviet government insisted for decades that the mission had come off without a hitch. Pages from the flight log recently made public, however, show that such was not the case: the flight had nearly ended in disaster. The notes describe how the spacecraft spun wildly out of control on descent. The capsule in which Gagarin was riding was finally saved when it separated from the lurching **rocket.**

Yuri Alexeyevich Gagarin was born in the Russian village of Klushino, in the marshy Smolensk region west of Moscow. Gagarin was the third of four children. His parents worked on a collective farm, where his father was a cabinetmaker, a carpenter, and a bricklayer. Neither of his parents had much formal education, but they worked hard to make sure Yuri would have one.

Gagarin grew up during World War II, a time when resources were scarce. His home town was invaded by Nazi German forces, and his house taken over by soldiers. As a result, the entire family had to dig a large hole, where they went into hiding. It was not enough, however, to keep the German soldiers from discovering them. They took away Gagarin's older brother and sister, who, along with many other young men and women of the village, were never seen again.

Gagarin's Career As a Pilot

After the war, Gagarin's family moved to the town of Gzhatsk, where he completed high school in 1949. Gagarin then enrolled in the Lyubertsy Agricultural Machinery School, where he was trained to work in an iron foundry. Two years later, he entered the Industrial Technical

Yuri Gagarin, the first human in space, in 1961.

School at Saratov on the Volga River. There Gagarin joined a flying club and became an amateur pilot, a move that changed the course of his life.

At the recommendation of an instructor, Gagarin was accepted to the Orenburg Aviation School in 1955. It was there, at a dance, that he met the woman who was to become his wife, Valentina Ivanovna Goryacheva, a worker at a telegraph office. On November 7, 1957, Gagarin graduated with honors and was given the rank of lieutenant. The next day, he put on his officer's jacket and proposed to Valentina. She accepted.

Gagarin then went off to the Arctic to train as a fighter pilot with the Soviet Northern Fleet. He was inspired by the successful 1959 flight of the Soviet satellite *Luna 3,* which orbited the moon. Soon thereafter he applied to be among the first group of **cosmonaut**s and was approved. For more than a year, he was involved in testing and training for space flight. Because of his outstanding personal traits and physical capabilities, Gagarin was chosen to pilot the first Vostok mission into space.

For the five years following that flight, Gagarin was kept busy with public appearances in the Soviet Union and abroad, training the next group of cosmonauts, administrative tasks, and political activities. In 1966, Gagarin finally began to prepare himself for another space mission on board a Soyuz spacecraft.

The first Soyuz flight took place the following year. The cosmonaut on board, Vladimir Komarov, was killed during re-entry into the Earth's atmosphere. Gagarin, however, continued training for a later Soyuz mission, but he never went into space again. During a training flight on March 27, 1968, his jet spun out of control and crashed to the ground. Gagarin, at the age of thirty-four, and his flight instructor were killed.

See also **Space race** and **Vostok program**

Galaxy

A **galaxy** is a huge grouping of stars, glowing **nebula**e, gas, dust, and empty space. Many scientists now believe that a **black hole** lies at the center of many galaxies.

Galaxies are as plentiful in the universe as grains of sand on a beach. The galaxy that contains our **solar system** is called the **Milky Way.** The Milky Way is part of a cluster of galaxies known as the Local Group, and the Local Group is part of a local supercluster that includes many clusters. Superclusters are separated by extremely large voids of space, with very few galaxies in between.

Galaxies can be spiral, elliptical, or irregular in shape. The Milky Way and nearby Andromeda galaxy are both spiral-shaped. That means they have a group of objects at the center (stars and possibly a black hole), surrounded by a **halo** and an invisible cloud of **dark matter,** with arms spiraling out like a pinwheel. The spiral shape is formed because the entire galaxy is rotating, with the stars at the outer edges forming the arms. Most of these galaxies have just one arm wrapped around the nucleus, although some have two or even three arms.

Spiral galaxies come in two kinds: barred and unbarred. In barred spirals, a thick band of stars crosses the center of the galaxy. Unbarred spirals have no such feature.

An **elliptical galaxy** contains mostly older stars, with very little dust or gas. It can be round or oval, flattened or spherical, and resembles the nucleus of a spiral galaxy without the arms. Astronomers do not yet know whether elliptical galaxies eventually form arms and become spirals, or if spiral galaxies lose their arms to become elliptical.

About one quarter of all galaxies are irregular in shape. Irregular shape may be caused by the formation of new stars in these galaxies or by the pull of a neighboring galaxy's gravitational field. Two examples of an irregular galaxy are the Large and Small Magellanic Clouds, visible in the night sky from the Southern Hemisphere.

Photo of a galaxy taken by the Hale Telescope at Palomar Observatory in 1961.

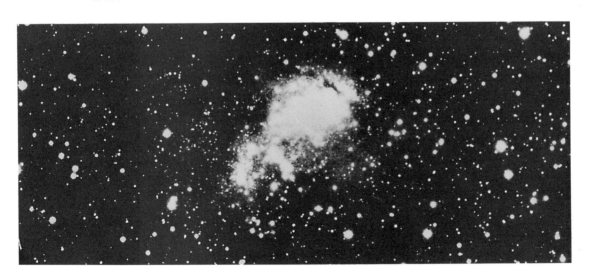

Some galaxies are variations of these types. There are **Seyfert galaxies,** violent, fast-moving spirals; bright elliptical galaxies of **supergiant**s that often consume other galaxies; ring galaxies that seem to have no nucleus; twisted starry ribbons formed when two galaxies collide; and others.

The Milky Way galaxy is a barred spiral about eighty thousand **light-year**s across. Its nucleus contains billions of old stars and maybe even a black hole. It has four spiral arms. Our solar system is located in the Orion arm, about twenty-eight thousand light-years from the center of the galaxy.

In ancient times, people looked into space and saw a glowing band of light. They thought it resembled a river of milk and called it the "Milky Way." In the late 1500s, Galileo Galilei first examined the Milky Way through a telescope and saw that the glowing band was made up of countless stars. As early as 1755, German philosopher Immanuel Kant suggested that the Milky Way was a lens-shaped group of stars, and that many other such groups existed in the universe.

Over the years, astronomers learned more about the shape of the Milky Way, but they continued to place the sun at the center. In 1918, American astronomer Harlow Shapley studied the distribution of star clusters and determined that our solar system was not at the center, but on the fringes of the galaxy.

In 1924, American astronomer Edwin Hubble first proved the existence of other galaxies. He used a very powerful 100-inch (254-centimeter) telescope at Mount Wilson Observatory to discover that a group of stars long thought to be part of the Milky Way was actually a separate galaxy, now known as the Andromeda galaxy. He then discovered many other spiral-shaped galaxies. Three years later, Dutch astronomer Jan Oort showed that galaxies rotate about their center.

In early 1996, the Hubble Space Telescope sent back photographs of fifteen hundred very distant galaxies in the process of formation, indicating that the number of galaxies in the universe is far greater than previously thought. Soon after this discovery, astronomers estimated the number of galaxies to be fifty billion.

See also **Andromeda galaxy**; **Elliptical galaxy**; **Milky Way galaxy**; **Seyfert, Carl**; **Shapley, Harlow**; and **Spiral galaxy**

Galilei, Galileo (1564–1642)

Italian mathematician and astronomer

Galileo lived at a time when scientific understanding of the physical world was in its infancy. He was a pioneer of the scientific method, which involves suggesting a hypothesis and then conducting strict and thorough experimentation to test the likelihood of that idea. For instance, most scientists of Galileo's day believed that the sun revolved around the Earth (the **geocentric,** or **Ptolemaic, model.**) The Christian Church followed and taught the same belief. Galileo found scientific evidence to support the idea that the Earth revolves around the sun (the **heliocentric,** or **Copernican, model.**) For the sake of these scientific truths, Galileo was willing to sacrifice his freedom.

Galileo was born in Pisa, Italy, and received his early education at home from his father. At age ten, he began attending school at a Jesuit monastery near Florence. When he expressed an interest in the idea of becoming a monk, his father removed him from the school. In 1581, when he was seventeen years old, Galileo went to the University of Pisa to study medicine. But after listening to a lecture on geometry one day, Galileo decided to switch fields and study mathematics.

Galileo Galilei.

Galileo ran out of money and had to leave college in 1585. He returned to Florence and continued his studies on his own. The next year he published a paper on specific **gravity.** Specific gravity tells whether a substance will sink or float in water. With this work he became known throughout Italy's scientific community.

A few years later, Galileo was offered a job as professor of mathematics at the University of Pisa. When his three-year contract at Pisa ended, he was hired to teach at the University of Padua, a position he held for eighteen years. While at his teaching posts, Galileo continued his research and made a number of important discoveries.

In one study, Galileo rolled two different-sized balls down an angled surface to demonstrate that falling objects speed up or slow down at an equal rate. He proved false Aristotle's theory that heavier objects fall at a faster rate than lighter objects, because the balls reached the bottom at the same time. His experiments laid the groundwork for Isaac Newton's laws of motion.

Galileo's Telescope Research

In the early 1600s, a Dutch lens-grinder named Hans Lippershey created the first telescope. In 1609, Galileo made his own telescope. It had two lenses and was strong enough for astronomical viewing, magnifying objects to thirty-two times their original size. (By today's standards, that level of magnification is not very impressive. A relatively inexpensive telescope today has a magnification fifty to five hundred times that of Galileo's.)

With his telescope, Galileo dispelled a number of false assumptions about the **solar system.** First, he found that the moon is not smooth, but has a bumpy surface. He also learned that the **Milky Way galaxy** is not a solid white band, but contains, as he described in a book on his sightings, "innumerable stars grouped together in clusters. . . . Many of them are rather large and quite bright, while the number of smaller ones is quite beyond calculation."

In addition, Galileo observed dark spots on the sun's surface, called **sunspot**s, and Saturn's rings, although he described them as "protuberances" (outward bulges) on either side of the planet. One of Galileo's most significant discoveries was that four moons are in orbit around Jupiter. This proved to him that the geocentric model, which states that everything revolves around the Earth, was incorrect.

In 1610, Galileo published the findings of his telescopic research in a book entitled *Sidereus Nuncius* (*The Starry Messenger*). Soon after, he arranged a meeting with the pope and other church officials to describe his findings. He left the meeting believing that he had convinced church officials of the heliocentric model. Yet, as it turned out, it was not so easy to change the church's centuries-long-held-beliefs, about the Earth's place in the solar system.

In 1616, after many debates over the meaning of new scientific findings, Nicholas Copernicus' book *De Revolutionibus Orbium Coelestium* (*Revolution of the Heavenly Spheres*) was banned. It had been published in 1543, and remained banned until 1835. Galileo was told that his opposition to the church's belief in the geocentric model was "false and erroneous" and he was forbidden to continue his support of Copernicus' ideas.

When a new pope was elected in 1624, Galileo traveled to Rome to have his case heard again. The new pope gave Galileo permission to write about the Copernican model, but insisted that he had to give equal treatment to the Earth-centered model.

In 1632, Galileo published his *Dialogo di Galilei linceo. . . sopra I due massimi sistemi del mondo* (*Dialogue Concerning the Two Chief World Systems*) about the heliocentric and geocentric solar system theories. By describing the geocentric model in unconvincing terms, he clearly did not represent the two equally. Galileo was brought before the Inquisition (the church's board that sought out and punished non-believers) and was found guilty of heresy, promoting opinions in conflict with those of the church. For his punishment, Galileo's book was banned and he was sentenced to house arrest for the rest of his life.

Galileo continued to work at his home until his death at age seventy-eight, but was forbidden to publish anything else.

See also **Ancient Greek astronomy**; **Copernicus, Nicholas**; **Planetary motion**; and **Sunspot**

Lamp at Midnight (1966)

This movie tells the story of three periods in the life of Galileo Galilei. In the first period, Galileo constructs his own telescope; in the second, he defends, before the Inquisition, his belief that the Earth revolves around the sun; and in the third, he publishes his book, *Dialogue on the Two Systems of the World*.

Galileo

After many delays, the *Galileo* **space probe** was launched from the **space shuttle** *Atlantis* in 1989. The 2.5-ton (2.3-metric ton), Jupiter-bound **probe** began its journey traveling in a direction to that opposite of its destination. It headed first for Venus and looped around it, using that planet's gravitational field to propel it towards Jupiter, a technique called **gravity assist.** In all, *Galileo* traveled two and one-half billion miles to reach its target, which is a half a billion miles away.

Galileo finally approached Jupiter in December 1995. On arrival, it dropped a barbeque-grill-sized mini-probe to the planet. The mini-probe entered Jupiter's atmosphere at a speed of 106,000 miles (170,550 kilometers) per hour. Within two minutes it slowed to 100 miles (161 kilometers) per hour. Soon after, it released a parachute. As it floated toward the planet's hot surface, intense winds blew it 300 miles (482 kilometers) horizontally. The mini-probe spent fifty-eight minutes taking extremely detailed pictures of the gaseous planet before being incinerated in the 3,400-degree-Fahrenheit (1,871-degree-Celsius) heat near the surface.

Galileo is the successor to the *Voyager 1* and *2* probes, which passed by Jupiter in 1979 and 1980 and took pictures of the planet's swirling colors, volcanic moons, and previously undiscovered ring. The *Voyager*s merely whet the appetite of the scientific community, which is now excitedly analyzing the information transmitted by *Galileo*. This information includes photos up to one thousand times more detailed than those taken by the *Voyager*s. In particular, scientists are looking for signs of water, which may sustain primitive life forms.

Galileo is controlled from afar by engineers at the Jet Propulsion Laboratory (JPL), operated by the California Institute of Technology in Pasadena, California. JPL is the National Aeronautics and Space Administration (NASA) organization responsible for space exploration missions. In the process of guiding *Galileo* to Jupiter, JPL staffers issued over a quarter of a million instructions.

Delays in the Launch of *Galileo*

The history of *Galileo* is full of ups and downs, shortfalls, and setbacks. The probe was initially set to be transported into space by a space shuttle flight scheduled soon after the doomed January 28, 1986, *Challenger* mission. After that explosion, however, the entire shuttle program was put on hold for the two years and eight months, during which time an investigation and safety upgrades to the remaining shuttles were completed.

By the time NASA was ready to send *Galileo* up, two new problems had arisen.

Artist's conception of the Galileo *probe descending to Jupiter.*

First, the powerful Centaur **rocket** that was originally going to send the probe directly to Jupiter had been pulled out of use due to safety concerns. Second, the positions of the planets had shifted, making *Galileo*'s initially intended path impossible. Thus, JPL engineers had to find another way to get *Galileo* to Jupiter. They eventually decided to use the gravity-assisted "slingshot" path described earlier, a journey that took six years to complete, compared to the direct course's estimated two and a half years.

Galileo's problems did not end there. Eighteen months into its voyage, the staff at JPL realized that the probe's antennas were jammed. It appeared that during the three-year delay in launch the spacecraft's lubricants had dried up. Without the use of its antennas, *Galileo* would be unable to send back its prized information about Jupiter. The control crew worked on the problem for two years and eventually reprogrammed the probe with new computer software. They were able only to partially repair the damage, however. Instead of the initially promised fifty thousand photographs, *Galileo* will now deliver only one thousand.

Despite its rocky beginnings, *Galileo* is still expected to provide some of the most valuable information to date about the outer half of our **solar system.** Even before reaching Jupiter, the probe yielded a wealth of data. It discovered lightning on Venus, found that an **asteroid** called Ida has a tiny moon, and mapped the north pole of the Earth's moon. *Galileo* will continue to orbit Jupiter and eight of its moons through late 1997.

See also **Jupiter** and **Voyager program**

Gamma ray astronomy

When we look out at the moon and stars, what we see is visible light. Most of the **electromagnetic spectrum,** however, is made up of radiation we cannot see, with wavelengths both longer and shorter than visible light. For instance, there are **radio wave**s, infrared, **X-ray**s, and **gamma ray**s, each of which can be detected only with specialized instruments and each of which gives us a different view of the sky. **Gamma ray astronomy** involves studying the picture of space created by gamma ray detection.

Gamma rays are high-energy subatomic particles formed either by the decay of radioactive elements or by nuclear reactions. Gamma rays can be observed here on Earth, but gamma rays produced in space do not penetrate the **ozone layer** and thus do not make it into the lower layers of the Earth's atmosphere. They are created by **nuclear fusion** reactions that occur within the core of stars and can be detected only in space.

Gamma rays in space, or cosmic gamma rays, were first discovered in 1967 by small satellites called Velas. These satellites had been put into orbit to monitor nuclear weapon explosions on Earth, but they found gamma ray bursts from outside our **solar system** as well.

Several other small satellites launched in the early 1970s gave pictures of the whole gamma ray sky. These pictures revealed hundreds of previously unknown stars and several possible **black hole**s. Thousands more stars were discovered in 1977 and 1979 by three larger satellites, called High Energy Astrophysical Observatories. They found that the

Gamma ray Observatory being released by the robot arm of the space shuttle Atlantis on April 8, 1991.

Milky Way looks much the same in gamma rays as it does in visible light.

Then, in 1991, the Compton Gamma Ray Observatory was carried into space by the **space shuttle** *Atlantis*. This satellite still orbits the Earth, giving us very detailed pictures of the gamma ray sky. It has provided us with new information about **supernova**s, young star clusters, **pulsar**s, possible black holes, and **quasar**s.

See also **Compton Gamma Ray Observatory** and **High Energy Astrophysical Observatories**

Gamow, George (1904–1968)
Russian-born American physicist

Best known for his work on **nuclear fusion** and the **big bang theory,** George Gamow was born in Russia and grew up during the Russian Revolution. His interest in astronomy began at age thirteen when his father gave him a telescope. Gamow went to the University of Leningrad and earned his Ph.D. in 1928.

George Gamow.

After graduation, Gamow went to Europe to work with physicists Niels Bohr and Ernest Rutherford. There he discovered how to break down an atomic nucleus by bombarding it with low-energy particles, a process known as the "tunnel effect."

When Gamow returned to Russia, the ruling Bolshevik Party tried to limit his travels. In 1933, while attending a conference in Belgium, he and his wife deserted their homeland and came to the United States. Here Gamow was welcomed onto the faculty of George Washington University in Washington D.C.

Gamow continued his work on nuclear physics, specifically studying how stars produce their energy. He discovered that as a star grows older and uses up its hydrogen in the fusion process, it actually becomes hotter, not cooler as previously thought. Carried one step further, this fact means that when the sun reaches the end of its life in four or five billion years, the Earth will burn up rather than freeze.

Next Gamow turned his attention to the origin of the **cosmos.** He helped popularize and further explain the big bang theory which had been proposed by Belgian astronomer Georges-Henri Lemaître in 1927. Lemaître had deduced that if the universe was expanding, then by going back in time one would find that everything had started from one point—a great "cosmic egg"—that exploded and expanded outward.

Gamow was interested in the particular question of how the universe could have been formed in a very short time following the big explosion. If a "bang" had occurred, he felt, it would have left traces of background radiation that could persist even after many billions of years. He estimated that the radiation, by the present time, would have cooled to just a few degrees above **absolute zero.**

Gamow was proven correct in 1965 when radio engineers Arno Penzias and Robert Wilson detected faint background radiation coming from all over the sky, matching that of an object radiating at the temperature predicted by Gamow. The presence of this background radiation remains the single greatest piece of evidence in support of the big bang.

Gamow died at age sixty-four in Boulder, Colorado. His work on the big bang theory contributed to making that theory the most widely accepted explanation of how the universe began.

See also **Bethe, Hans** and **Big bang theory**

Gauss, Carl (1777–1855)
German mathematician

It was obvious by the time Carl Friedrich Gauss was three years old that he was a genius. The young boy was doing arithmetic before he could even talk, the start of a lifelong fascination with numbers. During his lifetime, Gauss made important contributions to the fields of mathematics, physics, and astronomy.

Gauss came from a very poor family, so at age fourteen he received financial support from Duke Ferdinand of Brunswick to study science. While still in his teens, he made an important contribution to the field of geometry by discovering a simple way to construct equilateral polygons (figures with several equal sides). Gauss entered the University of Göttingen at age eighteen and four years later finished his doctoral degree.

Gauss went on to calculate an orbit for the **asteroid** Ceres, the famous first asteroid discovered by Sicilian monk Giuseppe Piazzi on January 1, 1801. Ceres had disappeared when it passed behind the sun and Gauss used information from Isaac Newton's law of gravitation and three observations made by Piazzi to predict where it would reappear. On December 31 of the same year, Ceres showed up very close to Gauss' predicted location, making Gauss famous throughout Europe. Gauss also made calculations based on planetary movements that helped in the discovery of Neptune.

From 1807 until his death forty-eight years later, Gauss served as director of the Göttingen Observatory. There he became interested in **geodesy,** the study of the size and shape of the Earth. To this end, in 1821 he invented the **heliotrope.** The heliotrope is an instrument that reflects sunlight over great distances to mark the positions of participants in a land survey. Gauss developed mathematical equations in this field that were later used by Albert Einstein to describe curved **spacetime** (where time and space intersect).

Carl Gauss.

Gauss' next area of study was the Earth's **magnetic field,** and he created the first specialized observatory for this purpose. With his colleague Wilhelm Weber (famous for his work with electricity), Gauss calculated the location of the Earth's magnetic poles and established the standard unit of measurement of magnetic force, later named the gauss.

In 1833, Gauss and Weber applied their knowledge of electromagnetism to build a telegraph. This machine consisted of a large coil placed over a magnet. The machine created an electrical current which moved a magnetic needle at the receiver and etched out coded messages. Gauss and Weber abandoned this project, however, when they ran out of funding for it.

Gauss is best known for the development of some important fundamental theorems of geometry and algebra. He was considered by most to be an eccentric genius, and has been called "Prince of Mathematicians" and "Father of Geodesy." His name lives on in asteroid number 1,001, which was christened Gaussia.

See also **Earth's magnetic field** and **Spacetime**

Gemini program

The Gemini program was the second phase in the U.S. history of piloted space flight. Gemini was an intermediate step between the earliest, short flights of American astronauts into space during the Mercury program and the moon-landing missions of the Apollo program.

The Gemini program, which covered the years 1964 to 1966, was operational at the height of the **space race,** the contest between the United States and the former **Soviet Union** for superiority in space exploration. In 1961, **cosmonaut** Yuri Gagarin accomplished the first piloted space flight, making the Soviets the victors in the first round of that race. In response, the U.S. space program went into high gear. Then-President John F. Kennedy vowed that not only would the United States match the Soviet accomplishment, but that by the end of the decade, the United States would put a man on the moon.

The first step toward this goal was a series of Mercury flights, six piloted missions launched between May 1961 and May 1963. Mercury spacecraft were small (only one astronaut at a time could fit in the tiny capsule) and capable of only the most basic functions. Gemini spacecraft, in contrast, were large enough to hold two astronauts and could be maneuvered in space. A Gemini vessel was capable of changing its orbit, linking with other spacecraft, and precisely controlling its re-entry and landing.

The Gemini program saw the launch of twelve spacecraft between April 1964 and November 1966. The first two were unpiloted flights, made in April 1964 and the following January, designed to test the spacecraft's launch and re-entry systems. The first piloted Gemini flight was made in March 1965 by Virgil "Gus" Grissom (making him the first man to fly in space twice) and John Young. *Gemini 3,* which stayed in orbit only five hours, marked the first time that astronauts used their controls to fire **rocket** motors in order to move their spacecraft from one orbit to another.

Gemini 4 was a much longer, highly publicized flight. Its June 1965 launch was broadcast to twelve European nations and watched by millions of people. During the mission's four days in space, astronaut Ed White undertook the first exercise outside of a spacecraft, called an **extravehicular activity (EVA).** White remained attached to a tether while orbiting the Earth at 18,000 miles (29,000 kilometers) per hour for twenty-one minutes.

On the *Gemini 5* flight of August 1965, astronauts Charles Conrad Jr. and Gordon Cooper Jr. circled the Earth 120 times. Their eight-day journey set a world record for endurance in space, a record that was broken by the very next Gemini flight.

Gemini 7, which remained in space for fourteen days, was launched on December 4, 1965. Eleven days after that, *Gemini 6* lifted off. The two ships rendezvoused (joined up) in space, coming within one foot of each other. They then flew in formation for over twenty hours. After that, *Gemini 6* returned to Earth while *Gemini 7* remained in space for three more days. *Gemini 7* proved that astronauts could withstand fourteen days in space without lasting physical problems, important information in planning for lunar landing missions.

Near Disasters in the Gemini Program

The next Gemini mission, launched in March 1966, was a near-disaster. Had things gone a little differently, Neil Armstrong would not have survived to become the first man to walk on the moon. He and crewmate David Scott had just achieved the first docking with another vessel in space (an Agena rocket), when the two crafts began spinning out of a control. Armstrong and Scott separated *Gemini 8* from the Agena, but the spinning only got worse. The two astronauts were nearing unconsciousness from spinning at one revolution per second when, as a last-ditch measure, Armstrong turned off the thrusters. That move saved their lives. *Gemini 8* then made an emergency landing in the Pacific Ocean. NASA investigators later found that the problem was caused by a thruster that had been stuck in the "open" position.

Gemini 9, launched in June 1966, also experienced difficulties that began even before it lifted off. First, the two astronauts originally slated for the mission, Elliot M. See and Charles A. Bassett, died in a plane crash and had to be replaced with a backup crew. Once in orbit, *Gemini 9* was

Opposite page: Astronauts Neil Armstrong (right) and David Scott, surrounded by pararescue men, look up at the USS Mason from inside the Gemini 8 *spacecraft after its emergency landing in the Pacific Ocean on March 22, 1966.*

unable to complete its planned docking with an Agena vessel because Agena's dock would not open. Then, during an EVA, astronaut Eugene Cernan's helmet became so fogged that he had to return to the spacecraft without trying out a new jet-powered backpack.

Concluding Successes in the Gemini Program

The tide turned for the next Gemini mission. During this three-day flight made in July 1966, *Gemini 10* successfully docked with the Agena rocket, broke the altitude record (at 458 miles [737 kilometers] above Earth), and even captured the ultraviolet light of stars on photographs. *Gemini 10* had an uneventful landing, splashing down within sight of the recovery ship.

Gemini 11 was launched two months later. On the first orbit of its three-day mission, the spacecraft successfully docked with an Agena. The crew then conducted a **gravity** experiment by connecting the two vessels with a tether, allowing each one to rotate around the other. That flight, which rose to a height of 853 miles (1,372 kilometers) over the Earth, broke its predecessor's altitude record.

The final mission of the series, *Gemini 12,* was commanded by *Apollo 13* astronaut Jim Lovell and piloted by *Apollo 11* astronaut Buzz Aldrin. The main accomplishment of that November 1966 flight was the performance of a lengthy EVA. Aldrin spent a total of five and one-half hours completing twenty simple spacecraft-maintenance tasks.

Two months later, the first Apollo mission was launched. And it was just two and one-half years after that, in July 1969, that *Apollo 11* landed on the moon.

See also **Apollo program**; **Conrad, Charles**; **Lovell, James**; **Mercury program**; and **Space race**

Giotto

In 1986, when Halley's **comet** reached its closest point to the sun (and Earth) in seventy-six years, it attracted a great deal of attention both among scientists and the general public. Over one thousand astronomers from forty countries coordinated the International Halley Watch. European, Soviet, and Japanese **space probe**s were sent toward the comet for a close look, while other telescopes—on board satellites and on the ground—were used for observation.

The space **probe** *Giotto,* sent by the European Space Agency (ESA), was the only probe to fly directly into the comet's nucleus. *Giotto* was named for the painter Giotto Ambrogio di Bondone, whose famous nativity scene "Adoration of the Magi," painted in 1304, depicted a comet that is believed to be Halley's.

Giotto was essentially a metal cylinder, 9 feet (2.7 meters) tall by 6 feet (1.8 meters) in diameter. It contained a television camera, a photopolarimeter to assess the brightness of the comet's nucleus, and **spectrometer**s to determine the chemical composition of the dust and gas in the comet's tail. *Giotto* also carried science experiments to study the effect of the **solar wind** on the comet's tail. Since the probe did not have enough power to store data, everything it learned was transmitted directly to Earth.

Giotto was launched on July 2, 1985, on an Ariane **rocket** and placed on a head-on intercept course with the comet. This project was a treacherous undertaking, given that the comet travels at a speed of 43 miles (69 kilometers) per second. Some people even called it suicidal, because if a probe were to encounter even a speck of dust traveling at that speed, it would explode like a hand grenade.

The 1,325-pound (602-kilogram) probe was given some protection by its two-layer dust shield. This covering was capable of absorbing the impact of the small particles, such as debris from the comet's dust cloud. Nothing could be done, however, to save *Giotto* from the larger objects it would encounter at the nucleus of the comet. *Giotto*'s designers could only hope the probe would accomplish its mission before being smashed apart.

The first spacecraft to fly past the comet were the Soviet *Vega 1* and *2*. Those vessels took photographs and relayed information to Earth on the comet's location. Based on that information, the ESA made last-minute adjustments to *Giotto*'s trajectory.

Giotto Encounters Halley's Comet

In the early morning of March 14, 1986, *Giotto* flew into the comet's inner coma (cloud of gas and dust surrounding the nucleus that looks like a fuzzy white "head"). The probe relayed television footage as well as scientific readings, to the ESA control station in Darmstadt, Germany. As *Giotto* entered the nucleus, it was showered by over two hundred dust particles per second. Then, just before it approached the very center, it was hit by a dust grain weighing only a third of an ounce that resulted in a loss of contact between the probe and Earth. After passing through the nucleus and emerging on the other side of the coma, the communications link with the probe was restored. From then on, however, only scientific data (no pictures) were transmitted.

Giotto's more than two thousand pictures showed the comet's never-before-seen nucleus to be a 9.3-mile-long (15-kilometer-long), 6-mile-wide (10-kilometer-wide), coal-black, potato-shaped object marked by hills and valleys. Two bright jets of gas and dust, each 9 miles (14 kilometers) long, shoot out of the nucleus. *Giotto*'s instruments detected the presence of water, carbon, nitrogen, and sulfur molecules. It also found that the comet was losing about thirty tons of water and five tons of dust each hour. This fact means that although the comet will survive for hundreds more orbits, it will eventually disintegrate.

ESA operators powered down *Giotto*'s systems following the mission, leaving it to coast along in orbit around the sun. That *Giotto* even survived its encounter with Halley's comet is more than most people expected. However, over half of its instruments were rendered unusable. The condition of its cameras was not known until *Giotto* was reactivated in 1990 and sent on a 1992 rendezvous with Comet Grigg-Skellerup. Astronomers then learned that *Giotto*'s camera had been damaged. Hence it was unable to film the comet.

See also **Comet**; **Halley's comet**; and **Vega program**

Glenn, John (1921–)
American astronaut and politician

On February 20, 1962, John Glenn was the first American to orbit Earth and became, in the process, a national hero. Today there is only one astronaut more famous, Neil Armstrong, the first man to walk on the moon. But back in 1962, all eyes were on Glenn. His space flight represented not just a technological achievement, but a political one. For in those days the **cold war** between the United States and the former **Soviet Union** was in full swing. Space had become an important arena in the conflict and in those early days, and the Soviet Union was winning the race.

Glenn's historic flight was part of the Mercury program, which was initiated by the National Aeronautics and Space Administration (NASA) to surpass what the Soviets had already accomplished in piloted space flight. Glenn traveled inside a capsule called *Friendship 7* for five hours on a journey that took him around the Earth three times. The two previous American piloted space missions had gone only beyond the Earth's atmosphere for a few minutes each and never into orbit. The Soviet **cosmonaut**s had both orbited Earth. The second to do so, German Titov, spent a whole day in space and completed seventeen orbits.

Glenn's flight was not entirely smooth. During his second orbit, NASA officials at the command center received signals that *Friendship*'s heat shield was loose. The heat shield is the portion of a spacecraft that prevents it from burning up as it re-enters the Earth's atmosphere. Glenn made some quick adjustments and hoped for the best. He had a frightening descent during which he watched pieces of flaming metal fly past his capsule window. But the heat shield held, and the capsule plunged into the ocean as planned.

Glenn's return was greeted with ticker-tape parades, and he quickly attained international celebrity status. Soon after the public appearances and travel had died down, however, Glenn made a career change. He shifted from astronautics to politics, beginning another chapter in his adventurous life.

Glenn's Early Life

John Herschel Glenn was born in Cambridge and raised in New Concord, both small towns in Ohio. His is the classic American story. His parents were hard-working, enterprising individuals with a strong moral foundation. The three things that mattered most to them were family, church, and neighborhood. During the hard times of the Great Depression, even young John chipped in to help make ends meet for the family. His childhood sweetheart was Annie Castor, the town dentist's daughter. Annie and John were eventually married.

Glenn graduated from high school in 1939 and went on to Muskingum College, New Concord's Presbyterian liberal arts school. There he majored in chemical engineering and played varsity football. Much to the dismay of his parents, he also enrolled in a pilot-training program.

When Japanese forces attacked Pearl Harbor in 1941, Glenn left college and enlisted in the Naval Aviation Cadet Program. He was later assigned to the Marines Fighter Squadron. During the final year of World

John Glenn practices climbing out of the top of a Mercury spacecraft as part of the then-new recovery technique, January 18, 1962.

War II, he flew fifty-nine combat missions. Glenn chose to stay in the military after the war and was stationed first in northern China and then Guam. In 1948, he returned to the United States as an instructor at Corpus Christi, Texas.

Two years later, Glenn was back on active duty in the Korean War. At the conclusion of his war service in 1954, Glenn moved to Maryland and attended the U.S. Naval Test Pilot School. During his third year at the school, he earned the title of "fastest pilot in America" by flying a jet across the United States in a record-setting three hours and twenty-three minutes.

A few months after that, in October 1957, came the launch of the world's first artificial satellite, the Soviet *Sputnik 1*. That event prompted officials of the U.S. space program to begin working toward piloted space flight. One step was to select a group of individuals to train as astronauts. In April 1959, Glenn was chosen to be among them. Glenn served a support role for the first two Mercury flights before his own historic flight in 1961.

Glenn's Political Career

In 1964, Glenn left NASA to pursue a political career, largely inspired by President John F. Kennedy. Kennedy had befriended Glenn after Glenn's space mission and had urged him to run for office. Despite Kennedy's 1963 assassination, Glenn decided to go ahead with this plan and entered the race for the Senate as a Democrat from Ohio. A few weeks into the campaign, however, he fell in his hotel room and suffered a head injury. Glenn decided to withdraw from the race and returned to an administrative post at NASA. Over the next few years, Glenn also worked in private industry and as a private investor, and he emerged a millionaire.

In 1970, Glenn again ran for the Senate and was defeated by Howard Metzenbaum. In 1974 he finally won a seat. He has been three times been re-elected in 1980, in 1986, and in 1992. In 1983, Glenn vied for the Democratic nomination for president, but his campaign was plagued with inefficiency and disorganization, and he was forced to withdraw from the race before the party convention.

As a politician, Glenn is considered left of center. His voting record is liberal on social and economic issues and centrist on foreign policy issues. For instance, he has been active in such racial justice concerns as the desegregation of schools, and has worked toward normalization of relations with China. Yet he remains a defender of a large military establishment. In the 1980s, Glenn successfully sponsored a government paperwork reduction act and a streamlined purchasing law. In the 1990s, he joined with the Republicans in supporting the unfunded mandates ban and congressional compliance with workplace laws. Glenn is also known for investigating government releases of radiation into the air. In 1994, Glenn voted against NAFTA, voted for the Brady bill to restrict handgun sales, and voted against cutting funds for defense missiles. In addition, for two decades Glenn has worked to stop nuclear proliferation. Above all, Glenn has achieved a reputation on Capitol Hill as a man who sticks to his ideals.

See also **Mercury program** and **Space race**

Goddard, Robert (1882–1945)
American physicist

Robert Goddard is the father of American rocketry. Ever since childhood, he had been fascinated by the prospect of space travel and as an adolescent began trying to figure out what it would take to launch a small **rocket.** In 1908, he entered Worcester College, in Massachusetts, to study physics and went on to a doctoral program at Clark University, also in Worcester. While still a student, Goddard determined that rocketry was the key to space flight. He came to this conclusion because he knew a rocket's thrusters could operate in vacuum, and therefore should also operate outside of the Earth's atmosphere.

When Goddard finished school, he worked briefly at Princeton University in New Jersey as a researcher before joining the faculty in physics back at Clark University. There he continued his research on rocketry and in 1919 published a now classic work on his ideas. Included in this book, *Method of Reaching Extreme Altitudes,* is the notion that a rocket could eventually be fired to the moon.

Journalists looking for a sensational story latched on to the moon-travel part of Goddard's paper and a headline in *The Boston Herald* read: "New Rocket Devised by Prof. Goddard May Hit Face of the Moon." The article made Goddard sound like some sort of lunatic. It resulted in many people contacting Goddard, asking him for rides to the moon. Goddard, a shy person, was extremely humiliated and from then on went about his work in secrecy.

In 1926, Goddard came to the conclusion that gasoline and liquid oxygen would make an effective rocket fuel. That same year he launched

Robert Goddard
with the first rocket
he ever built.

the world's first liquid-propelled rocket. This 10-pound (5-kilogram) rocket launched from a cabbage patch in Auburn, Massachusetts, was ridiculed by other scientists because it went up only 41 feet (12 meters) and traveled a distance of 184 feet (56 meters). What they did not realize was that the launch of this small rocket was the spark that would lead to the 1969 launch of the Saturn V rocket, which sent a man to the moon.

Three years later, Goddard launched another rocket, this time just outside of Worcester, Massachusetts, which exploded. As a result, the State Fire Marshal banned Goddard from testing more rockets. The launch attracted the attention of the famous aviator Charles Lindbergh, who sought Goddard out and helped him obtain funding to continue his rocket research.

Goddard's Early Rocket Tests

In 1930, Goddard moved to Roswell, New Mexico, to set up the world's first professional rocket test site. This task was not an easy one. Goddard and his poorly equipped crew encountered bad weather and dangerous insects. And because they were the first individuals to undertake such a project, they had to learn by trial and error.

Facing a shortage of funds and inadequate supplies, Goddard had to recover all the materials he could after each test flight. This limitation required the development of good parachutes so that a rocket would not come crashing down and be destroyed. The flights had other hazards as well. One rocket went off course and headed right for Goddard and his assistant, both of whom dived to the ground to avoid being hit. And they had to be constantly wary of explosions that would send pieces of metal flying in all directions. Nonetheless, in some of these test flights Goddard's rockets went as high as 1.25 miles (2 kilometers).

Goddard offered his services to the U.S. government when World War II broke out, but his work was not regarded seriously. Eventually, Goddard made some progress with U.S. Navy officials, who funded his research on small boosters that helped launch planes from ship decks. It was only toward the end of the war when the U.S. government discovered the power of Germany's extremely destructive V-2 rockets, that officials realized the importance of Goddard's rocketry work. From 1942 until his death three years later, Goddard worked for the U.S. Navy at Annapolis, Maryland.

Goddard greatly advanced the field of rocketry in his lifetime. He worked out systems for the various stages of rocket flight, from ignition and fuel systems, to guidance controls, to parachute recovery.

When *Apollo 11,* boosted by a Saturn V rocket, carried men to the moon in 1969, Goddard's widow Esther said, "That was his dream, sending a rocket to the moon. He would just have glowed."

See also **Rockets**

Gold, Thomas (1920–)

Austrian-born American astronomer

Best known as the originator of the **steady-state theory** of the origin of the universe, Thomas Gold was born in Vienna, Austria. He later moved to England and attended Cambridge University, from which he received a bachelor's degree in 1942 and a master's degree three years later. In 1956, he came to the United States and taught for one year at Harvard University before joining the faculty at Cornell.

Thomas Gold.

Gold is a cosmologist, that is, he studies the origins and structure of the universe. Cosmologists believe in the cosmological principle that the universe is essentially the same everywhere. They are convinced that the same objects and gasses fill the universe from end to end and that the view from one **galaxy** is not much different from the view from any other galaxy.

Gold applied this concept of **homogeneity,** or sameness, to time as well as space in developing the steady-state theory. He claimed that the universe should look the same, not only at all places, but at all times—past, present, and future.

Introduced in 1948, Gold's theory, stood in opposition to the other major theory of how the universe began, the **big bang theory.** In the late

1920s, Belgian astronomer Georges-Henri Lemaître suggested that the universe had originated as a great "cosmic egg," which exploded (with a "big bang") and expanded outward. This theory was bolstered by Edwin Hubble in 1929, who found proof that all matter in space is moving away from all other matter, and thus the universe is expanding and changing.

Gold explanation of Hubble's discovery was that as matter in space moves apart, new matter is created to fill in the gaps. And as older galaxies get pushed out of existence, new galaxies take their place. As a result, everything remains essentially the same.

For two decades, the steady-state and big bang theories were considered equally valid explanations for how the universe began. But then new evidence shifted the balance toward the big bang theory.

In 1964, while looking for sources of satellite message interference, radio engineers Arno Penzias and Robert Wilson detected background radiation at a temperature of 3 degrees above **absolute zero.** This temperature matched a prediction made by George Gamow some years earlier as the energy level remaining billions of years after the big bang.

The big bang theory was further reinforced in 1992, when evidence was found that the universe had indeed changed over time. In that year the National Aeronautics and Space Administration's *Cosmic Background Explorer* (*COBE*) satellite looked fifteen billion **light-year**s into space (the same as looking fifteen billion years into the past). It detected tiny temperature changes in the cosmic background radiation, which points to gravitational disturbances in the early universe. It is very possible that these ripples resulted in matter clumping together to form the stars, galaxies, and other pieces of the universe.

This last piece of evidence appears to have pushed the steady-state theory out of the running for the explanation of how the universe began, at least for now.

Gold is also known for his work in another area of astronomy, **pulsar**s. In August 1967, astronomy student Jocelyn Bell Burnell observed some strange, pulsating signals from her radio telescope. She and her professor, Antony Hewish, named the objects "pulsars" (short for "pulsating radio source"). Studying their data, they found several more pulsars, including some within **supernova** remains. Bell Burnell and Hewish hypothesized that the source of the pulsars were **white dwarf** stars or **neutron star**s.

Gold and fellow astronomer Franco Pacini investigated this problem and found that neutron stars must be the source. They came to this conclusion because neutron stars (the debris left after a supernova) are incredibly dense and rotate quickly. The spinning of a neutron star intensifies its **magnetic field,** causing the star to act as a giant magnet. It emits radiation from its magnetic poles. If the **magnetic axis** of the star is tilted in a certain way, the rotating star's on-and-off pulse is visible from Earth. More recent evidence has also pointed to neutron stars as the most likely source of pulsars.

See also **Bell Burnell, Jocelyn**; **Cosmology**; and **Hewish, Antony**

Gravity

Gravity is the force that keeps our feet on the ground, keeps the moon in orbit around the Earth, and keeps the planets in orbit around the sun. Over time, successive theories have brought us much closer to an understanding of how gravity works, yet we still do not know what causes it.

Around 1600, Italian mathematician Galileo Galilei determined that gravity acts equally on objects of any **mass** in a vacuum. He rolled two different-sized balls down an angled surface to demonstrate that falling objects speed up or slow down at an equal rate. He proved false Aristotle's earlier theory that heavier objects fall at a faster rate than lighter objects (as long as they are not subject to air resistance).

In 1687, English mathematician Isaac Newton, expanding on the work of Galileo, published *Philosophiae Naturalis Principia Mathematica* (*Mathematical Principles of Natural Philosophy*), containing his universal law of gravitation regarding the attraction between any two objects. Before Newton, gravity was thought to work only on Earth. Newton was the first to suggest that gravity worked throughout the **solar system** as well.

Newton explained that the gravitational force between any two objects depended on the mass of each object and the distance between them. The greater each object's mass, the stronger the pull, but the greater the distance between them, the weaker the pull. The relationship described in Newton's inverse square law is that gravitational force depends on the mass of each object divided by the square of the distance separating them.

The first measurement of gravitational force was made in 1798, when English physicist Henry Cavendish hung a pair of 2-inch (5-centimeter) lead balls near a pair of 12-inch (25-centimeter) lead balls. He then calculated the force of attraction between them, coming within 1 percent of today's accepted value.

Albert Einstein contributed to our knowledge of gravity in the early 1900s. He determined that in any reaction in which an object gives off energy, the object loses mass (the mass is turned into energy). This means that matter and energy are basically the same, they just exist in different forms. This discovery had a significant impact on Newton's inverse square law and all other equations concerning gravitational force.

In his **general theory of relativity,** Einstein explained how gravity works. He showed that the mass of an object causes space to curve around it. As a lighter object (like a planet) approaches a heavier object in space (like the sun), the lighter object follows the lines of curved space, which draw it near to the heavier object and into orbit.

Prior to Einstein, it was believed that since light has no mass, it

Astronauts Gerald P. Carr (left) and Edward G. Gibson (floating) show the effects of weightlessness aboard Skylab 4.

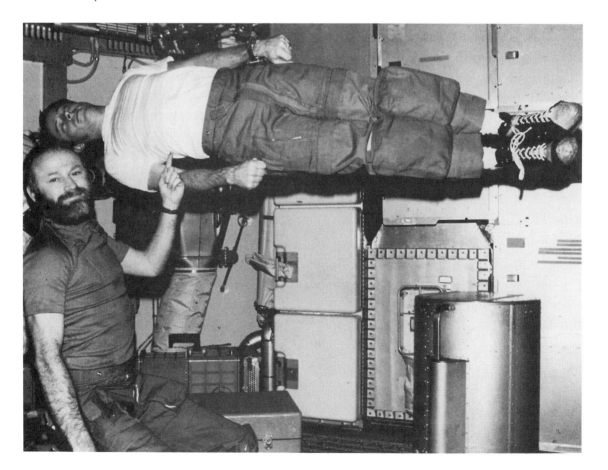

would not be influenced by gravity. Einstein argued that light should be affected by curved space the same way that matter is. In 1919, during a total eclipse of the sun, his theory was put to the test.

The **solar eclipse** gave scientists a rare opportunity to study stars while the sun is up. Normally sunlight blocks out the light of all other stars, but during an eclipse the sun is obscured and other stars are visible. The scientists carefully measured the positions of several stars that appeared close to the sun.

Six months later, the Earth had moved along its orbit to a point on the opposite side of the sun so that it was once again in line with the stars studied during the eclipse. The positions of those stars were again recorded and were found to differ slightly from their positions during the eclipse. The only explanation for this is that the stars' light had been bent by the sun's gravity.

The ultimate example of gravitational force is a **black hole.** A black hole (if indeed such an object exists) is the remains of a massive star that has used up its nuclear fuel and collapsed under tremendous force, into a single point. At this point, called the **singularity,** gravity is infinite. When anything (any object, or even light) gets too close to a black hole, it gets pulled in, stretched to infinity, and remains forever trapped.

The only way to detect a black hole is by seeing its effect on visible objects, such as neighboring stars. For example, some binary systems may contain one big star and a black hole. As they orbit around each other, the black hole would suck in matter from its companion.

Gravitation is the weakest known force in nature. For instance, it is many times weaker than magnetism. But its effect can be felt at far greater distances than any other force.

See also **Black hole**; **Einstein, Albert**; **Galilei, Galileo**; and **Newton, Isaac**

Greenhouse effect

The **greenhouse effect,** as its name implies, describes a warming phenomenon. In a greenhouse closed glass windows cause heat to become trapped inside. The greenhouse effect functions in a similar manner, on the scale of an entire planet. It occurs when a planet's atmosphere allows heat from sun to enter but refuses to let it leave.

A prime example of the greenhouse effect can be found on Venus. There solar radiation penetrates the atmosphere, reaches the surface, and is reflected back up. The re-radiated heat is trapped by carbon dioxide, the primary constituent of Venus' atmosphere. The result is that Venus has a balmy surface temperature of 900 degrees Fahrenheit (480 degrees Celsius). The greenhouse effect can also be found in the upper atmospheres of Jupiter, Saturn, Uranus, and Neptune, the giant planets.

On Earth, the greenhouse effect works in a similar way, yet to a much smaller degree. As on Venus, solar radiation passes through the atmosphere and strikes the surface. As it is reflected back up, some is absorbed by atmospheric gases (such as carbon dioxide, methane, chlorofluorocarbons, and water vapor), resulting in the gradual increase of the Earth's temperature. The rest of the radiation escapes back into space.

Human activity has been largely responsible for the buildup of these gases in the Earth's atmosphere, and hence the Earth's gradual warming. For instance, the burning of fossil-fuels (like coal, oil, and natural gas) and forest fires add carbon dioxide to the atmosphere. Methane buildup comes from the use of pesticides and fertilizers in agriculture. Chlorofluorocarbons (CFCs) are produced by aerosol spray-cans and coolants in refrigerators and air conditioners. Due to CFCs' role in the destruction of the **ozone layer,** most CFC sources have now been banned.) And large amounts of water vapor are emitted as an industrial by-product.

After a long winter, one may think that the greenhouse effect sounds like a good thing. Unfortunately the negative consequences far outweigh any benefit gained from slightly higher temperatures.

An atmosphere with natural levels of greenhouse gases (left) compared with an atmosphere of increased greenhouse effect (right).

Between the start of this century and 1970, the atmospheric carbon dioxide level rose 7 percent and that rate is on the increase. The resulting temperature increase has caused more water to evaporate from the oceans (as well as some ice to melt in the Arctic), which, in turn, increases the clouds in the atmosphere. While the greater cloud cover blocks some solar heat from entering our atmosphere, it also worsens the greenhouse effect by trapping in more of the heat that does make it down to the surface. With a slow but steady increase in the world's temperature, the Earth could, far in the future, become like the scorching Venus.

Grimaldi, Francesco (1618–1663)

Italian physicist

Francesco Maria Grimaldi was born in Bologna, Italy, to a fairly wealthy family. His father died when he was young, and his mother took over the family business. Grimaldi and his brother entered the Roman Catholic order of the Society of Jesus in 1632. There Grimaldi studied theology and philosophy for thirteen years. He earned his degree in 1645 and took the vows of priesthood in 1651. Grimaldi is best known for his description of the **diffraction** (bending) of light and his observation of the surface of the moon.

When Grimaldi finished his schooling, the Jesuits appointed him professor of philosophy and mathematics at the Jesuit College in Bologna. He remained in this post until his death at age forty-five.

Grimaldi became interested in astronomy as a student, when he worked as a research assistant for professor Giovanni Riccioli. In the early 1640s, Grimaldi helped Riccioli with experiments involving the speed of falling weights. Grimaldi also built a telescope with a very accurate **micrometer.** A micrometer is an instrument for measuring distances very precisely. Using this telescope, he made hundreds of drawings which he pieced together to form a map of the features of the moon's surface. For his efforts, Grimaldi has been honored by having a large crater on the moon named after him.

Grimaldi's most significant work, however, came later in the field of optics (the study of light). He was the first scientist to record the effects of light diffraction. He did this by allowing a beam of sunlight to pass first through one slit, then through a second slit, and onto a blank screen. What he found was that the light appearing on the screen was much wider than the final slit. This experiment indicated that the light had bent and spread out.

Grimald's discovery was important because it came at a time when light was believed to be made up of particles. But Grimaldi's findings indicated that light seemed to consist of waves. We now know that light can behave both as particles and waves.

Diffraction is a process found in all forms of waves. It allows for sound to be heard around corners and for water waves to fill a harbor. It works as follows: when a wave encounters a corner, a narrow hole, or a sharp edge, a new wave begins at that point and flows outward.

Grimaldi also noticed a band of color at the edge of a diffracted light beam. He carefully recorded these colored streaks, but was unable to determine what caused them. It was not until 150 years later that German optician Joseph von Fraunhofer discovered that these colored bands were made up of various wavelengths of light.

See also **Bell Burnell, Jocelyn**; **Big bang theory**; *Cosmic Background Explorer*; **Cosmology**; **Hewish, Antony**; **Hoyle, Fred**; **Neutron star**; **Pulsar**; and **Steady-state theory**

Hale, George (1868–1938)

American astronomer

As a youngster, George Ellery Hale had perhaps the greatest advantage any aspiring astronomer could have—wealth. His father recognized George's talent, interest, and hard work and decided to supply him with expensive equipment and even his own observatory, placed next to the family's Chicago, Illinois, home. This investment turned out to be a wise one on the elder Hale's part, as his son went on to found and direct two major U.S. observatories, to oversee the construction of the world's four largest telescopes (each surpassing its predecessor in size), and to make some of the most significant astronomical discoveries of his time.

As a teenager, Hale was given a 4-inch (8.6-centimeter) **refractor telescope,** which launched him on a career in astronomy. Soon thereafter, while attending the Massachusetts Institute of Technology (MIT), Hale was volunteering at the Harvard College Observatory.

It was during college, in 1889, that Hale invented the **spectrohelioscope,** a combined telescope and **spectroscope.** This instrument produces a colorful display of the sun's chemical components. For instance, hydrogen appears red and ionized calcium appears ultraviolet in a spectrohelioscope. Fifteen years later, **spectroheliograph**s—modified spectrohelioscopes capable of photographing the **spectra** they produced—would become a central component of the **solar telescope**s Hale set up at Mount Wilson Observatory.

Hale's father gave him a 12-inch (30.5-centimeter) refractor telescope as a graduation present, which Hale used in his private Kenwood

Observatory to conduct original research. In the meantime, Hale, who had accepted a position on the faculty of the University of Chicago, was closely following the efforts of Harvard astronomers who were attempting to set up a research station atop Mount Wilson in southern California. The researchers erected a 13-inch (33-centimeter) refractor and ordered the lens for a 40-inch (102-centimeter) refractor, which would have been the largest in the world at that time. Then, a harsh winter wreaked havoc on instruments and astronomers alike, causing workers to abandon the site.

Hale next learned that the 40-inch lens had already been cast and was available. This news prompted him to approach the president of the University of Chicago, William Rainey Harper, with the idea of raising funds to establish an observatory for the university. Hale suggested that the observatory have as its centerpiece the orphaned 40-inch instrument. He solicited from a wealthy donor, Chicagoan Charles Yerkes, a sum of money large enough for the construction of the telescope and a dome in which to house it. The site chosen for the Yerkes Observatory was Lake Geneva, Wisconsin, 80 miles (129 kilometers) northwest of Chicago.

Hale At Yerkes

Construction of the observatory was completed in 1897, and Hale became its first director. Under his tutelage, the facility became a center for solar research, as well as for the study of objects in the night sky. Hale's directorship lasted only five years. Yet during that time, he set Yerkes well on a course of becoming a world-class observatory.

In 1902, Hale learned that the Carnegie Institution had been established by multimillionaire Andrew Carnegie, to support scientific research. As one with a keen sense of money, as well as science, Hale was naturally drawn to the new organization. He joined the Institution's Advisory Committee on Astronomy and lobbied heavily for his concept of a "new astronomy." This new astronomy involved a combination of traditional astronomy (such as describing a star's motion and brightness) with physics (studying the physical properties of a star, such as learning how it moves, why it shines, and what it is made of). Hale named this new science "**astrophysics.**"

Hale also believed in the importance of solar research for, as he stressed, our sun is the only star that can be studied in detail. Although Hale had few supporters at first, he eventually got the funding he needed. The Carnegie Institution agreed to fund a solar observatory in the south-western United States, and Mount Wilson was selected as the site. Hale moved to California in 1903, taking most of the Yerkes staff with him.

Mount Wilson Telescopes

The following year, after Hale made countless trips on mule-back up the mountain with parts, the Snow Solar Telescope (named for wealthy Chicagoan Helen Snow, who helped fund its construction) was erected. (Solar telescopes are large, specialized instruments that break sunlight down into its component wavelengths and then photographs the resulting image.) The Snow Telescope mirror was 24 inches (61 centimeters) in diameter, three times as large as any existing solar telescope at the time. Sunlight entered the structure through a 29-foot-tall (8.8-meter-tall) tower and traveled through a wood-and-canvas tube to reach the subterranean mirror. The telescope was used primarily to observe **sunspot**s.

Hale's next project on Mount Wilson was begun in 1908. For the second time, he directed construction of the world's largest telescope. The new telescope exceeded his 40-inch Yerkes refractor by 20 inches (51 centimeters). The 60-inch (152-centimeter) mirror for this new **reflector** had been donated by Hale's father shortly before his death.

No sooner had the 60-inch telescope been completed than Hale was envisioning a larger one. The latest of Hale's projects was initially designed to have an 84-inch (213-centimeter) mirror. However, a grant from John D. Hooker, philanthropist and founder of the California Academy of Science, allowed for the construction of one with a 100-inch (254-centimeter) mirror. After facing delays due to World War I, the Hooker Telescope was completed in 1917. This time Hale had created a telescope that would remain the world's largest for the next thirty years.

In the meantime, two additional solar tower telescopes had been completed at the observatory. The first had a 60-foot (18-meter) tower and the second a 150-foot (45-meter) tower. Using these telescopes, Hale continued his exploration of sunspots and discovered, in their spectra, that magnetic forces were at work. Before this, no indication had been found that **magnetic field**s exist anywhere other than on Earth.

Under Hale's directorship, revolutionary scientific discoveries were commonplace on Mount Wilson. In addition to solving the mysteries of sunspots, Hale and the rest of the observatory staff determined the temperature and composition of numerous stars and advanced our knowledge of the structure of the universe.

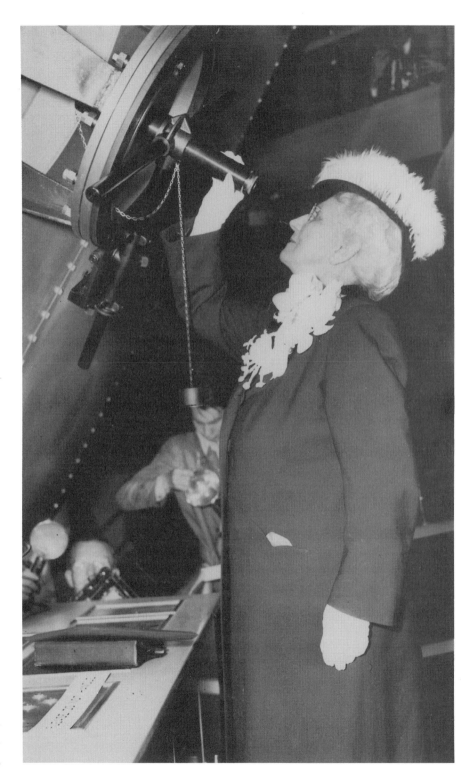

*George Ellery
Hale's widow looks
through the
eyepiece of the
giant 200-inch (508-
centimeter) Hale
Telescope at the
Palomar
Observatory on
June 3, 1948.*

As his last major accomplishment, Hale devised plans and raised money for what was to be, once again, for the world's largest telescope. This instrument was twice as big as the Hooker. The mirror for the 200-inch (508-centimeter) Hale Telescope was cast in 1934. Because of a long construction process, plus delays caused by World War II, this telescope was not erected at the Palomar Observatory until 1947, ten years after Hale's death. The Hale Telescope held the title of world's largest telescope for three decades. Many astronomers still consider it to be the finest instrument in the world, as well as a fitting monument to man who inspired it.

See also **Hale Telescope**; **Hooker Telescope**; **Mount Wilson Observatory**; **Palomar Observatory**; **Solar telescope**; **Sunspot**; and **Yerkes Observatory**

Hale Telescope

The Hale Telescope is a 200-inch-diameter (508-centimeter-diameter) instrument located at Palomar Observatory. For nearly three decades it held the distinction of being the largest optical telescope in the world. Christened in the late 1940s, the Hale Telescope has been used by legendary astronomers to unlock some of the great mysteries of the universe. Now, almost a half-century later, it remains one of the most powerful telescopes on Earth.

George Hale, the turn-of-the-century astronomer for whom the telescope is named, was the driving force behind its creation. While Hale was conducting research in the 1920s on the 100-inch-diameter (254-centimeter-diameter) Hooker Telescope at Mount Wilson Observatory, he recognized the need for a much larger instrument. Hale then made it his mission to raise the funds for this project. In 1928, he succeeded in securing a six million dollar grant from the Rockefeller Foundation.

The construction and erection of the Hale Telescope took thirteen years from start to finish. Following a series of technical problems associated with making such a large mirror, the telescope's Pyrex glass mirror was cast in December 1934 by the Corning Glass Works in New York. To save weight, a new design was used. This design involved a thinner-than-usual glass disc, reinforced by a ribbed backing. Even so, the mirror still weighed 20 tons (18 metric tons). The disk was left to cool for eight months before being transported by train to Pasadena, California. There it was ground, polished, and given a surface coating of aluminum.

In the meantime, construction at Palomar Observatory was underway on the twelve-story rotating dome that was to house the telescope. In 1941, when the structure was nearly complete, the United States entered World War II and the project was put on hold. Finally, in November 1947, the finished mirror was brought to the mountain and the telescope installed. The next year, scientific research began.

The Updated Telescope

This **reflector telescope** (an instrument that brings light rays into focus using a mirror) is still the primary research instrument at Palomar Observatory. It has been upgraded in recent years and now includes a **spectrograph**; an infrared filter, which detects **infrared radiation** in space; and high-speed computers that process data quickly.

More features are planned for the telescope in the future. One such addition is **adaptive optics.** Adaptive optics is a system that makes minute adjustments to the shape of the mirror within hundredths of a second of an arc, to correct distortions that result from disturbances in the atmosphere. This improvement should result in the production of near-perfect images.

Research conducted on the Hale Telescope over the decades has covered a broad range of studies, including **asteroid**s and **comet**s; stars at the far reaches of the **Milky Way**; and the extremely bright and distant objects known as **quasar**s. Astronomers have also investigated the life cycles of stars, the formation of the planets and sun, and questions pertaining to how the universe began.

Observing time at the Hale is divided among scientists from the California Institute of Technology (CalTech), which owns and operates Palomar Observatory; the National Aeronautics and Space Administration's Jet Propulsion Laboratory; and Cornell University.

See also **Hale, George** and **Palomar Observatory**

Halley, Edmond (1656–1742)
English astronomer

Over the course of his eighty-five-year lifetime, Edmond Halley created an unequaled legacy of astronomical achievements, from determining the

*John Edbon,
director of the
London
Planetarium, stands
with a wax figure of
Edmond Halley. The
figure was going on
show in the
planetarium as
Halley's comet was
set to pass by in
November 1985.*

paths of **comet**s and charting the movements of stars, to developing the first weather map and calculating the age of the Earth.

The son of a wealthy merchant, Halley was drawn to astronomy after seeing two comets as a child. By the age of eighteen, as a student at Oxford University, he was carefully plotting the positions of Jupiter and Saturn and writing about Johannes Kepler's laws of planetary motion.

In 1676, Halley left school. He traveled to Saint Helena, an island off the west coast of Africa, and established the first observatory in the Southern Hemisphere. There he made the first map of the southern **constellation**s, recording the positions of 381 stars. His work was warmly received when he returned to England. He was awarded an honorary master's degree from Oxford and was elected to England's Royal Society, an elite science club.

Halley became interested in the force that causes the planets to orbit the sun and in 1684 turned to his friend Isaac Newton for answers. He learned that Newton had already developed the laws of **gravity** but had never published his work. Halley convinced Newton to take this step and offered to pay for the publication of his book. Thus, three years later, Newton published *Philosophiae Naturalis Principia Mathematica* (*Mathematical Principles of Natural Philosphy*). Among other things, the book contains Newton's universal law of gravitation, which states that forces of gravity are at work throughout the entire universe and not just on Earth.

Halley's Research On Comets

At the age of thirty-nine, Halley turned his attention to comets. Although comets appeared free from the effects of gravity as they streaked through the sky, Halley wondered if, somehow, gravity might influence their movement.

Halley carefully calculated the paths traveled by twenty-four comets. With the help of Isaac Newton, he found three—those occurring in 1531, 1607, and one he viewed himself in 1682—with nearly identical paths. This discovery led him to conclude that comets follow a long, elliptical (oval-shaped) orbit around the sun, and thus reappear periodically. In 1695, Halley wrote in a letter to Isaac Newton, "I am more and more confirmed that we have seen that Comett now three times, since ye yeare 1531."

Halley predicted that the same comet would return in 1758 and published his findings in *A Synopsis of the Astronomy of Comets*. Although Halley did not live to see it, his prediction was correct and the comet was named after him.

Halley also made observations of the positions of stars and compared them with the positions of those same stars recorded by Alexandrian astronomer Ptolemy around the year A.D. 150. He found that these so-called fixed, or motionless, stars had moved a measurable distance over the years, even though no change in their position could be seen from year to year. Halley had discovered **proper motion,** the change in the position of a star with respect to other stars because of its movement in space.

Halley made many other accomplishments during his lifetime. First, he was instrumental in changing England's Royal Society from a scientific social club into a well-respected organization. Second, he estimated the age of the Earth by calculating the amount of salt the rivers had dumped into the seas over the years. Halley also spent two years crossing the Atlantic on a Royal Navy ship, studying the Earth's **magnetic field.**

Halley acted as chief science advisor to Russian czar Peter the Great when he visited England, helping to pass on the knowledge of the Western world to the developing Russian society. In 1719, Halley became England's Astronomer Royal and continued actively in this role until just before his death. Throughout all this time, he still found time to write poetry in Latin. Halley died in 1742 at the Greenwich Observatory.

See also **Comet**; **Gravity**; **Halley's comet**; and **Newton, Isaac**

Halley's comet

Halley's **comet** has been seen streaking through the sky periodically for over two thousand years. The first record of its appearance dates to 240 B.C. Since that date, its re-appearance has been documented every time it has passed by the Earth.

For example, in 240 B.C., the Chinese noted the comet's presence and blamed it for the death of an empress. Its appearance was also recorded by the Babylonians in 164 B.C. and 87 B.C. And in 12 B.C., the Romans thought the comet was connected with the death of statesman Marcus Vipsanius Agrippa. Several other sightings of the comet were recorded before Edmond Halley's observation in 1682.

Until Halley's study of comets, no one knew where comets came from or what paths they followed. Johannes Kepler observed Halley's comet in 1607, although it had not yet been given that name. Kepler concluded that comets follow straight lines, coming from and disappearing into infinity. Somewhat later, German astronomer Johannes Hevelius suggested that comets follow slightly curved lines. In the latter half of the 1600s, German astronomer Georg Samuel Dörffel suggested that comets follow a parabolic course, a curve with the shape of the nose cone of a **rocket.**

Although comets appeared free from the effects of **gravity** as they traveled through the sky, Halley wondered if gravity somehow influenced their movement. He carefully analyzed the paths of twenty-four comets. With the help of his friend, English mathematician Isaac Newton, he found three comets—those occurring in 1531, 1607, and the one he viewed himself in 1682—with nearly identical paths. This discovery led him to the conclusion that what observers had seen was really a single comet passing by the Earth three different times. It also suggested that comets follow a long, elliptical (oval-shaped) orbit around the sun.

Halley, however, found some problems with this theory. First, the period between the first and second sightings was a year longer than the period between the second and third sightings. Second, the comet was not found in the same place in the sky each time it re-appeared. To deal with these inconsistencies, Halley suggested that the comet's path was thrown a little off course by the gravitational fields of Jupiter and Saturn as it passed by those large planets.

Predicting the Comet's Orbit

After long, detailed calculations that took into account the influences of Jupiter and Saturn, Halley predicted that this same comet would return

*Halley's comet,
1910.*

in 1758. He published his findings in 1705 in *A Synopsis of the Astronomy of Comets*. Although Halley did not live to see it, his prediction was correct, and the comet was named after him.

After Halley's death in 1742, others continued to plot more accurately the course of Halley's comet. First, French mathematician Alexis Clairaut made precise calculations of the gravitational interactions between Jupiter, Saturn, Earth, and the comet. He was joined by French astronomers Joseph Lalande and Nicole-Reine Lepaute (the leading female astronomer in France at the time). Their results were so exact that their predictions were only a month different from the comet's actual return. They determined that Halley's comet completes one orbit in just over seventy-six years.

In 1986, when Halley's comet was scheduled to pass near the sun and Earth, it attracted a great deal of attention among both scientists and the general public. Over one thousand astronomers from forty countries coordinated the International Halley Watch. Soviet, Japanese, and European **space probe**s were sent to get a close look at the comet, while other spacecraft and telescopes were used for observation.

The European Space Agency's probe, *Giotto,* flew toward and took pictures of the comet's center. These pictures showed the nucleus to be a 9.3-mile-long, 6-mile-wide, (5.8 kilometers long and 3.7 kilometers wide) coal-black, potato-shaped object marked by hills and valleys. Two bright jets of gas and dust, each 9 miles (5.6 kilometers) long, shot out of the nucleus. *Giotto*'s instruments detected the presence of water, carbon, nitrogen, and sulfur molecules. It also found that the comet was losing about thirty tons of water and five tons of dust each hour. This fact means that although the comet will survive for hundreds more orbits, it will eventually disintegrate. Halley's comet is next due to pass by Earth in the year 2062.

See also **Comet** and **Halley, Edmond**

Harriot, Thomas (1560–1621)
English mathematician,
astronomer, and physicist

Thomas Harriot (also given as Hariot) was born in Oxford, England, where he later attended Oxford University. Shortly after graduation he was hired by Sir Walter Raleigh to go to Virginia and find out about the life, language, and customs of the New World. Harriot returned a year later and wrote a report detailing his findings.

Harriot spent the rest of his life exploring the different areas of science and math that fascinated him. In his early thirties he began working in astronomy. He calculated the distance between the celestial North Pole and the North Star. Harriot did this using a telescope and algebraic equations he had created himself.

In 1607, Harriot made observations of Halley's **comet** with another homemade telescope. A few years later, he conducted detailed studies of Jupiter's moons and **sunspot**s.

Harriot lived in Ireland for several years, where he studied the colors produced by a prism. He computed the refractive indexes (wavelength and change in **speed of light** as it leaves a prism) for green, orange, and red rays. He planned to write a book on this subject, but no record of such a book exists today.

Harriot is probably best known as a mathematician. He wrote an algebra textbook, published ten years after his death, that was widely used for many years. In this book he came up with a number of equations and notations that simplified algebra.

Harriot was also famous for not recording and publishing much of his work. One example of this pattern is that Harriot observed the moon with a telescope a few months before Italian astronomer Galileo Galilei did, but only Galileo charted the moon's features and did follow-up studies. Galileo, therefore, received the credit for discovering that the moon had craters.

Harriot died of cancer at age sixty-one.

Harvard-Smithsonian
Center for Astrophysics

The Harvard-Smithsonian Center for Astrophysics (CfA) was established in 1973 as a partnership between the Smithsonian Astrophysical Observatory and the Harvard College Observatory. It is headquartered in Cambridge, Massachusetts, and has three field stations: the Whipple Observatory near Tucson, Arizona; the Oak Ridge Observatory near Harvard, Massachusetts, and the George Agassiz Station near Fort Davis, Texas.

The Harvard College Observatory (HCO) was founded in 1839 on the Harvard campus. It is used primarily for teaching and research by Harvard astronomy faculty members. Its 15-inch (38-centimeter) **refractor telescope** dates back to 1847. At the time it was installed and for the twenty years that followed, this telescope was the largest in the United States. It still stands in its original building, the Sears Tower, which is located on Observatory Hill in Cambridge. In contrast to when it was erected, the tower today is surrounded by several building wings that have been added on to it.

The HCO also houses the largest collection of photographic plates in the world, over four hundred thousand of them. The plates are pictures of the sky that were taken between the 1880s and the 1980s. They constitute a valuable archive that is widely used by astronomers from around the world.

The Smithsonian Astrophysical Observatory (SAO) was established in 1890 in Washington, D.C., as part of the Smithsonian Institution. It was moved from the D.C. mall (where many of the national monuments are located) to Cambridge in 1955 and eighteen years later, formally merged with the HCO.

The SAO has traditionally been a clearinghouse for information about current astronomical phenomena. The observatory operates a subscription-based service via postcards and the computer, which provides astronomers with information on the current status of objects such as **comet**s, **asteroid**s, **nova**e, and **supernova**e. The SAO also contributes to an international computer database of information about all known astronomical objects.

Work of the Center for Astrophysics

Central to an understanding of the work done at CfA is a definition of **astrophysics,** the study of the physical properties and evolution of celestial bodies, particularly concerning the production and use of energy in stars and **galaxies.** Under the heading of astrophysics fall the branches of astronomy that deal with the distinct types of radiation along the **electromagnetic spectrum,** including **radio waves**, **infrared** and **ultraviolet radiation, X-ray**s, and **gamma ray**s.

The CfA is one of the country's largest astronomy centers, with a staff of over two hundred scientists and over three hundred technical and administrative personnel and one of the largest astronomical libraries in the world. It is internationally recognized for its achievements in ground-based **gamma-ray astronomy,** the study of stellar atmospheres, radio **interferometry,** planetary sciences, and the development of a wide variety of instrumentation for orbiting observatories in space. In addition to carrying out observations with ground-based telescopes, CfA researchers conduct experiments by placing instruments on balloons, **rocket**s, and satellites.

Much of the research done by CfA astronomers takes place at one of the three field stations. The largest CfA outpost is the Whipple Observatory. Research activities there include spectroscopic observations of stars and planets, gamma-ray astronomy, and solar energy research.

The Whipple Observatory is home to the Multiple Mirror Telescope, an instrument made of six individual **reflector telescopes,** each one with a primary mirror 71 inches (180 centimeters) in diameter. These telescopes are placed in an array, with an electronic guidance system that brings all six images into focus at the same time. The result is an instrument with the observing power of a 177-inch (450-centimeter) reflector. Construction is currently underway to replace the array with a single mirror, 265 inches (673 centimeters) in diameter.

Another telescope at Whipple is a 59-inch (150-centimeter) reflector, used mainly for determining the **spectra** of stars and galaxies. The observatory also has a 328-inch (833-centimeter) wide optical reflector, a honeycomb-shaped object made of 248 individual mirrors used to study **cosmic ray**s.

The Oak Ridge Observatory has a 61-inch (155-centimeter) reflector telescope that is used to observe comets and asteroids, as well as to track the apparent motion of stars across the night sky. Also at the site is an 84-foot (26-meter) **radio telescope** used in the ongoing SETI (Search for Extraterrestrial Intelligence) project.

Finally there is the Agassiz station, which maintains an 85-foot (26-meter) radio telescope, a link in the coast-to-coast chain of radio telescopes called Very Long Baseline Interferometry (VLBI). Each telescope in the chain is linked electronically so that the information collected by each one is transmitted to a central computer, which combines the data. The string of telescopes acts as a single telescope with a diameter equal to the distance separating them. The result is a radio picture with much finer detail than could be produced by any one telescope.

The CfA hosts an impressive series of public programs. For instance, on the third Thursday of every month, the CfA sponsors a free lecture, film, or video, followed by telescopic viewing from the Sears Tower. And viewing nights called "star parties" are held regularly at the Whipple Observatory, along with programs in both English and Spanish. The CfA also develops and distributes educational materials for use in elementary schools on up through high schools.

See also **Extraterrestrial life**; **Gamma-ray astronomy**; **Infrared astronomy**; **Ultraviolet astronomy**; **Whipple Observatory**; and **X-ray astronomy**

Hawking, Stephen (1942–)
English physicist and mathematician

Stephen William Hawking was born on January 8, 1942, three hundred years after the birth of Isaac Newton and three hundred years after the death of Galileo Galilei. He is similar to these two scientific geniuses in that he has a brilliant mind, and his theories have advanced our knowledge of the **cosmos.** His similarity to Newton even extends to academic appointments. Hawking is the Lucasian Professor of Mathematics at Cambridge University, a position once held by Newton.

Diagnosed with Lou Gehrig's disease, Stephen Hawking was given two and a half years to live thirty-three years ago.

Hawking grew up in the suburbs of London where his father, a research biologist, kept bees in the basement. By the age of fourteen, Hawking knew he wanted to study mathematics and physics. He attended college at Oxford University, where he had a reputation of being so smart that he did not need to study. Hawking's nights of playing bridge, however, caught up with him when it became questionable whether his final exam scores were good enough to get him into graduate school at Cambridge. Cambridge finally accepted him, and it was there that he earned his Ph.D in physics.

While at Cambridge, Hawking's motor skills began to deteriorate. For example, he had a tendency to slur his words and had trouble tying his shoes. He was taken to a specialist and

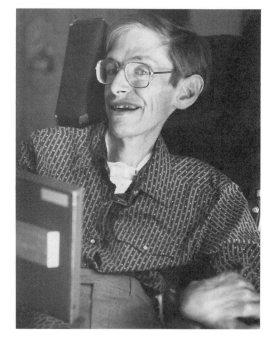

diagnosed with amyotrophic lateral sclerosis (also known as Lou Gehrig's disease). The disorder causes the muscles, but not the mind, to deteriorate. Hawking was told he had two years to live, which sent him into a terrible depression.

After two years, his condition stabilized. Although his body had become very frail and he was confined to a wheelchair, his mind remained as sharp as ever. Hawking learned to write using a specialized computer attached to his wheelchair and to speak through a machine called a speech synthesizer.

Hawking's Research On Black Holes

While in graduate school, Hawking met mathematician Roger Penrose who introduced him to the concept of **black hole**s, extremely dense objects in space with infinite **gravity.** This subject quickly became, and remains to this day, the focus of Hawking's life work.

Hawking believes that a black hole is the final stage of a massive star's life, but he proposes that they then continue to evolve by evaporating and giving off radiation.

Hawking's theory is based on the concept of virtual particles. Virtual particles can not themselves be detected but their presence is known by their effect on other objects. When approaching a black hole, one half of these particles gets sucked in while the other half evaporates, or radiates outward.

Through this process, the black hole loses **mass.** The smaller the black hole, the more quickly this occurs. Eventually the black hole completely evaporates away. In a black hole small enough, complete evaporation causes a violent explosion that gives off gamma radiation. Hawking is convinced that this energy, also known as Hawking radiation, will one day be detected and verify his theory.

In a large black hole, however, say the size of the sun, its complete evaporation would result in a huge explosion equal to a billion hydrogen bombs. However, it should be billions of years before any such event takes place.

Hawking is also exploring the possibility that numerous mini-black holes were formed right after the "big bang," the initial explosion in which the universe was probably formed. The basis for this prediction is that the same conditions existed then as exist when a massive star collapses. In particular, there is a huge amount of mass in a very small area. It is possible that these mini-black holes could still be scattered throughout the universe today.

Adding a strange twist to the **big bang theory,** Hawking has questioned whether the universe has any beginning at all in terms of space or time. He has suggested that as at the earliest stages of the universe, linear time (the orderly progression from past to future) did not exist. Like the Earth, which is round, time may be a circle. As Hawking stated, "Asking what happens before the Big Bang is like asking for a point one mile north of the North Pole."

Hawking is now working on his Grand Unified Theory, an effort to further explain the beginnings of space and time. Such a magnificent goal involves merging **quantum mechanics** with Einstein's theory of relativity, to produce a full quantum theory of gravity. This theory, if it can be worked out, would be as significant as Newton's laws of motion.

Hawking has written several best-selling books that explain concepts of astronomy in a non-technical way. His most famous book, *A Brief History of Time,* has even been made into a movie.

Throughout his illness Hawking has never lost his sense of humor. He jokes that his research into the birth of the universe is like trying to "know the mind of God."

See also **Big bang theory** and **Black hole**

Herschel, Caroline
(1750–1848)
German astronomer

Caroline Lucretia Herschel had an unusual upbringing for a girl of her time. Her father, an oboe player and amateur astronomer, arranged for her to be educated in areas outside of traditional women's work, such as cooking and knitting. When her father died in 1767, Herschel's mother tried to re-mold her teenage daughter into her idea of a proper young lady. But it was too late. Herschel's mind had already been opened to the world, and there was no going back. In 1772, she left home and joined her brother, organist, choirmaster, and amateur astronomer William Herschel, in England.

Caroline Herschel.

Herschel trained to become a professional singer while learning mathematics from her brother. She soon began to assist William in his astronomical studies by polishing and grinding mirrors for his telescope and copying his notes. Brother and sister found themselves dedicating more and more of their time to astronomy and less to music. Caroline once remarked, "If it had not been sometimes for the intervention of a cloudy or moon-lit night, I know not when my brother (or I either) should have got any sleep." In 1871, following William's discovery of the planet Uranus, the brother-and-sister team began receiving a yearly salary from King George III. This salary allowed them to become full-time astronomers.

Eventually Herschel began making her own contributions to astronomy. In 1783, she discovered three new **nebula**e (clouds of gas and dust), and over the next decade she discovered eight **comet**s. In 1787, King George decided to give Herschel her own salary, something very rare for a woman then.

Herschel went on to make a complete index of the star catalogue created by John Flamsteed, the first Astronomer Royal, England's honorary chief-astronomer.

When her brother William died in 1822, Herschel returned to Hanover, Germany, where she lived to the age of ninety-seven. She continued working with William's son, astronomer John Herschel, for whom she put together a new catalogue of nebulae.

Herschel was one of the first two women granted membership in the Royal Society, England's elite science club. She won the Gold Medal of the Royal Astronomical Society at age seventy-eight; was elected to the Royal Irish Academy at eighty-six; and won the King of Prussia's Gold Medal for Science at age ninety-six. She was a pioneer of women in the sciences and a true inspiration to a generation of girls.

See also **Herschel, William**

Herschel, William (1738–1822)

German astronomer

William Herschel was born in Hanover, Germany, at a time when that region was under English control. As a youngster he aspired to follow in his father's footsteps and become a musician in the Hanoverian army. But seeing the horrors of the Seven Years' War changed that ambition.

Herschel decided he wanted nothing to do with the military, and at age nineteen he moved to England. He found work as an organist and music teacher in the city of Bath, long-famous for its public baths and concert halls. He then became interested in the nature of sound, mathematics and optics.

Herschel's other interest was astronomy. An avid stargazer since his youth, he was always disappointed with the quality of telescopes available. He decided to make his own and, with the help of his sister Caroline, began to grind and polish lenses. His first telescope, one of the best of its kind, was a 6-foot-long (2-meter-long) **reflector.** This telescope was only the first of many he built. He turned practically every room in his house into a workshop and created telescope after telescope, each one more powerful than the last. In 1789, he built a huge, 40-foot-long (12-meter-long) telescope with a 49-inch (124-centimeter) mirror, through which he discovered two of Saturn's moons.

Herschel was conducting a general survey of the stars and planets in 1781 when he made another major discovery, the planet Uranus. It appeared as a disk'shaped object in the **constellation** Gemini. At first Herschel thought the object was a **comet.** But its orbit was not as elongated as a comet's; it was more circular, like that of a planet. Six months later he became convinced that this body was indeed a planet. He calculated its orbit and found it was twice as far from the sun as the next closest planet, Saturn. Thus, the discovery of Uranus doubled the known size of the **solar system.**

William Herschel.

Upon confirmation that he had discovered a new planet, Herschel was made a member of the prestigious science club called the Royal Society. The discovery also came to the attention of King George III, who appointed Herschel to be the King's Astronomer. The position included a small salary, which enabled Herschel to study the skies full-time.

Herschel's Other Astronomical Accomplishments

Herschel's main field of interest was the order and nature of the stars and planets. He

mapped out 848 pairs of stars and discovered that a force of attraction exists between stars. He also theorized that stars originally were randomly scattered throughout the universe and that over time they had come together in clusters.

Herschel was the first astronomer to conduct a scientific survey of the **Milky Way.** He and his sister discovered numerous **nebula**e (clouds of dust and gas that exist between stars). Herschel even studied the sun and learned that what we see is not the sun itself, but clouds of gases over its surface. And when Father Giuseppi Piazzi discovered the first **asteroid** in 1801, Herschel suggested the name for this class of small, starlike bodies.

Herschel is well-known for his study of the planets Mercury, Venus, Mars, Jupiter, and Saturn. For each one he measured the time it took to complete a rotation, the angle at which it was tilted, its shape, and the nature of its atmosphere. He carefully observed Saturn and at first argued that its rings were solid, but later found that they were composed of floating particles.

Herschel came to believe that other solar systems outside our own may exist. He challenged the popular notion that the Milky Way was the center of the universe and suggested that our **galaxy,** and Earth itself, were quite insignificant pieces of an immense puzzle.

See also **Herschel, Caroline**

Hertzsprung, Ejnar (1873–1967)
Danish astronomer

Ejnar Hertzsprung, born in Frederiksberg, Denmark, studied chemical engineering in college. He later switched to astronomy and was hired as a professor at the University of Göttingen, in Germany. Hertzsprung is credited with charting the brightness and temperature of stars, and showing the relationship between these factors.

Hertzsprung first sought to find a way to measure the brightness of stars, regardless of their distance from Earth. A star farther from Earth naturally would appear dimmer than one closer to Earth. But two stars the same distance from Earth could have different brightnesses, too.

To determine a star's true brightness, in 1905 Hertzsprung devised a measure called the **absolute magnitude** of a star. He defined absolute magnitude as the brightness of a star at a constant distance from Earth of 32.5 **light-year**s. Using this standard, he measured the brightness of several stars and learned that their color was related to their brightness. For instance, blue stars are brighter than yellow ones, and red stars are the dimmest stars of all.. And given that a star's color is an indication of its temperature, it must also be true that a star's temperature and brightness are linked. Hertzsprung made a diagram of his results, which he then tucked away in his desk.

Hertzsprung did not realize the importance of his diagram until ten years later, when American astronomer Henry Russell produced a similar piece of work on his own. Today the graph showing the relationship among the color, brightness, and temperature of stars (probably the most

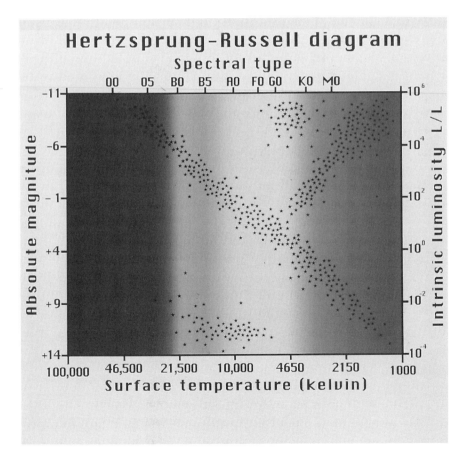

The Hertzsprung-Russell diagram plots the brightness (vertical axis) and temperature (horizontal axis) of stars. The clusters in the top right are supergiants, and the bottom clusters are white dwarfs.

famous diagram in astronomy) is called the **Hertzsprung-Russell diagram.**

The Hertzsprung-Russell Diagram

This graph has brightness on the vertical axis and temperature (or
color) on the horizontal axis. When groups of stars are plotted, a clear pattern arises. The majority of the stars appear on the diagonal line that runs
from hot, bright, blue stars on the upper left to the cool, dim, red stars on
the lower right. The diagonal line is often called the main sequence. Some
stars, however fall outside of this path. Examples of these are **supergiant**s
and giants (very large, bright stars), and **white dwarf** stars (cool remnants
of exploded stars).

A star spends most of its lifetime at one position on the main sequence, depending on its brightness and temperature. As it reaches the
end of its life, it becomes a **red giant,** and later a white dwarf (or, if it's
large enough, a **black hole**) and moves to a place off the main sequence. Thus, the distribution of stars on the diagram tells us a lot about
both the life cycle of an individual star and the characteristics of a type
of stars.

In 1913, Hertzsprung, with the help of American astronomer Henrietta Swan Leavitt, began calculating the distances to certain stars
known as **cepheid variables.** Cepheid variables are pulsating yellow supergiant stars, called "astronomical yardsticks" because the rate at which
they pulsate is directly related to their brightness at a constant distance
from Earth. That is, the brighter a cepheid variable is, the longer its rate
of pulsation.

Using a cepheid variable as a marker, Hertzsprung made the first cal-
culation of the distance to an object outside of the **Milky Way,** the Small
Magellanic Cloud. Although he greatly underestimated this distance,
Hertzsprung had established a method of measurement that was improved
on and used to greater accuracy by later astronomers, such as American
Harlow Shapley, who measured the size of our **galaxy.**

In 1935, Hertzsprung was made director of the observatory at Leiden, in the Netherlands. He retired ten years later and died in Denmark at
the age of ninety-four.

See also **Cepheid variables**; **Leavitt, Henrietta Swan**; **Russell,
Henry**; and **Uranus**

Sources

Books

Abbott, David, ed. "Seyfert, Carl Keenan," *The Biographical Dictionary of Scientists: Astronomers,* New York: P. Bedrick Books, 1984.

Abell, George O. *Realm of the Universe,* 3rd edition, Philadelphia: Saunders College Publishing, 1984.

Anderson, Julie. "Edward Mills Purcell," *Notable Twentieth-Century Scientists,* Volume 3, Ed. Emily J. McMurray, Detroit: Gale Research, 1995.

Apfel, Necia H. *Astronomy Projects for Young Scientists,* New York: Prentice Hall Press, 1984.

Asimov, Isaac. *Isaac Asimov's Library of the Universe: Ancient Astronomy,* Milwaukee: Gareth Stevens Publishing, 1989.

Asimov, Isaac. *Isaac Asimov's Library of the Universe: Projects in Astronomy,* Milwaukee: Gareth Stevens Publishing, 1990.

Bali, Mrinal. *Contemporary World Issues: Space Exploration,* Santa Barbara, CA: ABC-CLIO, Inc., 1990.

Barone, Michael and Grant Ujifusa. *The Almanac of American Politics 1996,* Washington, D.C.: National Journal Inc., 1995, pp. 1032-36.

Beck, R. L. and Daryl Schrader. *America's Planetariums & Observatories,* St. Petersburg, FL: Sunwest Space Systems, Inc., 1991.

Bernstein, Joanne E. and Rose Blue. *Judith Resnik: Challenger Astronaut,* New York: Lodestar Books, 1990.

Blaauw, Adriaan. *ESO's Early History,* Garching bei München, Germany: European Southern Observatory, 1991.

Blaauw, Adriaan. "Sitter, Willem de," *Dictionary of Scientific Biography,* Volume XII, Ed. Charles Coulston Gillispie, New York: Charles Scribner's Sons, 1973.

Bonnet, Robert L. and G. Daniel Keen. *Space and Astronomy: 49 Science Fair Projects,* Blue Ridge Summit, PA: Tab Books, 1992.

Booth, Nicholas. *Encyclopedia of Space,* London: Brian Trodd Publishing House Limited, 1990.

Brecher, Kenneth and Michael Feirtag, eds. *Astronomy of the Ancients,* Cambridge, MA: The MIT Press, 1979.

Carroll, Peter N. *Famous in America: The Passion to Succeed,* New York: Dutton. 1985.

Cassut, Michael. *Who's Who in Space: The First 25 Years,* Boston: G. K. Hall & Co., 1987.

Cornell, James. *The First Stargazers: An Introduction to the Origins of Astronomy,* New York: Charles Scribner's Sons, 1981.

Couper, Heather and Nigel Henbest. *How the Universe Works,* Pleasantville, NY: Reader's Digest Association, Inc., 1994.

Davies, J. K. *Space Exploration,* Edinburgh: W & R Chambers Ltd., 1992.

Davies, Kay and Wendy Oldfield. *The Super Science Book of Time,* New York: Thomson Learning, 1992.

D'Occhieppo, Konradin Ferrari. "Oppolzer, Theodor Ritter Von," *Dictionary of Scientific Biography,* Volume X, Ed. Charles Coulston Gillispie, New York: Charles Scribner's Sons, 1973.

Drake, Frank D. *Is Anyone Out There?: The Scientific Search for Extraterrestrial Intelligence,* New York: Delacorte Press, 1992.

"Drake, Frank Donald," *American Men and Women of Science,* 18th edition, Vol. 2, New Providence, New Jersey: R. R. Bowker, 1972.

Eastwood, Bruce S. "Grimaldi, Francesco Maria," *Dictionary of Scientific Biography,* Volume V, Ed. Charles Coulston Gillispie, New York: Charles Scribner's Sons, 1973.

Friedman, Herbert. *The Astronomer's Universe,* New York: W.W. Norton & Company, 1990.

Gatland, Kenneth. *The Illustrated Encyclopedia of Space Technology,* New York: Crown Publishers, Inc., 1981.

Goldsmith, Donald. *The Astronomers,* New York: St. Martin's Press, 1991.

Graham, Judith, ed. "Jemison, Mae C.," *Current Biography Yearbook 1993,* New York: H.W. Wilson, 1993.

Gray, Chris Hables. "Carl Sagan," *Notable Twentieth-Century Scientists,* Volume 3, Ed. Emily J. McMurray, Detroit: Gale Research, 1995.

Gump, David P. *Space Enterprise: Beyond NASA,* New York: Praeger, 1990.

Hadingham, Evan. *Early Man and the Cosmos,* New York: Walker and Company, 1984.

Haskins, Jim and Kathleen Benson. *Space Challenger: The Story of Guion Bluford,* Minneapolis: Carolrhoda Books, Inc., 1984.

Hathaway, Nancy. *The Friendly Guide to the Universe,* New York: Penguin Books, 1994.

Hawking, Stephen W. *A Brief History of Time: From the Big Bang to Black Holes,* Toronto: Bantam Books, 1988.

Heidman, Jean. *Extraterrestrial Intelligence,* Cambridge, England: Cambridge University Press, 1995.

Hoffleit, Dorrit. "Mitchell, Maria," *Dictionary of Scientific Biography,* Volume IX, Ed. Charles Coulston Gillispie, New York: Charles Scribner's Sons, 1973.

Hunley, J. D. "Hermann Oberth," *Notable Twentieth-Century Scientists,* Volume 3, Ed. Emily J. McMurray, Detroit: Gale Research, 1995.

Ilingworth, Valerie, ed. *The Facts on File Dictionary of Astronomy,* 3rd edition, New York: Facts on File, Inc., 1994.

Itard, Jean. "Legendre, Adrien-Marie," *Dictionary of Scientific Biography,* Volume VIII, Ed. Charles Coulston Gillispie, New York: Charles Scribner's Sons, 1973.

Kaufmann, William J., III. *Discovering the Universe,* 3rd edition, New York: W. H. Freeman and Company, 1993.

Kippenhahn, Rudolf. *Bound to the Sun: The Story of Planets, Moons, and Comets,* New York: W. H. Freeman and Company, 1990.

Kirby-Smith, H.T. *U.S. Observatories: A Directory and Travel Guide,* New York: Van Nostrand Reinhold Company, 1976.

Kopal, Zdenek. "Römer, Ole Christensen (or Roemer, Olaus)," *Dictionary of Scientific Biography,* Volume XI, Ed. Charles Coulston Gillispie, New York: Charles Scribner's Sons, 1973.

Kragh, Helge. "Lemaitre, Georges," *Dictionary of Scientific Biography,* Volume 18-Supplement II, Ed. Charles Coulston Gillispie, New York: Charles Scribner's Sons, 1990.

Krauss, Lawrence M. *The Physics of Star Trek,* New York: BasicBooks, 1995.

Lerner, Eric. *The Big Bang Never Happened,* New York: Times Books, 1991.

Lévy, Jacques R. "Le Verrier, Urbain Jean Joseph," *Dictionary of Scientific Biography,* Volume VIII, Ed. Charles Coulston Gillispie, New York: Charles Scribner's Sons, 1973.

Lohne, J. A. "Harriot (or Hariot), Thomas," *Dictionary of Scientific Biography,* Volume VI, Ed. Charles Coulston Gillispie, New York: Charles Scribner's Sons, 1973.

MacDonald, D.K.C. *Faraday, Maxwell, and Kelvin,* Garden City, NY: Doubleday & Company, Inc., 1964.

Mallas, John H. and Evered Kreimer. *The Messier Album: An Observer's Handbook,* Cambridge, MA: Sky Publishing Corp, 1978.

Marsden, Brian G. "Newcomb, Simon," *Dictionary of Scientific Biography,* Volume X, Ed. Charles Coulston Gillispie, New York: Charles Scribner's Sons, 1973.

Marx, Siegfried and Werner Pfau. *Observatories of the World,* New York: Van Nostrand Reinhold Company, 1982.

McDonald, Avril. "Grote Reber," *Notable Twentieth-Century Scientists,* Volume 3, Ed. Emily J. McMurray, Detroit: Gale Research, 1995.

Moore, Patrick. *Fireside Astronomy: An Anecdotal Tour through the History and Lore of Astronomy,* Chichester, England: John Wiley & Sons, 1992.

Moore, Patrick. *The Guinness Book of Astronomy,* Middlesex, England: Guinness Publishing Ltd., 1988.

Moore, Patrick. *The International Encyclopedia of Astronomy,* New York: Orion Books, 1987.

Moore, Patrick. *Patrick Moore's History of Astronomy,* 6th edition, London: MacDonald & Co. Ltd., 1983.

Moyer, Don F. "Langley, Samuel Pierpont," *Dictionary of Scientific Biography,* Volume VIII, Ed. Charles Coulston Gillispie, New York: Charles Scribner's Sons, 1973.

Multhauf, Lettie S. "Olbers, Heinrich Wilhelm Matthias," *Dictionary of Scientific Biography,* Volume X, Ed. Charles Coulston Gillispie, New York: Charles Scribner's Sons, 1973.

Munitz, Milton K., ed. *Theories of the Universe,* Glencoe, IL: The Free Press, 1957.

Neal, Valerie, Cathleen S. Lewis and Frank H. Winter. *Spaceflight: A Smithsonian Guide,* New York: Macmillan • USA, 1995.

Newton, David E. "Martin Ryle," *Notable Twentieth-Century Scientists,* Volume 3, Ed. Emily J. McMurray, Detroit: Gale Research, 1995.

North, John. *The Norton History of Astronomy and Cosmology,* New York: W. W. Norton & Company, Inc., 1995.

O'Connor, Karen. *Sally Ride and the New Astronauts: Scientists in Space,* New York: Franklin Watts, 1983.

Office of Technology Assessment. *Civilian Space Policy and Applications,* Washington, D.C.: U.S. Government Printing Office, 1982.

O'Neil, W. M. *Early Astronomy from Babylonia to Copernicus,* Sydney, Australia: Sydney University Press, 1986.

Parker, Barry. *Stairway to the Stars: The Story of the World's Largest Observatory,* New York: Plenum Press, 1994.

Pasachoff, Jay M. *Contemporary Astronomy,* 4th edition, Philadelphia: Saunders College Publishing, 1989.

Pasachoff, Jay M. *Journey Through the Universe,* Fort Worth, TX: Saunders College Publishing, 1992.

Pendick, Daniel. "Clyde W. Tombaugh," *Notable Twentieth-Century Scientists,* Volume 4, Ed. Emily J. McMurray, Detroit: Gale Research, 1995.

Riabchikov, Evgeny. *Russians in Space,* Garden City, New York: Doubleday & Company, Inc., 1971.

"Rocket and Rocket Engine," *Science and Technology Illustrated: The World Around Us,* Volume 22, Chicago: Encyclopedia Britannica, Inc., 1984.

Ronan, Colin A. *The Natural History of the Universe,* New York: MacMillan Publishing Company, 1991.

Sagan, Carl. *Cosmos,* New York: Random House, 1980.

Schmittroth, Linda, Mary Reilly McCall, and Bridget Travers, eds. *Eureka!* 6 Volumes, Detroit: U•X•L, 1995.

Smith, Julian A. "Valentina Tereshkova," *Notable Twentieth-Century Scientists,* Volume 4, Ed. Emily J. McMurray, Detroit: Gale Research, 1995.

Smith, Julian A. "Vera Cooper Rubin," *Notable Twentieth-Century Scientists,* Volume 3, Ed. Emily J. McMurray, Detroit: Gale Research, 1995.

Smith, Robert W. *The Space Telescope: A Study of NASA, Science, Technology and Politics,* Cambridge, MA: Cambridge University Press, 1993.

Stuewer, Roger H. "Gamow, George," *Dictionary of Scientific Biography,* Volume V, Ed. Charles Coulston Gillispie, New York: Charles Scribner's Sons, 1973.

Swenson, Loyd S. Jr. "Michelson, Albert Abraham," *Dictionary of Scientific Biography,* Volume IX, Ed. Charles Coulston Gillispie, New York: Charles Scribner's Sons, 1973.

Swift, David W. *SETI Pioneers: Scientists Talk About Their Search for Extraterrestrial Intelligence,* Tucson, AZ: The University of Arizona Press, 1990.

Thurston, Hugh. *Early Astronomy,* New York: Springer-Verlag, 1994.

Travers, Bridget, ed. *The Gale Encyclopedia of Science,* 6 Volumes. Detroit: Gale Research, 1996.

Travers, Bridget, ed. *World of Invention,* Detroit: Gale Research, 1994.

Travers, Bridget, ed. *World of Scientific Discovery,* Detroit: Gale Research, 1994.

Tucker, Wallace H. *The Star Splitters: The High Energy Astronomy Observatories,* Washington, D.C.: National Aeronautics and Space Administration, 1984.

Walter, William J. *Space Age,* New York: Random House, 1992.

Wilson, Colin. *Starseekers,* New York: Doubleday & Company, Inc., 1980.

Wilson, Philip K. "Allan R. Sandage," *Notable Twentieth-Century Scientists,* Volume 4, Ed. Emily J. McMurray, Detroit: Gale Research, 1995.

Zeilik, Michael and John Gaustad. *Astronomy: The Cosmic Perspective,* 2nd edition, New York: John Wiley & Sons, Inc., 1990.

Articles

Acton, Scott. "Untwinkling Our Own Star," *Sky & Telescope,* June 1994: 26-27.

"Allan Sandage Receives 1991 Crafoord Prize," *Physics Today,* December 1991: 91.

Allen, Jane E. "Probe Finds Jupiter Surprisingly Windy, Drier Than Expected," *Detroit Free Press,* 23 January 1996: A1.

Allen, Jane E. and Russell Grantham. "By Jupiter! Probe's Findings Surprise Scientists," *The Ann Arbor News,* 23 January 1996: A3.

"Americans Get the Mir Experience," *Astronomy,* April 1995: 28.

"Astronaut at Home on Mir," *The Ann Arbor News,* 26 March 1996: A4.

"Astronomers Are Closer to Agreeing on the Age of the Universe," *Chronicle of Higher Education,* 17 May 1996: A10.

Banke, Jim. "The Story of Apollo 13: The Movie," *Ad Astra,* March/April 1995: 50.

Bartusiak, Marcia. "Head in the Stars," *The New York Times Book Review,* 10 December 1995: 22.

Bond, Bruce. "100 Years on Mars Hill," *Astronomy,* June 1994: 28-39.

Boyd, Robert S. "Astronomers See Potential for Life on Newly Found Planets," *Detroit Free Press,* 18 January 1996: A3+.

Boyd, Robert S. "Exploring the Big Bang and Beyond," *Detroit Free Press,* 7 January 1996: H1+.

Boyd, Robert S. "Origin of Life on Earth Eludes Scientists," *Detroit Free Press,* 7 January 1996: H4.

Boyd, Robert S. "Somewhere, Some Other Planet Must Sustain Life," *Detroit Free Press,* 7 January 1996: H4.

Broad, William J. "Could Life on Loose Bit of Mars Survive a Short Cut to Earth?" *The New York Times,* 12 March 1996: C1.

Broad, William J. "Russian Space Momentos Show Gagarin's Ride Was a Rough One," *The New York Times,* 5 March 1996: B12.

Browne, Malcolm W. "'Neutrino Bomb' Idea Expands Debate on Human Extinction," *The New York Times,* 23 January 1996: D4.

Brunier, Serge. "Temples in the Sky," *Sky and Telescope,* February 1993: 18-24.

Bruning, David. "Hubble: Better Than New," *Astronomy,* April 1994: 44-49.

Chang, Kenneth. "Two More Planets Found Near Stars Similar to the Sun," *The Los Angeles Times,* 18 January 1996: A3.

Chartrand, Mark. "A Measure of Space," *Ad Astra,* November/December 1993: 52.

Clary, Mike. "U.S. Woman Will Spend Months in Mir," *The Los Angeles Times,* 21 March 1996: A18.

"COBE Mission Launched," *Astronomy,* February 1990: 16+.

Cole, Richard. "NASA Mission May Unlock a Few Cosmic Secrets," *The Detroit News,* 3 December 1995: A2.

Cowley, Anne. "The Catherine Wolfe Bruce Medal to Maarten Schmidt," *Mercury,* November-December 1992: 197-98.

"Dr. Mae Jemison Becomes First Black Woman in Space," *Jet,* 14 September 1992: 34-38.

Drago, Mike. "Shuttle Retrieves NASA Probe," *The Ann Arbor News,* 16 January 1996.

Dunn, Marcia. "Female Astronaut Settles In on Mir," *USA Today,* 25 March 1996: A3.

Dunn, Marcia. "Shuttle, Mir Are Linked After Tricky Docking," *The Boston Globe,* 16 November 1995: A3.

Dyson, Freeman. "Hidden Worlds: Hunting for Distant Comets and Rogue Planets," *Sky & Telescope,* January 1994: 26-30.

Eicher, David J. "Descent Into Darkness," *Astronomy,* April 1995: 66-69.

Friedlander, Blaine P. Jr. "The Comet With Two Tails," *The Washington Post,* 6 March 1996: B5.

"Gamma-Ray Telescope Takes Shape," *Astronomy,* July 1995: 26.

Gauthier, Daniel James. "One Hundred Stars of Space," *Ad Astra,* July/August 1991: 8+.

Goldman, Stuart J. "Astronomy On the Internet," *Sky & Telescope,* August 1995: 21-27.

Grantham, Russell. "By Jupiter! Instruments From U-M to Explore It," *The Ann Arbor News,* 6 December 1995: B1+.

Grantham, Russell. "Expert Shares Jupiter Surprises," *The Ann Arbor News,* 8 February 1996: B3.

Grantham, Russell. "Hyakutake Brightest Comet in Sky Since 1976," *The Ann Arbor News,* 20 March 1996: B1+.

Grantham, Russell. "New Technology Has Accelerated Advances In Field of Astronomy," *The Ann Arbor News,* 11 April 1996: D1+.

Grantham, Russell. "Star Potential," *The Ann Arbor News,* 11 April 1996: D1+.

Gurshtein, Alexander. "When the Zodiac Climbed into the Sky," *Sky & Telescope,* October 1995: 28-33.

Hathaway, David H. "Journey to the Heart of the Sun," *Astronomy* January 1995: 38-43.

Horgan, John. "Beyond Neptune: Hubble Telescope Spots a Vast Ring of Ice Protoplanets," *Scientific American,* October 1995: 24+.

Hotz, Robert Lee. "Quest for Ice: Polar Prospecting." *The Los Angeles Times,* 14 January 1996: A1.

Hoversten, Paul. "Hubble's Time Travel Finds Galaxies," *USA Today,* 16 January 1996: A1.

"Hubble Observes the Violent Birth of Stars," *Astronomy* October 1995: 22.

Jaroff, Leon. "Listening for Aliens," *Time,* 5 February 1996: 55+.

"Jemison, Endeavour Crew Return To Earth After Successful Science Mission," *Jet,* 5 October 1992: 9.

Johnson, George. "Dark Matter Lights the Void," *The New York Times,* 21 January 1996: E1+.

Knight, Tony. "To Explore Strange New Worlds—Galileo Streaks Toward Jupiter," *Daily News of Los Angeles,* 27 November 1995.

Lemonick, Michael D. "Astronomers Have Detected Water-Bearing Planets Around Nearby Stars. Now They're Focused on a Deeper Mystery: Where Are the Friendly, Earthlike Worlds?" *Time,* 5 February 1996: 53+.

Lemonick, Michael D. "Beyond Pluto," *Time,* 28 September 1992: 59.

Luxner, Larry. "Southern Space: Down South Looks To The Stars," *Ad Astra,* November/December 1992: 46-47.

Mallon, Thomas. "Galileo, Phone Home," *The New York Times Magazine,* 3 December 1995: 57+.

Mann, Paul. "Spacelab's Demise?" *Aviation Week & Space Technology,* 1 August 1994: 23.

McDonald, Kim A. "A Great Comet," *The Chronicle of Higher Education,* 5 April 1996: A10.

Nash, Nathaniel C. "Starry-Eyed But Resolute: Astronomers in Race," *The New York Times,* 6 January 1994: A4.

"New Life for McMath Solar Telescope," *Sky & Telescope,* October 1990: 346.

Nicholson, Thomas D. "Observatory Hill," *Natural History,* April 1991: 78+.

"100-Inch Mount Wilson Telescope to Reopen," *Astronomy,* January 1988: 86-87.

O'Toole, Thomas. "The Man Who Didn't Walk On the Moon," *The New York Times Magazine,* 17 July 1994: 26+.

Owen, Tobias. "Ice in the Solar System: How the Earth Got its Atmosphere," *Ad Astra,* November/December 1995: 26-29.

Powell, Andrew. "Spaced Out," *Harper's Bazaar,* September 1994: 332-36.

Preston, Richard. "Beacons in Time: Maarten Schmidt and the Discovery of Quasars," *Mercury,* January-February 1988: 2-11.

Recer, Paul. "And It's Colder Than Michigan in March: Hubble Telescope Captures First Surface Images of Remote, Frozen Pluto," *The Ann Arbor News,* 8 March 1996: A6.

"Rendezvous in Space," *Astronomy,* October 1995: 23.

"Report: Insulation Puncture Caused Tether Failure," *The Ann Arbor News,* 5 June 1996: A4.

Ressmeyer, Roger H. "Tradition & Technology at Yerkes Observatory," *Sky & Telescope,* September 1995: 32-34.

Robinson, Cordula. "Magellan Reveals Venus," *Astronomy,* February 1995: 32-41.

Roylance, Frank D. "'Right Stuff' Old Stuff to Him; 'I Love Space': A 29-Year Astronaut, Dr. Storey Musgrave at 61 Will be the Oldest Human to Fly in Space When Columbia Takes Off in November," *The Baltimore Sun,* 26 April 1996: 1A.

Rudich, Joe. "The Electronic Frontier," *Ad Astra,* September/October 1995: 32-36.

Sawyer, Kathy. "Space Fleet Stares Deep Into Sun," *The Washington Post,* 20 May 1996: A3.

Sawyer, Kathy. "'Tadpoles' In Nebula Suggest Presence of Rogue Planets," *The Washington Post,* 20 April 1996: A3.

Shibley, John. "Glow Bands & Curtains," *Astronomy,* April 1995: 76-81.

"Space Flight: Endeavor Is a Symbol of Dreams," *The Ann Arbor News,* 14 January 1996.

Stephens, Sally. "The End of Hubble's Troubles," *Ad Astra,* March/April 1994: 50-52.

Stephens, Sally. "Telescopes that Fly," *Astronomy,* November 1994: 46-53.

Stern, Alan. "Chiron: Interloper From the Kuiper Disk?" *Astronomy,* August 94: 26-33.

Stevens, William K. "One Hundred Nations Move To Save Ozone Shield," *The New York Times,* 10 December 1995: A6.

"Subrahmanyan Chandrasekhar (1910-1995)," *Astronomy,* December 1995: 32.

"Taking the Long View: Hubble Images Shed Light On the Unknown, the Unseen," *Detroit Free Press,* 18 January 1996: F8.

Tyson, Neil de Grasse. "Romancing the Mountaintop," *Natural History,* January 1995: 70-73.

Watson, Traci and William J. Cook. "A New Solar System?" *U.S. News & World Report,* 30 October 1995: 69-72.

Weissman, Paul R. "Comets At the Solar System's Edge," *Sky & Telescope,* January 1993: 26-29.

Wilford, John Noble. "Ear to Universe Is Plugged by

Budget Cutters," *The New York Times,* 7 October 1993: B12.

Wilford, John Noble. "Found: Most of Missing Matter Lost Around Edges of Universe," *The New York Times,* 17 January 1996: A1+.

Wilford, John Noble. "Gifts Keep Alive Search for Other Life In Universe," *The New York Times,* 25 January 1994: C5.

Wilford, John Noble. "Life in Space? Two New Planets Raise Thoughts," *The New York Times,* 18 January 1996: A1+.

Wohleber, Curt. "The Rocket Man," *Invention & Technology,* Summer 1996: 36-45.

Websites

About La Silla. [Online] Available http://lw10.ls.eso.org/lasilla/generalinfo/html/aboutls.html, April 7, 1996.

Allen, Jesse S. The Uhuru Satellite: December 1970-March 1973. [Online] Available http://heasarc.gsfc.nasa.gov/docs/heasarc/missions/uhuru.html, June 5, 1996.

Altschuler, Daniel. General Information on Arecibo Observatory. [Online] Available http://www.naic.edu/, April 4, 1996.

Arnett, Bill. Pluto. [Online} Available http://seds.lpl.arizona.edu/billa/tnp/pluto.html, March 14, 1996.

Astronaut Alan B. Shepard, Jr. News & Photo Archives, NASA Ames Public Affairs Home Page. [Online] Available http://ccf.arc.nasa.gov/dx/basket/storiesetc/Shepa.html, May 9, 1996.

Bartlett, Don. A Practical Guide to GPS. [Online] Available http://www.fys.uio.no/~kjetikj/fjellet/GPS1.html, June 25, 1996.

Beatty, J. Kelly. Life from Ancient Mars? *Sky & Telescope's Weekly News Bulletin: Special Edition.* [Online] Available http://www.skypub.com/news/marslife.html, August 8, 1996.

Behr, Bradford. Big Bear Solar Observatory. [Online] Available http://astro.caltech.edu.observatories/bbso/bluebook.html, July 26, 1996.

Behr, Bradford. Palomar Observatory. [Online] Available http://astro.caltech.edu.observatories/palomar/, May 27, 1996.

Bell, Edwin V. Cassini. [Online] Available http://nssdc.gsfc.nasa.gov/planetary/cassini.html, March 18, 1996.

Bell, Edwin V. Pluto Express. *NSSDC Master Catalog Display Spacecraft.* [Online] Available http://nssdc.gsfc.nasa.gov/cgi-bin/database/www-nmc?PFF, July 22, 1996.

Biography of Dr. Buzz Aldrin. [Online] Available http://www.nss.org/askastro/biography.html, April 3, 1996.

Capt. Charles 'Pete' Conrad, Jr. (Ret.). [Online] Available http://www.nauts.com/astro/conrad/conrad.html, May 8, 1996.

Columbia Lands in Florida. [Online] Available http://shuttle.nasa.gov/sts-75, May 8, 1996.

Dettling, J. Ray. Beyond Hubble. [Online] Available http://ori.careerexpo.com/pub/docs/hubble.html, July 22, 1996.

Donahue, Bob. Mount Wilson Observatory. [Online] Available http://www.mtwilson.edu/, April 7, 1996.

Double Nucleus of the Andromeda Galaxy M31. [Online] Available http://galaxy.einet.net/images/galaxy/m31c.html, May 1, 1996.

Dr. Buzz Aldrin. *The National Space Society and the Space, Planetary, and Astronomical Cyber-Experience Present...Ask An Astronaut.* [Online] Available http://www.nss.org/askastro/#question, April 3, 1996.

Duarte, Luis Sánchez. SOHO-Solar and Heliospheric Observatory Home Page. [Online] Available http://sohowww.nascom.nasa.gov/, July 17, 1996.

Dumoulin, Jim. Space Shuttle Orbiter Atlantis. [Online] Available http://www.ksc.nasa.gov/shuttle/resources/orbiters/atlantis.html, April 6, 1996.

Dumoulin, Jim. Space Shuttle Orbiter Challenger. [Online] Available http://www.ksc.nasa.gov/shuttle/resources/orbiters/challenger.html, April 6, 1996.

Dumoulin, Jim. Space Shuttle Orbiter Columbia. [Online] Available http://www.ksc.nasa.gov/shuttle/resources/orbiters/columbia.html, April 6, 1996.

Dumoulin, Jim. Space Shuttle Orbiter Discovery. [Online] Available http://www.ksc.nasa.gov/shuttle/resources/orbiters/discovery.html, April 6, 1996.

Dumoulin, Jim. Space Shuttle Orbiter Endeavour. [Online] Available http://www.ksc.nasa.gov/shuttle/resources/orbiters/endeavour.html, April 6, 1996.

Educator's Guide to Convection. [Online] Available http://bang.lanl.gov/solarsys/edu/convect.html, April 22, 1996.

Educator's Guide to Eclipses. [Online] Available http://bang.lanl.gov/solarsys/edu/eclipses.html, April 22, 1996.

Frommert, Hartmut. M31: The Andromeda Galaxy. [Online] Available http://ftp.seds.org/messier/m/m031.html, April 30, 1996.

George Ellery Hale. *The Bruce Medalists-Brief Biographies.* [Online] Available http://yorty.sonoma.edu/people/faculty/tenn/BM2H-L.html#13, June 5, 1996.

Goldstein, Bruce E. Welcome to the Ulysses Mission Home Page! [Online] Available http://ulysses.jpl.nasa.gov/ULSHOME.html, May 30, 1996.

Grote Reber. *The Bruce Medalists-Brief Biographies.* [Online] Available http://yorty.sonoma.edu/people/faculty/tenn/BM2Q-R.html#55, June 5, 1996.

Haizen's Astrology FAQ. [Online] Available http://www.sedona.net/nen/haizen/faq.html, April 12, 1996.

Hamilton, Calvin J. Chronology of Space Exploration. [Online] Available http://bang.lanl.gov/solarsys/craft2.html, April 22, 1996.

Hamilton, Calvin J. Magellan Mission to Venus. [Online] Available http://bang.lanl.gov/solarsys/magellan.html, April 22, 1996.

Hamilton, Calvin J. Neptune. [Online] Available http://bang.lanl.gov/solarsys/neptune.html, July 11, 1996.

Hamilton, Calvin J. Saturn. [Online] Available http://bang.lanl.gov/solarsys/saturn.htm#stats, March 26, 1996.

Hamilton, Calvin J. Sun. [Online] Available http://bang.lanl.gov/solarsys/sun.html, April 22, 1996.

Hamilton, Calvin J. Uranus. [Online] Available http://bang.lanl.gov/solarsys/uranus.html, April 22, 1996.

Hamilton, Calvin J. Venus Introduction. [Online] Available http://bang.lanl.gov/solarsys/venus.html, April 22, 1996.

Hamilton, Calvin J. Venusian Impact Craters.[Online] Available http://bang.lanl.gov/solarsys/vencrate.html, April 22, 1996.

Hamilton, Calvin J. Venusian Volcanic Features. [Online] Available http://bang.lanl.gov/solarsys/venvolc.html, April 22, 1996.

Hamilton, Calvin J. Voyager Uranus Science Summary: December 21, 1988. [Online] Available http://bang.lanl.gov/solarsys/vgrur.html, April 22, 1996.

Harris, Pete. Star Facts: The Andromeda Galaxy—The Most Distant Thing Human Eyes Can See. [Online] Available http://ccnet4.ccnet.com/odyssey/sfa995.html, April 30, 1996.

Harvard-Smithsonian Center for Astrophysics (CfA). [Online] Available http://sao~www.harvard.edu/hco~home.html, July 17, 1996.

Hathaway, David H. Skylab. [Online] Available http://ally.ios.com/~skylab19/skylab19.html, March 22, 1996.

Hill, Frank. The National Solar Observatory at Kitt Peak. [Online] Available http://www.nso.noao.edu/nsokp/nsokp.html, July 17, 1996.

Hoffman, Kay. Shuttle/Mir. [Online] Available http://shuttle-mir.nass.gov/, May 8, 1996.

The Infrared Space Observatory (ISO). [Online] Available http://isowww.estec.esa.nl/ISO/ISO.html, March 27, 1996.

Intelsat. [Online] Available http://www.intelsat.int:8080/info/html/intelsat.html, May 21, 1996.

International Space Station: Frequently Asked Questions. [Online] Available http://issa-www.jsc.nasa.gov/ss/sshpt.html, March 28, 1996.

International Ultraviolet Explorer Satellite. [Online] Available http://inewwww.gsfc.nasa.gov/iue/iue_homepage.html, March 27, 1996.

Introduction to SOHO. [Online] Available http://vulcan.sp.ph.ic.ac.uk/SOHO/soho/html, July 22, 1996.

Irving, Don. Mt. Hamilton and Lick Observatory. *XPLORE Tours.* [Online] Available http://www.ucolick.org/, June 5, 1996.

James Clerk Maxwell. [Online] Available http://www~groups.dcs.st~and.ac.uk/~history/Mathematicians/, June 5, 1996.

Jenkins, Dawn. Maya Astronomy Page. [Online] Available http://www.astro.uv.nl/michielb/maya/astro.html, July 25, 1996.

Johannesson, Anders. Big Bear Solar Observatory www page. [Online] Available http://sundog.caltech.edu/, July 26, 1996.

JPL Space Very Long Baseline Interferometry Project. [Online] Available http://sgra.jpl.nasa.gov/mosaic_v0.0/svlbi.html, June 3, 1996.

Judith Resnik. *STS 51-L (Challenger) Crew Biography.* [Online] Available http://flight.osc.on.ca/documentation/judy.html, May 9, 1996.

Judith A. Resnik: Biography. *The Challenger Accident: January 28, 1986.* [Online] Available http://www.dartmouth.edu/~wsk/challenger/resnik.html, May 9, 1996.

King, J. H. Pioneer 10. *NSSDC Master Catalog Display Spacecraft.* [Online] Available http:nssdc.gsfc.nasa.gov/cgi-bin/database/www-nmc?72-012A, June 18, 1996.

King, J. H. Pioneer 11. *NSSDC Master Catalog Display Spacecraft.* [Online] Available http:nssdc.gsfc.nasa.gov/cgi-bin/database/www-nmc?73-019A, June 18, 1996.

King, J. H. Voyager Project Information. [Online] Available http:nssdc.gsfc.nasa.gov/planetary/voyager.html, June 18, 1996.

Kitt Peak. [Online] Available http://www.noao.edu/kpno/pubpamph/pub.html, April 7, 1996.

Launius, Roger D. Chronology of Selected Highlights in the First 100 American Spaceflights, 1961-1995. [Online] Available http://www.hq.nasa.gov/office/pao/History/Timeline/100flt.html, April 4, 1996.

Levine, Deborah A. Brief Introduction to IRAS. [Online] Available http://www.gsfc.nasa.gov/astro/iras/iras_home.html, March 27, 1996.

Liebacher, John. Global Oscillation Network Group. [Online] Available http://www.gong.noao.edu/, July 17, 1996.

Lyndon B. Johnson Space Center. Biographical Data: Shannon W. Lucid. [Online] Available http://www.jsc.nasa.gov/Bios/htmlbios/lucid.html, May 9, 1996.

Maarten Schmidt. *The Bruce Medalists-Brief Biographies.* [Online] Available http://yorty.sonoma.edu/people/faculty/tenn/BM2S.html#85, June 5, 1996.

MacRobert, Alan. When, Where, and How to See Comet Hyakutake. [Online] Available http://www.skypub.com, March 23, 1996.

Malin, David. General Information About the AAO. [Online] Available http://www.aao.gov.au/general.html, April 4, 1996.

Mariner Space Probes. [Online] Available http://www.hq.nasa.gov/office/pao/History/mariner.html, May 30, 1996.

Mars 96. [Online] Available http://www.iki.rssi.ru/mars96/mars96hp.html, July 2, 1996.

Mauna Kea Observatories. [Online] Available http://www.ifa.hawaii.edu/mko/mko.html, April 7, 1996.

McClaughlin, Siobhan. Anglo-Australian Observatory. [Online] Available http://www.aao.gov.au/aaohome-page.html, April 4, 1996.

McCurdy, Andrea and Mark Stokes. Jim Lovell: An Astronaut's Story. [Online] Available http://www.mcn.org/Apollo 13/Home.html, May 9, 1996.

McDonald Observatory Visitors Center Home Page. [Online] Available http://vulcan.as.utexas.edu//vc/vc_home.html, June 5, 1996.

McDonnell Douglas Spacelab Homepage. [Online] Available http://hvsun21.mdc.com:8000/~mosaic/main.html, July 15, 1996.

Napier, Beth. Activity: Precession of the Equinoxes. [Online] Available http://cea-ftp.cea.berkeley.edu/Education/beth/precess.html, April 12, 1996.

NASA Headquarters. International Space Station. [Online] Available http://www.dfrc.nasa.gov/PAIS/HQ/HTML/FS-004-HQ.html, May 8, 1996.

NASA Headquarters. An Overview of NASA. [Online] Available http://www.dfrc.nasa.gov/PAIS/HQ/HTML/FS-001-HQ.html, May 8, 1996.

National Solar Observatory. [Online] Available http://argo.tuc.noao.edu/, March 22, 1996.

Naumann, Michael. ESO Telescopes, Instrumentation & Detectors. [Online] Available http://www.hq.eso.org/telescopes-instruments.html, April 7, 1996.

Nemiroff, Robert and Jerry Bonnell. Astronomy Picture of the Day. M31: The Andromeda Galaxy. [Online] Available http://antwrp.gsfc.nasa.gov/apod/ap950724.html, May 1, 1996.

Neufeld, Christopher. The Physics of Solar Sailing. [Online] Available http://caliban.physics.utoronto.ca/neufeld/sailing.txt, March 21, 1996.

Pluto Express Home Page. [Online] Available http://www.jpl.nasa.gov/pluto/, July 22, 1996.

Project Mercury. [Online] Available http://www.osf.hq.nasa.gov/mercury/, May 8, 1996.

Rapp, Michael. Dr. Carl Sagan Honorary Page. [Online] Available http://wwwvms.utexas.edu/~mrapp/sagan/sagan.html, March 18, 1996.

Reflection. [Online] Available http://covis.atmos.uiuc.edu/guide/optics/html/reflection.html, June 14, 1996.

Refraction. [Online] Available http://covis.atmos.uiuc.edu/guide/optics/html/refraction.html, June 14, 1996.

Rudd, Richard. Voyager Project Home Page. [Online] Available http://vraptor.jpl.nasa.gov/voyager/voyager.html, July 2, 1996.

Sally Kristen Ride. Juanita Kreps Award. [Online] Available http:www.jcpenney.com/nrelease/jkreps/content/sride.html, May 9, 1996.

Sargent, Wallace W. Caltech Astronomy: Keck Observatory. [Online] Available http://astro.caltech.edu/observatories/keck/bluebook.html, April 7, 1996.

Satellite Tracking of Threatened Species. [Online] Available http://sdcd.gsfc.nasa.gov/ISTO/satellite_tracking/satelliteDRO.html, June 25, 1996.

Search for Extraterrestrial Radio Emissions from Nearby Developed Intelligent Populations (SERENDIP). [Online] Available http://albert.ssl.berkeley.edu/serendip/, April 12, 1996.

Simmons, Michael. The History of Mount Wilson Observatory. [Online] Available http:www.mtwilson.edu/history/history.html, June 5, 1996.

Simon Newcomb. *The Bruce Medalists-Brief Biographies*. [Online] Available http://yorty.sonoma.edu/people/faculty/tenn/BM2MN.html#1, June 5, 1996.

Smith, Woody. The Flights of Project Gemini. [Online] Available http://www.osf.hq.nasa.gov/gemini/, May 8, 1996.

Smith, Woody. STS-71 Press Kit: The Space Station Mir. [Online] Available http://www.osf.hq.nasa.gov/shuttle/sts71/mir.html, May 8, 1996.

Smithsonian Astrophysical Observatory. [Online] Available http://cfa~www.harvard.edu/sao~home.html, May 27, 1996.

SOHO Ultraviolet Coronagraph Spectrometer-UVCS. [Online] Available http://sao~www.harvard.edu/uvcs/, July 17, 1996.

SOHO-CDS at Imperial College. [Online] Available http://www.sp.ph.ic.ac.uk/SOHO/, July 22, 1996.

Solar and Heliospheric Observatory (SOHO). [Online] Available http://www.hq.nasa.gov/office/oss/enterprise/II/ii-soh82.html, July 22, 1996.

Space Shuttle Launches. [Online] Available http://www.ksc.nasa.gov/shuttle/missions/missions.html, July 15, 1996).

Space Telescopes. [Online] Available http://meteor.anu.edu.au/anton/astro_space.html, March 27, 1996.

Spacecraft: SOHO Brief Description. [Online] Available http://www~istp.gsfc.nasa.gov/ISTP/soho.html, July 22, 1996.

Spacelab. [Online] Available http://www.ksc.nasa.gov/shuttle/technology/sts-newsref/spacelab.html, July 15, 1996.

Spend an Out-of-this-World Evening at McDonald Observatory. [Online] Available http://numedia.tddc.net/hot/bigbend/mdo, June 5, 1996.

Stanton, Ed. Six Reasons Why America Needs the Space Station. [Online] Available http://issa-www.jsc.nasa.gov/ss/prgview/prgview.html, March 28, 1996.

STS-75 Payloads: TSS-1R, USMP-3 & MGBX. [Online] Available http://liftoff.msfc.nasa.gov/sts-75/welcome.html, May 8, 1996.

Tethered Satellite System (TSS-1R). [Online] Available http://liftoff.msfc.nasa.gov/sts-75/tss-1r/tss-1r.html, May 8, 1996.

Tribute to Carl Sagan. [Online] Available http://wea.mankato.mn.us:80/tps/sagan.html, March 18, 1996.

Urbain Jean Joseph Le Verrier. [Online] Available http://www~groups.dcs.st~and.ac.uk/~history/Mathematicians/, June 5, 1996.

Weisstein, Eric. Janksy, Karl (1905-1950). *Eric's Home Page*. [Online] Available http://www.gps.caltech.edu/~eww/bios/jnode2.html#SECTIONO, June 5, 1996.

Welcome to CTIO! [Online] Available http://www.ctio.noao.edu/ctio.html#visitors, April 7, 1996.

Welcome to Lowell Observatory.[Online] Available http://www.lowell.edu/, May 27, 1996.

Welcome to the Yerkes Observatory Virtual Tour! [Online] Available http://astro.uchicago.edu/vtour/, June 5, 1996.

What is the VLA? [Online] Available
http://www.nrao.edu/doc/vla/html/VLAintro.html,
June 5, 1996.

Wirth, Fred. Pioneer Project Home Page. [Online] Available
http://pyroeis.arc.nasa.gov/pioneer/PNhome.html,
July 2, 1996.

Wyoming Infrared Observatory. [Online] Available
http://faraday.uwyo.edu/physics.astronomy/
brochures/wiro.html, July 17, 1996.

Yerkes Observatory, University of Chicago. [Online]
Available http://astro.uchicago.edu/Yerkes.html,
June 5, 1996.

Index

Italic type indicates volume numbers;
boldface type indicates entries and their page numbers;
(ill.) indicates illustrations.

A

Aberration of light *1:* 70; *3:* 514, 612
Absolute magnitude *1:* 86, 219; *2:* 318; *3:* 631
Absolute zero *1:* 192; *2:* 267, 439; *3:* 494
Absorption lines *2:* 298; *3:* 610
Accretion *2:* 448
Achromatic lens *2:* 432
Adams, John Couch *1:* **1-2,** 1 (ill.), 119-20; *2:* 325, 407, 444
Adaptive optics *1:* 204; *2:* 250, 393, 401
Adel, Arthur *2:* 335
Adenosine triphosphate (ATP) *3:* 522
Adilade *1:* 39
"Adoration of the Magi" *1:* 183
Advanced X-ray Astrophysics Facility *1:* **2-4,** 3 (ill.); *3:* 591, 696
Aerobee rocket *3:* 662, 695, 697
Aerodrome *2:* 309
Agassiz station *1:* 212
Agena rocket *1:* 35, 107, 180; *2:* 400
Agrippa, Marcus Vipsanius *1:* 207
Airy, George *1:* 2
Akiyama, Toyohiro *2:* 383
Al-Sufi *1:* 19
Albrecht, Andreas *2:* 268
Aldrin, Buzz *1:* **4-7,** 5 (ill.), 23, 35, 182; *2:* 302, 330, 345, 391; *3:* 582, 596
Alexander the Great *1:* 32-33
Alfvén, Hannes Olof Göst *2:* 450-52
ALH 84001 *2:* 356
Almagest *2:* 459
Alnilan *1:* 11
American Academy of Arts and Sciences *2:* 385
American Astronomical Society *3:* 536
American Ephemeris *2:* 414-15

American Ephemeris and Nautical Almanac *2:* 386
Ames, Joseph *2:* 399
Ames Research Center (ARC) *2:* 399
Ampere, André *1:* 29
Analytical Mechanics *2:* 308
Anaxagoras *1:* 12
Anaximander *1:* 12
Ancient Chinese astronomy *1:* **7-9**
Ancient Egyptian astronomy *1:* **9-11**
Ancient Greek astronomy *1:* **11-14**
Ancient Mayan astronomy *1:* **16-17**
Anderson, Carl *1:* 22
Andromeda galaxy *1:* **17-20,** 18 (ill.), 49, 168-69; *2:* 254, 256, 312, 373, 382, 404, 436; *3:* 504, 551, 614, 704
Anglo-Australian Observatory *1:* **20-21**
Anglo-Australian Telescope (AAT) *1:* 20-21
Anti-matter *1:* **21-22,** 106; *2:* 268
Apache Point Observatory *3:* 701
Apogee *3:* 324
Apollo objects *1:* 38
Apollo program *1:* 7, **22-24,** 35, 100, 107, 161-62, 179, 182; *2:* 343, 369, 372, 399; *3:* 532, 534, 548, 565, 582, 589, 596, 600, 604-05, 689
***Apollo-Soyuz* Test Project** *1:* **24-25,** 24 (ill.); *2:* 324, 370; *3:* 578, 583, 634
Apollo Telescope Mount *3:* 548, 587
Apollo 1 *1:* 23; *3:* 682, 689
Apollo 7 *1:* 23; *2:* 345
Apollo 8 *1:* 6, 23, 76; *2:* 331, 345; *3:* 512, 532
Apollo 9 *1:* 23
Apollo 10 *1:* 23; *3:* 592
Apollo 11 *1:* 6, 23, 35, 182; *2:* 353, 391, 426; *3:* 532, 582, 595 (ill.), 596, 605
Apollo 12 *1:* 108; *2:* 345

Apollo 13 *1:* 23, **25-28,** 27 (ill.), 182; *2:* 329, 331, 345
Apollo 14 *2:* 331, 345; *3:* 544-45
Apollo 15 *2:* 345, 347
Apollo 16 *2:* 345, 347
Apollo 17 *1:* 24; *2:* 345, 347; *3:* 583
Apollo 18 *1:* 6, 27; *2:* 324; *3:* 583
Apparent solar time *3:* 642
Arabsat *2:* 337
Arachnoids *3:* 673
Arago, Dominique-Francois-Jean *1:* **28-29,** 28 (ill.)
Arecibo Observatory *1:* **29-31,** 30 (ill.), 130; *3:* 494, 498, 675
Argos *2:* 403
Ariane rocket *1:* 154 (ill.), 155, 183; *2:* 247, 316
Ariel *1:* 51; *3:* 656
Aristarchus *1:* 14, 112, 118; *2:* 445
Aristotle *1:* 13, **32-33,** 32 (ill.), 71, 98, 131, 171, 193; *2:* 260
Armagh Observatory *1:* 50
Armillary sphere *1:* 72
Armstrong, Neil *1:* 6, 23, **33-36,** 34 (ill.), 180, 184; *2:* 302, 331, 345, 391; *3:* 582, 596
Artsimovich, Lee *2:* 450
Association for the Advancement of Women *2:* 385
Association of Universities for Research in Astronomy (AURA) *2:* 299, 400
Asteroid belt *2:* 443
Asteroid Gaspra *1:* 37 (ill.)
Asteroids *1:* **36-39,** 99, 119, 174, 204, 211-12, 218; *2:* 271, 300, 308, 335, 356, 374, 376, 389, 406-07, 414, 427, 437, 443, 454; *3:* 506, 562, 565-66, 602, 646-47, 656, 659
Astrolabe *1:* **39-40,** 39 (ill.), 72; *2:* 265, 402
Astrology *1:* 14, **40-42,** 71; *2:* 294, 460

Astrometric binary star *1:* 53, 63; *3:* 623

Astrometry *3:* 658

Astronomer Royal *1:* 69, 207, 216

Astronomical Almanac 3: 659

Astronomical Society of the Pacific *3:* 536

Astronomical unit (AU) *1:* 85; *2:* 305

Astronomy 3: 557

Astronomy websites *1:* 15

Astrophysical Journal 3: 501

Astrophysics *1:* 94, 200

AT&T *1:* 104

Attila the Hun *1:* 98

Atlantis 1: **42-44,** 43 (ill.), 90, 96, 106, 127, 149, 172, 176; *2:* 336-37, 349, 385, 395; *3:* 580, 586, 591, 607, 636

Atlas rocket *2:* 316, 369

Atmospheric Compensation Experiment *2:* 394

Atomic bomb *1:* 55, 145

Aurora australis *1:* 44, 117

Aurora borealis *1:* 44, 45 (ill.), 117

Aurorae *1:* 9, **44-45**; *3:* 573, 630, 638, 662

Autumnal equinox *1:* 152

B

Baade, Walter *1:* 19, **47-50,** 48 (ill.); *2:* 256, 421, 436; *3:* 704

Ballistic missile. *See* Intercontinental ballistic missile (ICBM)

Barnard, Edward E. *3:* 701

Barnard Observatory *3:* 539

Barred spiral galaxy *1:* 168; *3:* 615

Barringer meteor crater *2:* 375 (ill.)

Bassett, Charles A. *1:* 180

Baum, L. Frank *1:* 129

Bean, Alan *1:* 108

Bell Burnell, Jocelyn *1:* 47, **50-52,** 192; *2:* 244-45, 412, 461; *3:* 494, 520

Bell Telephone Laboratories *1:* 104

Belyayev, Pavel *2:* 323; *3:* 680

Bennett, David *1:* 124

Benzenberg, Johann *2:* 376

Beregovoy, Georgi *3:* 576

Berlin Observatory *1:* 2; *2:* 325

Bessel, Friedrich *1:* **52-53,** 52 (ill.), 62, 70; *2:* 428

Bethe, Hans *1:* **53-56,** 54 (ill.), 140

Big bang theory *1:* 31, **56-59,** 57 (ill.), 61, 113, 117, 120, 176-77, 191-92; *2:* 250, 256, 262, 267, 320, 410, 438-39, 449, 451-52; *3:* 489, 494, 498, 515, 546, 619

Big Bear Solar Observatory *1:* **59-60**; *2:* 402

Big bore theory *1:* 60

Big crunch theory *1:* **60-61,** 125

Big dipper *1:* 159; *2:* 445; *3:* 570

Billion-channel Extra-Terrestrial Assay *1:* 159

Binary star *1:* **62-63,** 66; *2:* 328, 387, 419; *3:* 541, 621-22, 651, 676, 694, 696

Binary star system *1:* 62 (ill.)

Biot, Jean-Baptiste *2:* 376

Black dwarf star *1:* 61, 123; *2:* 394, 398-400; *3:* 506, 513, 532, 580, 586, 593, 596-97, 599, 605, 636-38, 653, 691, 705

Black hole *1:* 3, 18, 22, 61, **63-66,** 64 (ill.), 93, 106, 123, 140, 167, 169, 175-76, 195, 214, 220; *2:* 274, 311, 314, 328, 380, 411, 417, 420-21; *3:* 488, 503, 589, 614, 622, 631, 651, 676, 691, 695, 697, 701, 705

Bloch, Felix *2:* 463

Blue-shift *3:* 504, 552

Bluford, Guion *1:* **66-68,** 90

Bode, Johann Elert *1:* 37, **68-69,** 68 (ill.), 111

Bode's Law *1:* 37, 68-69

Bohr, Neils *1:* 176

Bolometer *1:* 147; *2:* 309

Bolshevik Revolution *3:* 648

Bonaparte, Napoleon *2:* 308

Bondi, Hermann *1:* 121; *2:* 250

Bondone, Giotto Ambrogio di *1:* 183

Borman, Frank *3:* 545

The Boston Herald 1: 188

Bradley, James *1:* **69-70,** 69 (ill.); *3:* 514, 612

Brahe, Tycho *1:* **70-73,** 71 (ill.), 85, 119; *2:* 294, 390, 420, 446; *3:* 553

Brand, Vance *1:* 27

Brandes, Heinrich *2:* 376

Braun, Wernher von *1:* **73-76,** 74 (ill.), 156; *2:* 425; *3:* 513, 532, 665

Brezhnev, Leonid *1:* 27; *2:* 323

A Brief History of Time 1: 215

Brown dwarfs *1:* 61, **76-77,** 77 (ill.), 123; *2:* 300, 406-07; *3:* 624, 659, 705

Brownian movement *1:* 143

Brunhes, Bernard *1:* 138

Bunsen, Robert *2:* 297

Bureau of Longitudes *1:* 28

Burke, Bernard *1:* 494

Burney, Venetia *3:* 646

Burrell-Schmidt telescope *2:* 299

Butler, Paul *1:* 159; *2:* 445; *3:* 569

Bykovsky, Valery *3:* 635

C

C. Donald Shane Telescope *2:* 328

C-141 Starlifter *2:* 302

Caesar, Julius *1:* 79, 98

Calendar *1:* 8, 10-11, 14, **79-81,** 80 (ill.); *2:* 453, 459; *3:* 514, 625

Calendar of Works and Days, 1281 1: 9

Callipus *1:* 13

Caloris Basin *2:* 368

CalTech Submillimeter Observatory *2:* 362

Cambridge Observatory *1:* 2, 140; *2:* 325; *3:* 517

Cannon, Annie Jump *1:* **81-83,** 82 (ill.)

Cape Canaveral *1:* 24; *2:* 293, 337, 398; *3:* 505

Capture trajectory *3:* 604

Carnegie, Andrew *1:* 200; *3:* 516

Carnegie Institution *1:* 152; *2:* 391, 437; *3:* 515-16, 661

Carpenter, Scott *2:* 369, 371

Carter, Jimmy *3:* 658, 686

Cassini, Gian Domenico *1:* **83-85,** 84 (ill.); *3:* 513, 530

Cassini 3: 531, 581

Cassini Division *1:* 85; *3:* 530

Catherine Wolfe Bruce Medal *3:* 536

Cavendish, Henry *1:* 193

Cavendish Laboratory *1:* 54

Celestial mechanics *2:* 319

Celestial Mechanics 2: 311, 413

Celestial Police *1:* 69

Celestial sphere *1:* 42, 108

Centaur rocket *1:* 174; *2:* 317, 400; *3:* 510 (ill.)

Centaurus A *2:* 449

Cepheid variables *1:* 19, 49, **85-87,** 220; *2:* 248, 254, 318, 404, 436; *3:* 541-42, 618, 632, 666

Ceres *1:* 36-37, 119, 178; *2:* 427; *3:* 566

Cernan, Eugene *1:* 182

Cerro Tololo Interamerican Observatory *1:* **87-89,** 88 (ill.), 130, 152; *2:* 298, 313, 400, 402

Cesarsky, Catherine *2:* 274

CGRO. *See* Compton Gamma Ray Observatory

Chaffee, Roger *1:* 23; *3:* 596, 689

Challenger 1: 36, 44, 66, **90-92,** 91 (ill.), 94, 96, 114, 125, 127, 134, 149, 161-63, 173; *2:* 257, 316, 395; *3:* 505-07, 513, 585 (ill.), 586, 592, 653, 685

Chandrasekhar, Subrahmanyan *1:* **92-94,** 93 (ill.), 140; *2:* 417, 421; *3:* 701

Chandrasekhar's limit *1:* 93; *2:* 421

Chang-Diaz, Franklin *1:* 96

Charged coupling device (CCD) *1:* 20; *2:* 440

Charon *2:* 305, 388, 456-57; *3:* 659

Chiron *1:* 38

Chladni, E. F. F. *2:* 375

Christian constellations *1:* 111

Christian IV *1:* 73

Christy, James *3:* 659

Chromatic aberration *2:* 432

Chromosphere *2:* 394; *3:* 555-56

Chronometer *2:* 402

Interferometry 2: **277-78,** 361, 379, 433

Internal Constitution of the Stars 1: 92

International Geodetic Association 2: 431

International Geophysical Year 3: 582, 665

International Halley Watch 1: 99, 182, 209; 3: 668

International Solar Polar Mission 3: 653

International Space Station 1: 151, 156; 2: **278-79,** 383, 385; 3: 526, 551, 584, 589, 607, 638

International Telecommunications Satellite Organization. *See* Intelsat

International Ultraviolet Explorer 2: **279-80;** 3: 590, 653

Internet. *See* Astronomy websites

Intersputnik 1: 105

Interstellar medium 1: 148; 2: **281-82,** 304, 386, 404, 428; 3: 579, 652, 685

Inverse square law 2: 419

Io 3: 684

Ionosphere 1: 137; 3: 616

Irregular galaxy 1: 148, 168; 3: 614

Is Anyone Out There?: The Scientific Search for Extraterrestrial Intelligence 1: 130

Isochronicity 2: 263

It Is I, Sea Gull: Valentina Tereshkova, First Woman in Space 3: 636

Italian Space Agency 3: 636

J

James Clerk Maxwell Telescope 2: 362

Jansky, Karl 2: **283-85,** 284 (ill.); 3: 491-92, 498-99, 518

Japanese Space Agency 3: 605

Jemison, Mae 1: 151; 2: **285-88,** 286 (ill.)

Jet Propulsion Laboratory (JPL) 1: 173; 2: 399

Jewitt, David C. 2: 306

Johnson, Caldwell 1: 162

Johnson, Lyndon B. 2: 385

Johnson Space Center (JSC) 1: 162; 2: 398

Julian calendar 1: 79

Juno 1 1: 76, 156; 3: 512

Jupiter 1: 9, 13, 37, 45, 68-69, 76, 83, 128, 134, 171-72, 174, 196, 206, 208, 210, 218; 2: 280, **288-91,** 289 (ill.), 296, 304, 306, 310, 328, 335, 337, 366, 386, 407, 409, 440, 443, 445, 455, 458; 3: 494, 513, 528, 530-31, 546, 551, 561, 565-66, 568, 573, 580, 612, 646, 653, 655, 676, 683-84

Jupiter-C rocket 1: 76, 156; 2: 399; 3: 512, 599 (ill.), 665

K

Kaiser Wilhelm Physical Institute 1: 144

Kant, Immanuel 1: 169; 2: 382; 3: 569

Kapteyn, Jacobus Cornelius 3: 546

Keck Telescope 1: 20, 153; 2: 314, 328, 361, 364, 373, 433; 3: 699

Kennedy, John F. 1: 22-23, 35, 179, 187; 2: 274, 293, 369; 3: 582, 594, 596, 681

Kennedy Space Center 2: **293-94,** 337, 398 (ill.); 3: 505, 602

Kenwood Observatory 1: 199

Kepler, Johannes 1: 37, 73, 85, 98, 112-13, 119, 131, 206-07; 2: **294-96,** 295 (ill.), 390, 416, 446; 3: 553, 568, 660

Kepler's Star 2: 296

Kerr, Roy 1: 65

Kerridge, John F. 2: 357

Khrunov, Evgeni 3: 576

King of Prussia's Gold Medal for Science 1: 216

King's Astronomer 1: 217

Kirchhoff, Gustav 1: 119; 2: **297-98,** 297 (ill.)

Kirchhoff's Law 2: 298

Kirkwood, Daniel 1: 38

Kirkwood Gaps 1: 38

Kitt Peak National Observatory 1: 89, 130; 2: **298-300,** 299 (ill.), 400-01; 3: 572

Knowledge of the Times 2: 372

Köhne, Dorothea 2: 427

Komarov, Vladimir 1: 167; 2: 324; 3: 576, 680

Königsberg Observatory 1: 52; 2: 428

Korean War 1: 35, 187

Korolëv, Sergei 2: **300-02,** 301 (ill.), 317, 340; 3: 512, 538, 575, 616

Krushchev, Nikita 2: 358

Kua, Shen 1: 9

Kubasov, Valerly 1: 27; 2: 324

Kuiper, Gerard 1: 99; 2: 304-05, 409; 3: 656, 701

Kuiper Airborne Observatory 2: **302-04,** 303 (ill.); 3: 701

Kuiper belt 1: 99; 2: **305-06, 458**

L

La Palma Observatory 3: 572

Lagoon nebula 2: 282

Lagrange, Joseph Louis 2: **307-08,** 307 (ill.), 310

Lagrange points 2: 308

Laika 3: 593

Lalande, Joseph 1: 209

Lamp at Midnight 1: 172

Lampland, Carl 2: 335

Lang, Fritz 2: 425

Langley, Samuel 2: **308-10,** 309 (ill.)

Langley Air Force Base 2: 310

Langley Research Center (LRC) 2: 310, 399

Langmuir, Irving 2: 450

Laplace, Pierre-Simon 1: 64; 2: **310-11,** 310 (ill.), 413, 427; 3: 569

Large and Small Magellanic Clouds 1: 168; 2: **312-13**

Large Magellanic Cloud (LMC) 1: 4, 89, 168; 2: 312 (ill.), 421; 3: 542

Las Campanas Observatory 1: 152; 2: **313-14,** 433

Lassell, William 3: 656

Last quarter moon 3: 640

Launch vehicle 1: 76; 2: **314-17,** 315 (ill.), 351; 3: 532, 575, 597

Lavoisier, Antoine-Laurent 2: 310

Law of universal gravitation 2: 415, 418-19, 447

Laws of motion. *See* Newton's laws of motion

"Leadership and America's Future in Space" 3: 509

Learmonth Solar Observatory 2: 402

Leavitt, Henrietta Swan 1: 86, 220; 2: 245, **317-18;** 3: 541, 666

Legendre, Adrien-Marie 2: **319**

Leibniz, Gottfried 2: 416-17

Leiden Observatory 1: 220

Lemaître, Georges-Henri 1: 56, 120, 177, 192; 2: **320-21,** 320 (ill.); 3: 619

Leo 2: 377

Leonid meteor shower 2: 377

Leonid meteor swarm 1: 2

Leonov, Alexei 1: 27; 2: **321-24,** 322 (ill.); 3: 680

Lepaute, Nicole-Reine 1: 209

Leverrier, Urbain 1: 2, 120; 2: **325-26,** 325 (ill.), 407, 444

Levison, Harold F. 2: 306

Lewis Research Center (LRC) 2: 400

Liberty Bell 2: 370

Liberty Bell 7 3: 594

Lichtenberg, G. F. 2: 375

Lick, James 2: 326

Lick Observatory 2: **326-28,** 415; 3: 542

Lick Telescope 2: 327 (ill.)

Light-year 1: 17, 19, 86-87, 159, 219; 2: 254, 282, 305, 312, 381-82, 404, 407, 445; 3: 488, 527, 535, 541-42, 569, 607, 612, 620, 627, 676, 694

Lindbergh, Charles 1: 190

Linde, A. D. 2: 268

Linnaeus, Carl 1: 32

Lippershey, Hans 1: 171

Local Group 1: 17, 167-68; 2: 382

Lost Moon 1: 26

Lou Gehrig's disease 1: 214

Louis XIV 1: 83; 2: 308

Penzias, Arno *1:* 58, 114, 177, 192; *2:* **438-39,** 438 (ill.); *3:* 494, 620

Perihelion *2:* 457

Period-luminosity curve *3:* 541

Perkins Observatory *2:* 335

Perseid meteor shower *2:* 377

Perseus *2:* 377

Perth Observatory *2:* 335

Peter the Great *1:* 207

Peterson, Donald *2:* 395

Philip II *1:* 32

Philolaus *1:* 14

Philosophiae Naturalis Principia Mathematica *1:* 131, 193; *2:* 417-18, 447

Phobos *2:* 355; *3:* 657

Pholus *1:* 36

Photoelectric effect *1:* 143

Photometry *2:* **439-40**

Photopolarimeter *1:* 183

Photosphere *3:* 555-56, 561, 627, 630

Physics *1:* 55; *2:* 439, 450, 463-64; *3:* 520

Piazzi, Father Giuseppe *1:* 37, 119, 218; *2:* 427

Pierce, John *1:* 104

Pioneer program *2:* 344, 399, **440-44**; *3:* 523, 629

Pioneer-Venus Multiprobe *2:* 443

Pioneer-Venus Orbiter *2:* 443

Pioneer 1 *2:* 442

Pioneer 3 *3:* 664

Pioneer 4 *2:* 344, 442

Pioneer 5 *2:* 442; *3:* 629

Pioneer 6 *3:* 629

Pioneer 7 *3:* 629

Pioneer 8 *3:* 629

Pioneer 10 *2:* 441 (ill.), 443; *3:* 580, 604, 683, 685

Pioneer 11 *2:* 443; *3:* 580, 604, 683, 685

Plages *3:* 556, 627

Planet X *2:* 334, **444-45,** 454; *3:* 566, 644

The Planetary Hypothesis *3:* 460

Planetary motion *1:* 9, 73, 131; *2:* 294, **445-48**

Planetary Society *1:* 159; *3:* 523, 685

Planetesimals *1:* 37; *2:* 305; *3:* 568

Planetesimals and protoplanets *2:* **448-49**

Plasma *1:* 44, 61; *2:* 359, **449-51,** 452; *3:* 561, 572-73, 606, 630, 638, 683

Plasma theory *1:* 61; *2:* **451-52**

Plateau theory *1:* 60

Plato *1:* 12, 32; *2:* 390

Pleiades star cluster *1:* 4, 129; *2:* **452-53**

Plinth *1:* 14; *2:* 460

Pluto *1:* 69; *2:* 261, 304-05, 331, 366, 388, 407, 409, 443-45, **453-56,** 454 (ill.), 457-58; *3:* 565, 579-81, 644, 646, 659

Pluto Express *2:* 456, **457-58,** 457 (ill.); *3:* 494, 620

Population I stars *1:* 49

Population II stars *1:* 49

Poseidon *1:* 134

Positional astronomy *3:* 658

The Primeval Atom *2:* 321

Probes *1:* 108, 155, 172, 174, 182; *2:* 288, 316, 333, 338, 342, 345, 349, 351, 353, 357-59, 368, 390, 399, 440, 443, 457; *3:* 553, 582, 592, 602, 628, 647, 654-55, 667-68, 676, 683

Proceedings of the Institute of Radio Engineers *3:* 499

Progress *3:* 525

Project Matterhorn *3:* 661

Project Orbiter *3:* 665

Project Ozma *1:* 129

Project Paperclip *1:* 75

Project Pathfinder *1:* 160

Prominence *1:* 45; *3:* 556, 571, 573, 627

Proper motion *1:* 207

Proton rocket *3:* 575

Protoplanetary systems *2:* 449

Protoplanets *3:* 568

Proxima Centauri *2:* 305; *3:* 607-08, 627

Ptolemaic model. *See* Geocentric model

Ptolemy *1:* 14, 42, 110, 112, 118, 131, 207; *2:* 445, **458-460,** 457 (ill.); *3:* 567

Pulitzer Prize *3:* 521

Pulsar *1:* 3-4, 31, 47, 50, 106, 176; *2:* 246, 405, 412, **460-61;** *3:* 494, 496, 498-99, 520, 590, 651, 688, 695, 697, 705

Purcell, Edward *2:* **461-64,** 462 (ill.); *3:* 493

Pythagoras *1:* 12

Q

Quadrant *1:* 72

Quantum mechanics *1:* 215

Quantum physics *1:* 92

Quasars *1:* 3-4, 21, 50, 65, 106, 121, 176, 204; *2:* 244, 252, 271-72, 280, 300, 328, 412, 437, 461; *3:* **487-89,** 488 (ill.), 495, 526-27, 534, 536, 539, 591, 620, 651-53, 695

Quasi-stellar radio source *3:* 527, 534

Queloz, Didier *1:* 159; *2:* 445; *3:* 569

R

Rabi, Isidor Isaac *2:* 463

Radiation *1:* 3, 20, 30, 105, 114, 174, 214; *2:* 243, 247, 267, 270, 273, 279, 337, 406, 439, 452, 460; *3:* 491, 494, 589, 620, 652, 695-96

Radiative zone *3:* 561, 627

Radio astronomy *1:* 30-31; *2:* 244, 283, 285, 429, 438, 463; *3:* **491-94,** 492 (ill.), 495-96, 518, 520

Radio galaxies *1:* 20; *3:* 493, 519

Radio interferometer *2:* 278, 361; *3:* 493, **494-96,** 499, 519, 674

Radio interferometry *1:* 212; *2:* 433; *3:* 520

Radio telescope *1:* 30, 89, 129, 153, 158-59; *2:* 244, 382, 431, 449, 461, 464, 487, 491; *3:* 493-95, **496-99,** 497 (ill.), 498-501, 518, 668, 674

Radio wave *1:* 105, 146-47, 174; *2:* 298, 363, 402, 412, 429, 439; *3:* 491, 493-94, 539, 652, 695

Radioisotope thermal generator (RTG) *2:* 458; *3:* 581 (ill.)

Raleigh, Walter *1:* 210

Ranger probes *2:* 344, 399; *3:* 579

Reagan, Ronald *2:* 278

Reber, Grote *2:* 285; *3:* 492, 498, **499-501,** 500 (ill.), 518

Red dwarf *2:* 406; *3:* 517

Red giant star *1:* 220; *2:* 282, 404, 419; *3:* **502-03,** 502 (ill.), 517, 622, 624, 628, 666, 691

Red-shift *2:* 256, 261, 272, 428; *3:* 487, **503-04,** 527, 535, 552, 688

Redstone rocket *1:* 75; *2:* 369, 399; *3:* 512, 532

Reflection of light *2:* 460

Reflector telescope *1:* 59, 128, 204, 212; *2:* 249, 314, 392, 431, 435; *3:* 659, 687, 699

Refraction of light *2:* 311, 460

Refractive indexes *1:* 210

Refractor telescope *1:* 59, 199-201, 211; *2:* 249; *3:* 644, 659, 699

Reines, Frederick *2:* 410

Relay *1:* 104

Resnik, Judith *1:* 127; *2:* 337; *3:* **504-06,** 505 (ill.)

Retrograde motion *1:* 9, 13; *3:* 568

Return to Earth *1:* 7

Revolution of the Heavenly Spheres *1:* 112-13, 119, 171

Riccioli, Giovanni *1:* 83, 197

Richer, Jean *1:* 85

Ride, Sally *1:* 90; *2:* 337; *3:* **506-09,** 508 (ill.), 633

The Right Stuff *3:* 545

Ring galaxy *1:* 169

Ring nebula *2:* 404

Rocket fuel *1:* 188

Rocketry *1:* 73, 75, 188, 190; *2:* 300, 329, 398-99, 423, 425; *3:* 509, 511, 648

Rockets *1:* 23, 35, 73, 114, 155, 174, 180, 188, 190, 212; *2:* 247, 294, 300, 316-17, 329, 346, 369, 398, 400, 423, 425-26; *3:* 506, **509-13,** 532, 534, 564, 575, 591, 597, 602-03, 648, 651, 661, 665, 695, 697

Rockoon technique *3:* 662

Roemer, Olaus *1:* 83; *3:* **513-14,** 514 (ill.), 612

Roosevelt, Franklin D. *1:* 55

ROSAT satellite *1:* 4

Royal Astronomical Society *1:* 2, 216

Royal Irish Academy *1:* 216

Royal Observatory *1:* 21, 51

Royal Radar Establishment *3:* 519

Royal Society of Edinburgh *2:* 364

Royal Society of London *2:* 364

RR Lyrae stars *3:* 666-67

Rubin, Vera *1:* 125; *3:* **515-17**

Rudolph II *1:* 73

The Rudolphine Tables *2:* 296

Russell, Henry *1:* 219; *3:* **517-18,** 517 (ill.), 541

Russian Space Agency *2:* 458

Rutherford, Ernest *1:* 176

Ryle, Martin *1:* 51; *2:* 244-45; *3:* 493, **518-20,** 519 (ill.)

S

Sacramento Peak Observatory *2:* 400-01

Sagan, Carl *1:* 130, 159; *2:* 357; *3:* **521-23,** 522 (ill.), 685

Sagittarius *2:* 282, 285; *3:* 500

Salyut program *2:* 324, 340; *3:* **523-26,** 578, 583

Salyut 1 *2:* 383; *3:* 523, 525, 576, 587

Salyut 2 *3:* 524

Salyut 3 *3:* 524

Salyut 4 *3:* 525

Salyut 5 *3:* 524

Salyut 6 *3:* 525, 587

Salyut 7 *3:* 525, 587

Sandage, Allan *3:* 487, **526-28,** 534

Saturn *1:* 2, 9, 13, 38, 45, 68, 112, 119, 134, 171, 218; *2:* 262, 310, 333, 335, 364, 366, 386, 409, 440, 443, 445; *3:* **528-31,** 529 (ill.), 565, 567-68, 580, 604, 655, 683-85

Saturn I rocket *3:* 532

Saturn IB rocket *3:* 532

Saturn V rocket *1:* 23, 76, 190; *3:* 513, **532-34,** 533 (ill.)

Schiaparelli, Giovanni *2:* 333, 357, 377

Schiller, Julius *1:* 111

Schirra, Walter *2:* 371

Schmidt, Maarten *3:* 488, **534-36**

Schmidt telescope *2:* 433

Scientific American *2:* 306

Search for Extraterrestrial Intelligence (SETI) *1:* 158 (ill.), 159-60

Seasat *1:* 134

Seasons *3:* **536-38,** 537 (ill.)

See, Elliot M. *1:* 180

Service module *1:* 22

SETI. *See* Search for Extraterrestrial In-telligence (SETI)

Seven Sisters *2:* 453

Sextant *1:* 40

Seyfert, Carl *3:* **539-40**

Seyfert galaxies *3:* 539-40

Shapley, Harlow *1:* 86, 220; *2:* 254; *3:* **540-43,** 540 (ill.)

Sharpe, Mitchell *3:* 636

Shepard, Alan *2:* 331, 370; *3:* **543-46,** 544 (ill.)

Shooting stars *2:* 376

Shuttle Autonomous Research Tool for Astronomy (SPARTAN) *2:* 337

Sidereus Nuncius *1:* 171

Sigma *2:* 371

Sitter, Willem de *1:* 56, 120; *3:* **546-48,** 547 (ill.)

61 Cygni *1:* 52

Sky & Telescope *3:* 705

Skylab space station *1:* 108; *2:* 394, 399; *3:* 534, **548-51,** 549 (ill.), 583-84, 587, 589, 601, 629

Slayton, Donald "Deke" *1:* 27

Slipher, Vesto Melvin *3:* 548, **551-53,** 551 (ill.)

Small Astronomical Satellite 1 *3:* 651

Small Magellanic Cloud (SMC) *1:* 4, 86, 89, 168, 220; *2:* 312, 318; *3:* 542

Smithsonian Astrophysical Observatory (SAO) *3:* 687

Smithsonian Submillimeter Array *2:* 362

Snell, Willebrord *3:* **552-53**

Snell's law *3:* 553

Snow, Helen *1:* 201

Snow Solar Telescope *1:* 201; *2:* 391, 393-94

Society for Space Travel *1:* 73

Society of Jesuits *1:* 197

Soft X-rays *1:* 3; *3:* 695, 697

Sokolov, Andrei *2:* 324

Solar and Heliospheric Observatory *3:* **553-55,** 629

Solar atmosphere *3:* **555-57**

Solar chromosphere *1:* 29

Solar eclipse *1:* 12, 13, 45; *2:* 243, 246, 340, 374; *3:* 556, **557-60,** 559 (ill.), 570

Solar energy transport *3:* **560-62**

Solar flare *1:* 45, 59, 106, 137; *2:* 246; *3:* 550, 556, 571, 573, 588, 627, 629-30

Solar Maximum Mission *3:* 592, 629

Solar rotation *3:* **562-63**

Solar sail *3:* **563-65,** 564 (ill.)

Solar system *1:* 9, 13-14, 24, 37, 56, 99, 111, 118-19, 131, 134, 138, 140, 167, 171, 174, 193, 207, 217; *2:* 253, 273, 290, 295, 305-06, 308, 310-11, 334, 342, 354, 366, 368, 376, 381, 397, 399, 406-09, 411, 417, 429-30, 438, 440, 443-45, 448, 454, 456-57, 459; *3:* 488, 494, 513, 527, 535, 551,

553, 557, 562, 564, **565-70,** 567 (ill.), 572, 579, 583, 591, 596, 598, 602, 604, 626, 652, 655, 683, 685

Solar telescope *1:* 199; *2:* 298, 391-92, 394, 400; *3:* 525, **570-72**

Solar wind *1:* 44, 98, 116, 137, 158, 183; *2:* 347, 352, 442, 449, 553; *3:* 557, 566, **572-73,** 627, 629, 654

Solstice *1:* 9, 14, 151; *3:* **573-75,** 625

Sommerfeld, Arnold *1:* 53

Sosigenes *1:* 79

South magnetic pole *1:* 137

South pole *3:* 574

Southern lights *1:* 117; *3:* 573, 630, 638

Soyuz program *1:* 167; *2:* 278; *3:* **575-79,** 605, 679-80

Soyuz T series *3:* 578

Soyuz TM series *3:* 578

Soyuz TM-11 *3:* 577 (ill.)

Soyuz 1 *2:* 323; *3:* 575-76

Soyuz 2–9 *3:* 576

Soyuz 10 *3:* 524, 576

Soyuz 11 *3:* 524, 576

Soyuz 12 *3:* 578

Soyuz 17 *3:* 578

Soyuz 19 *1:* 6, 27; *2:* 324; *3:* 578, 583

Space age *2:* 442

Space Infrared Telescope Facility *3:* 591

Space probe *1:* 24, 172; *2:* 301, 354, 368, 390; *3:* **579-81,** 586, 653-54, 673-74

Space race *1:* 26, 179; *2:* 302, 321, 343, 351, 369; *3:* 513, 523, 543, **582-84,** 586, 593, 616, 665, 679, 681

Space shuttle *1:* 6, 24, 42, 66-67, 90, 94, 96, 114, 125, 127, 134, 149, 161, 172-73, 176; *2:* 257-58, 276, 278, 287, 291, 294, 316, 331, 336-37, 349, 384; *3:* 505, 507, 564, 583, **584-86,** 592, 601, 604, 606, 685

Space Shuttle Orbiter *1:* 162

Space sickness *2:* 288; *3:* 682

Space station *1:* 127, 156; *2:* 247, 278, 317, 324, 336, 338, 340, 359, 382, 394, 425; *3:* 511, 523-24, 534, 548, 551, 575-76, 578, 583-84, **586-89,** 591-92, 596, 602, 605, 629

Space telescope *3:* **589-91**

Space-time continuum *1:* 144

Space trash *3:* **591-93**

Spacecraft, piloted *3:* **593-96**

Spacecraft design *3:* **596-99**

Spacecraft equipment *3:* **601-02**

Spacecraft voyage *3:* **602-05**

Spacelab *1:* 67, 90, 96, 155; *2:* 288, 399; *3:* 586, **605-07**

Spacelab 1 *3:* 606

Spacelab 2 *2:* 395; *3:* 606

Spacelab 3 *3:* 606

Spacesuits *1:* 101; *2:* 394; *3:* 598, 601, 605, 680

V

V-2 rockets *1:* 190; *2:* 425; *3:* 512, 662
Vacuum Solar Telescope *2:* 401
Vacuum tower *3:* 572
Valle Marineris *2:* 355
Van Allen, James *1:* 116, 156; *3:* **661-63,** 662 (ill.)
Van Allen belts *1:* 44, 116, 129, 137, 156; *3:* 661, **663-64,** 664 (ill.)
Van de Hulst, Hendrik *2:* 429
Vanguard program *1:* 156; *3:* **665-66**
Variable stars *1:* 85-86; *2:* 248, 318; *3:* **666-67**
Vega program *3:* 580, **667-68**
Vega 1 *1:* 183; *3:* 667
Vega 2 *1:* 183; *3:* 668
Velas *1:* 106, 175
Venera program *3:* 580, **668-71**
Venera 1 *3:* 670
Venera 2 *3:* 670
Venera 3 *2:* 301; *3:* 669 (ill.)
Venera 4 *3:* 670
Venera 5–14 *3:* 671
Venera 15 *3:* 670-71
Venera 16 *3:* 670-71
Vengeance Weapon 2 *1:* 75
Venus *1:* 13, 31, 68, 135, 172, 174, 196, 218; *2:* 290, 296, 301, 333, 340, 349, 351, 368, 440, 443, 445, 458; *3:* 498, 506, 521, 564-65, 567-68, 579-80, 592, 667-68, **672-74,** 672 (ill.)
Venus Orbiting Imaging Radar *2:* 349
Venus Radar Mapper (VRM) *2:* 349
Vernal equinox *1:* 80, 152
Verne, Jules *2:* 423
Very Large Array *1:* 130; *2:* 278; *3:* 493, 495, **674-76,** 675 (ill.)
Very Long Baseline Array (VLB) *2:* 361; *3:* 496
Very Long Baseline Interferometry (VLBI) *1:* 212; *3:* 495
Vesta *1:* 38; *2:* 356, 428
Viking program *2:* 317; *3:* 523, **676-79**
Viking 1 *2:* 356; *3:* 579, 677-79, 677 (ill.)
Viking 2 *2:* 356; *3:* 579, 677-78
Virtual particles *1:* 65
Visible light *1:* 147; *2:* 412

Visual binary star *1:* 53, 62; *3:* 623
VLBI Space Observatory Program (VSOP) *3:* 496
Volkov, Vladislav *3:* 578
Voskhod program *3:* **679-80**
Voskhod 1 *3:* 680
Voskhod 2 *2:* 321; *3:* 680
Vostok program *1:* 165, 167; *2:* 317; *3:* 633, 679, **680-83**
Vostok 1 *1:* 165; *2:* 301; *3:* 543, 594, 633, 680, 682
Vostok 2 *3:* 682
Vostok 3 *3:* 635, 682
Vostok 4 *3:* 682
Vostok 5 *3:* 635, 682
Vostok 6 *3:* 633, 635, 681 (ill.), 682
Voyager program *1:* 85; *2:* 317, 366, 399; *3:* 523, **683-86**
Voyager 1 *1:* 45, 173; *2:* 291, 349, 458; *3:* 528, 530-31, 580, 598, 604, 683-85, 684 (ill.)
Voyager 2 *1:* 173; *2:* 291, 349, 407, 458, 528; *3:* 530, 573, 580, 598, 604, 655-56, 683-85
Vulcan *2:* 326; *3:* 566

W

Wakata, Koichi *1:* 151
Waldheim, Kurt *3:* 686
Waning crescent phase *2:* 348
Waning gibbous phase *2:* 348
Washington Monument *2:* 415
The Washington Post *3:* 555
Waxing crescent phase *2:* 348
Waxing gibbous phase *2:* 348
Ways to Spaceflight *2:* 425
Weber, Wilhelm *1:* 178
Weightlessness *1:* 194 (ill.)
Weiler, Edward *2:* 259
Westar *1:* 105
Wheeler, John A. *1:* 65
Whipple, Fred L. *3:* 687
Whipple Observatory *1:* 210, 213; *3:* **687-89**
Whirlpool galaxy *2:* 273
White, Edward *1:* 23, 180; *3:* 596, **689-90,** 689 (ill.)
White dwarf star *1:* 47, 51, 53, 61, 65, 93-94, 123, 140, 192, 220; *2:* 245,

335, 411, 419, 461; *3:* 503, 518, 622, 628, 631, **690-91,** 691 (ill.), 694, 701, 705
William III *1:* 52
Wilson, Robert *1:* 58, 114, 177, 192; *2:* 438-39; *3:* 494, 620
WIMPs *1:* 123
Winter solstice *3:* 573, 575
Woodward, Charles *3:* 694
World Ocean Circulation Experiment *1:* 134
World War I *1:* 201; *2:* 249, 254, 320, 379, 393, 423
World War II *1:* 26, 166, 185, 190, 203-04; *2:* 293, 301, 335, 337, 399, 424-25, 429, 463; *3:* 493, 495, 498, 501, 512, 519, 532, 535, 543, 545, 633, 661-62, 703
World Wide Web. *See* Astronomy web-sites
Wyoming Infrared Observatory *3:* **692-94,** 693 (ill.)

X

X-ray astronomy *2:* 246, 337; *3:* 494, 605, 651, **695-96**
X-ray stars *2:* 363; *3:* **696-98,** 697 (ill.)
X-ray telescope *1:* 4; *3:* 695, 697

Y

Yeager, Chuck *2:* 371
Yegorov, Boris *3:* 680
Yeliseyev, Aleksei *3:* 576
Yerkes, Charles *1:* 200; *3:* 701
Yerkes Observatory *1:* 94, 200; *2:* 249, 432; *3:* **699-701,** 700 (ill.)
Yohkoh *3:* 629
Young, John *1:* 179
Young, Judy *3:* 516
Young, Thomas *2:* 264

Z

Zodiac *1:* 42 (ill.)
Zwicky, Fritz *1:* 47, 124; *2:* 421, 436; *3:* 516, **703-05,** 704 (ill.)